The White Sari

The White Sari

A Life of Delicate Courage

by

WILFRID RUSSELL

Lower Cole Press

British Library Cataloguing in Publication Data
A catalogue record for this book is available from the British Library

ISBN 0-9549942-0-5
ISBN 978-0-9549942-0-4

Typeset by Amolibros, Milverton, Somerset
This book production has been managed by Amolibros
Printed and bound by T J International Ltd, Padstow, Cornwall, UK

About The White Sari

This unusual book is written as informally as Wilfrid Russell's previous seven books, two of which were slim volumes of poetry. It is the author's memorial to his wife, Sheila, who was a truly exceptional person.

Sheila Sawhny was born in Rawalpindi (then part of India) on 16th December 1920. She died aged eighty-three in the village of Rock on the North Coast of Cornwall. This book recalls their long shared life and their many friends.

Joanna Lumley has written the foreword. Her grandfather, Colonel Weir, was the first Resident, representing the British government of India to the Dalai Llama at Lhasa, also the Kings of Bhutan and Nepal. Her grandmother was the first white woman in that remote country. The Weirs owned the mountain chalet in Gulmarg next door to that of the Sawhny family, so the two families and the author have been friends for three generations.

Both Sheila and Wilfrid had a great gift for friendship. In his Cambridge days, he had met Paul Mellon, an art lover from whose generosity both Clare College and the University greatly benefited. Another long friendship was with Leonard Cheshire. Having both served in the RAF, they linked up later and Wilfrid did much voluntary work for the Cheshire Foundation.

In India, Sheila's brother, Leslie, married Rodabeh Tata, younger sister of J R D Tata, Chairman of the largest industrial group in India. After the war, Leslie joined Tata Sons Ltd and would probably have succeeded J R D Tata as head of the Tata Group, but for his death at the age of forty-three.

When civil war erupted after the partition of India and the creation of the new Islamic State of Pakistan, Wilfrid was one of four managing directors in charge of fourteen cement factories. These factories were now in two separate countries, the workers comprising a mixture of Hindus, Sikhs and Muslims. Wilfrid promptly chartered a Dakota with its crew and flew it himself for a week, transferring Muslim employees from India to

Pakistan and Hindus and Sikhs from the Pakistan factories to India. On the last flight from Pakistan, Wilfrid and his crew flew Sheila, and her mother, Mrs Amy Sawhny, to safety. They had been holidaying in the Sawhny mountain chalet at Gulmarg.

These pages record the mixed marriage of Sheila's mother and father in 1904, when she eloped by climbing over the wall of Government House in Lahore where she had been working for several months as a nanny, to marry Sheila's barrister father.

This book contains much recent history and the atmosphere of four countries – India, England, America and France. The silken thread connecting them is *The White Sari* of Sheila Edwardes Russell. The book ends with a remark made in Sheila's drawing room when Wilfrid asked Sue Walsham, her best friend in England, "What would you say was Sheila's greatest virtue?" Without hesitation she said, "Her delicate courage."

His commitment to the country increased dramatically when the war came, and he was called up, having been in the Cambridge University Air Squadron before the war. Because of his knowledge of things Indian, the RAF sensibly asked him to instruct young Indians to fly, ultimately to fight the Japanese.

Wilfrid was an intensely social person and in India in the 1930s he was well known on the party circuit. Although he was very traditional in his views, he mixed with a broad range of Indians – Hindus, Muslims, Parsees and Sikhs. This openness was not a common feature amongst his contemporaries and led him to become a Member of Parliament for Bombay in one of the colonial power's experiments with limited home rule prior to Independence.

Wilfrid Russell

Renaissance man has been defined as a soldier, scholar and courtier. Wilfrid Russell was very much a Renaissance man. He was not a soldier in a conventional sense, but he fought when his country requested, in a very special way. At the outbreak of the Second World War, he was responsible for training young Indian pilots and became involved with that wonderfully named squadron 'The Friendly Firm', Number 194 which supplied the

Chindits operating behind Japanese lines in Burma. He was a fighter in the broadest sense, from total commitment on all sorts of different sports fields, to fighting for causes he passionately believed in – like his beloved Cheshire Homes.

Wilfrid Russell was born in Egypt where his father's accountancy business was based. He was educated first at Lambrook, then at Marlborough and onto Clare College, Cambridge, where his father had been before him and where he was proud to have skied for the University.

After Cambridge, Wilfrid emigrated to India as a clerk in a shipping company in 1935. He threw himself with zest into Indian life, moving around the country as a freelance manager working for firms of managing agents.

In 1942 he married outside of his own community into an Anglo-Indian family, the Sawhnys, which caused consternation amongst his own family in England, the Newbolts and Macphersons. However, his personality and will-power overcame this suspicion and the families came to respect each other. In 1944 Wilfrid and Sheila came back to London for a year and then back to India again – to a very different India. During the turmoil of Partition he used his determination, influence and flying skills to get his family and many of his Hindu employees out of West Pakistan and into India. Had he not done this, many would have perished in what turned out to be the bloodiest movement of peoples in peace-time.

In 1956 Wilfrid and Sheila with their two young children returned to England. He joined the Commonwealth Development Finance Company Ltd in whose employ he travelled the world. He retired from business in 1970 and settled in Rock on the North Cornish Coast.

Wilfrid had a long and in the main happy retirement in Cornwall, periods of it blighted by his daughter's and his wife's deaths, but he pulled through and his last few years were spent at full speed despite his physical disabilities. His keenness to live life to the full infected everyone around him and although rooted in the past, he was still resolutely looking forward.

His scholarliness was amazing. His love of poetry was rooted in a deep knowledge of the classics. He was also very interested in art and his own watercolour painting of a Moghul temple shows considerable skill. He was equally conversant in German and French. His knowledge of history was extraordinary and he remained an avid consumer of political biography.

He was an enthusiastic writer, with seven books to his credit, ranging from poetry to military history to autobiography with a large slice of political commentary. He continued to write, up to his death — indeed *The White Sari* was in the process of being sent to the publishers when he passed away.

Contents

Acknowledgements

On behalf of the author, his son would like to thank the following publishers, individuals and organizations for their kind permission to reproduce quotations from works for which they hold copyright:

The Society of Authors as the Literary Representative of the Estate of Alfred Noyes for a short extract from 'Forty Singing Seamen'; The Society of Authors as the Literary Representative of the Estate of John Masefield for a short extract; The Society of Authors as the Literary Representative of the Estate of A E Housman for a short extract from 'Loveliest of trees'; short extract from the work of Sir John Betjeman, from *John Betjeman's Collected Poems* published by John Murray reproduced by permission of John Murray; 'Dedicatory Ode' from *Complete Verse* by Hilaire Belloc (copyright © the estate of Hilaire Belloc 1970) reproduced by permission of the estate of Hilaire Belloc; a short extract from the work of Jan Struther reproduced with permission of Curtis Brown Group Ltd, London, on behalf of the Estate of Jan Struther, Copyright © Jan Struther; Sir Michael & Lady Rose for letters and extracts from the work of John Masters; A P Watt on behalf of The National Trust for Places of Historic Interest or Natural Beauty for a short extract from the work of Rudyard Kipling; excerpt from *Peter Pan* by J M Barrie, reproduced by kind permission of Great Ormond Street Hospital, London. Extensive effort has been made to track copyright holders of the following and permission is still being sought: Alan Whicker; Lord Deedes; Field Marshall Lord Wavell; Stephen Vincent Benet; Alice Duer Miller; Sarojini Naidu; Jerry Speer.

List of Illustrations

Foreword

This is a most human account of an extraordinary time in history, encompassing the Second World War, straddling the Partition of India and recording a way of life that has largely vanished.

Central to its theme is Sheila Sawhny, the figure in the white sari, Wilfrid Russell's beautiful and accomplished Indian wife whom he married when such unions were rare. Indeed, it is also part of my own family's history, linking us as neighbouring friends of the Sawhnys in the hill station of Gulmarg.

Russell may well have dropped supplies from a "medieval" aircraft to my father far below, fighting as a Chindit in Burma's jungles: my uncle, Ivor Jehu, was Russell's boss in Delhi during his stint in public relations in the air force in 1940.

But above all and through the book runs the silken thread of Sheila, whose delicate courage inspired this reflective and touching tribute.

As the days and years speed by, and present world events eclipse the recent past, it is good to remember the time when chaps drank burra pegs before lunch, tenants in Tibet paid their taxes in barley or gold and carrier pigeons replaced unreliable radio sets.

The White Sari is a very personal history; but one the reader shares with the greatest pleasure.

Joanna Lumley
20th December 2004

Preface

"She is by far the best of them all."

This forthright statement was made by Mrs Tony Hesketh, the smart, attractive, thirty-something wife of Captain Claude Hesketh of Probyns Horse, one of the smartest and most attractive cavalry regiments of the old Indian Army. The place where it was made was on the polo ground of Gulmarg (Meadow of Roses), which, in my view, at 8,000 feet above sea level was the most beautiful and exhilarating hill station the British (who had a genius for this kind of thing) had created. It lay above the most beautiful valley in India, itself the most beautiful country, overlooked to the north-west by Nanga Parbat, the third highest mountain in the world.

The "them all" in that opening statement were the many smart and pretty girls of the English fishing fleet who had been lucky enough to get to Gulmarg in that July of 1940. And there was only one Indian girl and that was "she"; her first name was Sheila, her surname Sawhny and she had never been out of India. We were married in May 1942 and lived happily ever after; ever after was the ensuing sixty years. This book is an effort to explain why Sheila Sawhny was a truly exceptional person.

Part One

Prologue

"Surely in toil or fray
Under an alien sky,
Comfort it is to say:
'Of no mean city am I!'" –

Rudyard Kipling

I crept onto the promenade deck of the *City of Venice* in the early hours of 5th February 1935 and tiptoed across the empty deck to the capstan, close to the bow, as we took on the pilot and continued at about ten knots into the magnificent harbour that opened up before us. There were many of Kipling's world-end steamers waiting at their moorings.

To the north-east there was a low horizon of buildings; in its centre a dome that stood out, not unlike the Duomo in Florence. But where were the minarets and the temples with their bells? Not having planned to seek my fortune in India, I only had a vague idea of what it would look like at close quarters.

The air was clear and calm, but where was the heat? I felt as fresh as a daisy. England was everywhere – the English bungalow on the top of Malabar hill, the chintzes in the drawing room of my English hostess, the young English ex-public schoolboys to whom I had been introduced that morning in the English-looking office building, the address of which was Home Street, Fort, Bombay. At lunch, my hostess, the wife of the partner of Killick Nixon who had met me at Ballard Pier, warned me that we were going in a party to the Bombay Yacht Club that night. "Black tie," she had said.

There must have been twenty people in the party that night, my first in India, all of them very English. The Yacht Club overlooking the immense harbour, whose placid waters shimmered in the silver light of a winter moon,

3

seemed larger and more imposing than those of its distant royal cousin at Cowes. There was an army of Indian servants who carried trays laden with drinks of every kind across the polished ballroom dance floor; every now and then, one of them paused to unclog a slow-moving ceiling fan where the dancers had thrown streamers of coloured paper which choked the fans to death.

We got home at one o'clock – it was cold and I was told to be up and ready at five for a forty-mile drive to the point-to-point race meeting of the Bombay and Poona Hunt, founded in 1832 and still going strong.

"You'll meet everyone and we'll fix you up with a chummery." I asked someone about the building with a dome that I had seen from the bow of the *City of Venice*. "Oh, that's probably our local hotel, the Taj. It belongs to the Tatas – Indians. They own everything here."

Next morning, I was driven forty miles outside Bombay through a suburban countryside on roads choked with bullock carts, motor cars and buses galore, to the base of Cathedral Rock, a mini rock of Gibraltar. There were half a dozen races; the jumps were prickly pear hedges. There were picnic baskets everywhere and empty champagne bottles.

I was introduced to a dozen young chaps, all of whom invited me to join one or other of their chummeries on the morrow. I supposed there would be time to move in to one of them before the races at Mahalaxmi in the afternoon. Within days I was a member of one such chummery. There were about half a dozen occupants and they lived in large houses just out of town near the sea. They each had an army of servants. I had my own servant, my own room and within a month my own horse and groom. Whisky was nine rupees a bottle, in my first exchange transaction I had bought thirteen of them for a single pound note.

All talk that was not about money, games and home was about the impending war with Germany. The only Indian name I heard mentioned was Tata. What did Tatas Deferred fetch last night on the Bombay Stock Exchange? Where and what was India? I very soon found out.

Hitler and his armies invaded Poland on 1st September 1939. A week later, thanks to my membership at Cambridge of the University Air Squadron, I found my application for a commission in the RAF was accepted on the spot. I was told to report as soon as possible to a place called Risalpur near the Khyber Pass in the North West Frontier Province of India, two thousand miles away.

I took my best friend, a German, as a passenger in my new car – a Ford. Rudi von Leyden came with me for the first eight hundred miles, to Delhi. I soon knew a fair amount about India, the real India of the Mahrattas and the Moghuls, with its division of India into millions of Hindus and millions of Mohammedans. It seemed to me then, on that first day, to be one of the most beautiful and stimulating countries in the world. I was told I would have to drive a long way to find an aeroplane to fly and as it turned out some very fine Englishmen to show me how to fly them.

27 Squadron of the regular air force had been turned overnight into a Flying Training School. They, too, were Englishmen. They and their predecessors had guarded the North West Frontier of India since April 1918 when the RAF was born.

I

Love is a Many Splendoured Thing

"You held a wild flower in your fingertips
Idly you pressed it to indifferent lips
Idly you tore its scarlet leaves apart,
Alas, it was my heart…"

Sarojini Naidu

We first met in the Meadow of Roses, at a cocktail party given by a "burra sahib", as senior English businessmen were then called in India. Jack Thomas was head of a firm of tea-brokers in Calcutta, Thomas & Co. He had a chalet (they were called Huts) in Gulmarg and he was taking his annual holiday playing golf and climbing hills at 8,000 feet rather than stew in the humid heat of Bengal. His youngest brother, Mervyn, was an old friend. We had skied against each other at St Moritz in 1932 in the Varsity ski match, and we had just finished our six months' flying training at the RAF station at Risalpur, near the Khyber Pass. We had left our cars at the bottom of the hill below Gulmarg to transfer onto the local ponies (tats) for the last leg (2,000 feet up to Gulmarg).

As pilot officers on probation (RAFVR) we both had a fortnight's leave before reporting for duty to our respective squadrons. Mervyn was on his way to Calcutta and I was going to Bombay, each about 2,000 miles away. Mervyn asked me to go to his brother's party where the fishing fleet was well represented and, blow me down, there she was, a lovely Indian girl. She was wearing a white sari.

2

The Tar Brush

*"East is East and West is West
and Never the Twain shall meet."*

Rudyard Kipling

At the end of that wonderful holiday, the first of many, I drove through the Punjab, Rajputana and Maharashtra, through the deserts down to Bombay where I reported to Gordon Lancaster. He had been in business in Bombay, as I had been, and then did his flying training at Habbaniya, in Iraq.

He was soon to be posted to England where later in the war he was to sink two U-boats in the Atlantic, win two DFCs and, tragically, lose his life and those of his passengers flying in bad weather into a hillside in the centre of France. He was flying Air-Chief-Marshal Sir Trafford Leigh-Mallory to take over command of the RAF in India.

The rest of that year, 1940, and through to March 1941 I spent flying patrols and escorting convoys from our tiny airfield at Juhu, ten miles north of Bombay, in twelve-year-old Wapiti biplanes, cast-offs from the regular RAF. Their maximum speed was 100 m.p.h. It was in November that I took over command of 2 Flight IAFVR (Indian Air Force Volunteer Reserve) from Gordon. The Flight (in my view) was in fact a Squadron, as were its fellow formations in the Wing, whose Headquarters were in Bombay. The only excitement was the occasion in the monsoon when I landed in a large puddle of water and did a cartwheel, landing upside down, thereby wrecking the poor old Wapiti. Happily the two 250lb bombs we carried underneath the lower wings dropped harmlessly into the mud, harmless since they were not fused.

During these early months of my RAF career I wrote numerous letters to Sheila in Lahore, to most of which she replied. Then a wonderful thing happened – I was posted as Chief Ground Instructor to the new Elementary Flying Training School, suddenly created by Air Head Quarters, to initiate the many new Indian recruits into the new Indian Air Force. By a stroke of luck AHQ had sited it at Lahore, capital of the Punjab Province, Sheila's home town.

AHQ in Delhi had taken over another headquarters, that of the Punjab Boy Scouts. Here there was a senior scout, a tough fifty-year-old Scotsman called Hogg. They had changed his title from the Reverend to Wing Commander, bought him the correct light blue uniform of the RAF and, "hey presto", they had themselves an EFTS. They gave him enough government money to build the necessary mini-barracks to house 400 young Indian cadets who, every six weeks, would be pushed through his Presbyterian hands towards their six months' flying training at an RAF FTS when the next lot would follow them; hopefully the single squadron of the IAF, whose first pilots had been trained at Cranwell would then be replaced by a regular Air Force of ten Squadrons commanded by the original Indian Cranwellians. My Number Two was an athletic Indian Air Force Flight Lieutenant of twenty-two, called Laurie Shaffi, who had played tennis for India in the Davies Cup. He had played at Wimbledon.

I lived in a tent on the spacious lawn of the old Boy Scout campus and gave lectures on the Theory of Flight, Navigation and Physical Training; I was rather like a house prefect at an English public school, trying to turn Indian youths into tough young officers who would understand the meaning of the word "leadership". We were only partially successful. In such spare time as I could wangle, I telephoned Sheila and we played golf together. I met her father and mother, her two brothers, her black Boston bull terrier and the family bulldog who looked like the ITV advertisement for Churchill Car Insurance. Her family exuded the comfortable atmosphere of an English family, yet was entirely Indian. Her mother was English, her father Hindu. Her two brothers, Reggie and Leslie (nicknamed Sonny and Duggie), were making their careers in the Indian Navy and Indian Army respectively. Her father was a barrister. Sheila was the only one who wore Indian dress – saris; Duggie and Sonny were in a strange way Indian and English at the same time in what were highly politicised days. They, together with their sister, were non-political Indian patriots. Sheila and I played golf twice a week, she wore strikingly smart shorts and shirts. I remember her shoes – white and black brogues. Wherever she was, whatever she was wearing, her taste and her sense of dress were equally immaculate.

✳

By this time Sheila had told me about as much as she could remember of her childhood and, more especially, about her father and her mother's marriage. How it happened and how they coped with a mixed marriage at a time when even mixed socialising between English and Indians was frowned upon, let alone mixed marrying, I cannot imagine. Later I shall describe how in fact they did manage. But before this I must explain by means of two anecdotes how the prevailing and widely held anti-social attitude had appalled me very soon after arriving in India in February 1935.

My mother had known a Conservative MP who had known Lord Brabourne, Governor of Bombay. The friendly MP dropped a line to his Excellency asking if he would keep an eye on me. I was duly invited to a cocktail party at Bombay's beautiful Government House, set on a promontory overlooking Back Bay. Having no car, I hitched a ride from a fellow guest who, as it so happened, had to leave early. When the time came to go home I gratefully accepted a lift from two English memsahibs, neither of them attractive in any way; but they did, surprisingly, have a chauffeur-driven car and, what's more, the chauffeur knew where I lived. I was squeezed onto the back seat between them. As we turned out of the splendid Government House gates shining black and gold, the tougher-looking of the two turned to me and said in a lofty voice, "Thank God there were none of those dreadful Wogs at that party. What do you think of them, Mr Russell?" (Wogs was short for "Worthy Oriental Gentlemen", a phrase much in use by the English married women of Bombay at that time.)

I thought for a moment and then I said, "My best friend at Cambridge was an Indian." The rest of the drive took place in silence.

The undergraduate of whom I was thinking was Muzaffar Ali Qizilibash, who actually lived in Lahore; later we discovered he was a friend of Sheila's.

The other story, slightly more subtle, but no less nasty for all that, concerned a junior partner of the firm, a Pukka Sahib. The partners of Killick Nixon & Co, founded in 1856 and still going very strong, were a group of good-hearted English and Scottish men, who had built on to the fifth floor of Killick building a tiffin room (lunch room) where the partners and assistants (as we juniors were called) could get a good free lunch which ensured that we put in a full day's work. The partners usually came up at two p.m. for their lunch, just as we juniors were returning to our offices. On this particular day I was the last of the juniors to go downstairs, when Victor Noel-Paton (later Lord Ferrier, on his retirement) told me of an Englishman in a competing firm about whom he was not at all complimentary. He finished up his story about this chap with the supercilious observation; "Well, he can't help it, poor fellow, after all everyone knows he has a touch of the tar brush."

3

Climbing over the Wall

"He is Father of the fatherless, and defendeth the cause of the widows; even God in his holy habitation. He is the God that maketh men to be of one mind in an house, and bringeth the prisoners out of captivity, but letteth the runagates continue in scareness."

The Book of Common Prayer

To return to 1941 and the Lahore Golf Course, Sheila felt she knew me well enough by this time to tell me how her parents had got married. She thought it must have been about the turn of the century when Des Raj and his cousin, Ram Lall, had come back to India, after four years at Trinity College, Cambridge.

The English Governor of the Punjab was a widower with three teenage daughters; he badly needed a nanny, an English nanny. So he advertised for one in *The Times*. Amy Edwardes, a youngish Englishwoman who lived in the country answered the advertisement.

I have always assumed from her tweed skirts and sensible shoes that her background must have been what one could describe with the epithet "farming" and the noun "yeoman". The Governor snapped her up and within weeks she was settling into her first job, 7,000 miles from her home.

Sheila was never able to tell me how her mother met the smart, westernised, up-and-coming young Indian barrister, but she could tell me that they fell in love and that Des Raj climbed over the wall of Government House, Lahore to take her away to the Indian equivalent of an English Registry Office, where they were married. If the dashing young man had been Amy's grandson, Robin, they would probably have made their getaway on a 1,000cc Yamaha motor-bike. As it was, I imagine the getaway was made in a tonga, pulled by a tired Punjabi pony with scarcely any horsepower. But they did it. Des Raj's promising practice at the bar came to a full stop. The Indian community was more horrified than the British. His briefs dried up.

There was money from the Sawhny lands away to the South but much of his share was trousered by a dishonest manager, so Sheila said; Des Raj, with great courage – a family trait – decided that they must accept the offer of help made by Motilal Nehru, a family friend and the best known barrister in the country. He was the father of Jawarharial Nehru, also the good friend of Rab Butler's father, the Governor of the United Provinces – help was on the way so that he could make a fresh start in the law.

This diversion meant that Des Raj had been forced to take his English bride to Allahabad 1,000 miles further east, where there were scarcely any English women and where a young English wife who never in her life spoke a word of an Indian language was understandably unhappy.

Forty years later Sheila took me to her family house in Lahore, where Des Raj was far from well. By this time Amy was almost a second mother to me; I fell for Des Raj's all-embracing charm as he sat before a fire. Six weeks later he died; Duggie was responsible for his father's funeral. Some years later he described to me this orthodox and mournful Hindu ceremony.

4

The Mother of all Holy Places

"So let me sing of names rememberèd
Because they, living not, can ne'er be dead
Or long time take their memory quite away
From us poor singers of an empty day…"

Wm Morris

Duggie had to take his father's body to the holiest place of all, after Benares, on the holiest river of all, the Ganges – Ganga to the Brahmins. Near to the place where the great river flowed from its source in the Himalayas to the great plains of India stands Hardwar, a small country town, its single industry holiness.

Duggie was then a Second Lieutenant in the 16th Light Cavalry, the only all-Indian cavalry regiment save for its CO (an English Lieutenant Colonel). He had to seek out the Sawhny clan's own Brahmin priest. This was a task in itself for the holy man had to be found from among the crowd of his colleagues, all dressed in white and squatting on the banks of the river, surrounded by constantly moving crowds of bearded Sikhs from the Punjab, groups of turbaned Afghans and Pathans from the frontier and their Rohilla cousins from the Ganges plains, for the Hindus were more liberal than the Muslims in allowing non-Hindus into their holy places. This very special Brahmin kept the names of every eldest Sawhny son from his particular section of the clan inscribed on rolls of vellum which had to be replaced by the name of the successor. The Sawhny family were Kshartrayas (warriors), the second rung of the caste system (the upper fifth, as it were).

Having found his man, Duggie then had to organise the funeral pyre, light it and say farewell to the beloved Duke, his father's nickname, wade into the muddy waters of the Ganga and cast the ashes to the winds and the waters.

When thinking of the strange contrast between this eastern scene and its western equivalent, I came to the conclusion that one reason at least why Sheila and her brothers understood instinctively the meaning of the word discipline was because they had been sent to English boarding schools. They had not been brought up as spoiled and softened children as most orthodox Hindu children were. This thought is not intended to contain any element of distaste for Hinduism but it partially explains, I think, the magic that Sheila and her family possessed for they were able to be English while remaining, if only subconsciously, Indians.

5

Education

*"I will point ye out the right path of a virtuous
and noble Education."*

John Milton

Sheila was baptised into the Church of England when she was twelve. I
don't know whether this long wait was because of any differences of view
between her father and mother; somehow I think not. Des Raj was miles
away from orthodox Hinduism and Amy Edwardes was by no means
churchy, yet she certainly went to church. Anyway Sheila went to a
Protestant Girls Boarding School in Simla when she was about fourteen.
She received a first-class secondary school education at this school which
was run by the Grey Ladies of Wantage.

There was no heating. This made its stone-walled dormitories excessively
cold in winter at 3,000 feet above sea level and I suspect the food was not
much better than mine at my prep school, Lambrook near Ascot.

One of the advantages, although not immediately apparent to her, must
have been Simla itself, with its Vice-Regal connections and its imperial English
atmosphere. Pretty well every other English woman she came across was a Mrs
Hawksbee, and the ghost of Rudyard Kipling haunted every street of this,
the best known hill station in the British Empire. Sheila, who missed her
dogs almost more than her parents, longed to pick up Lady Willingdon's
pekes every Sunday morning when their paths crossed momentarily at
Matins. Lady Willingdon's pekes were handed grandly on their leashes to a
waiting ADC as Her Ladyship entered the west door of the Simla Church.

Sheila spent four years at St Lawrence's before going home where she spent a year teaching at the Punjab University in Lahore. Duggie and Sonny were sent to the Bishop Cotton School for boys, also at Simla. I don't think she ever saw them there and had to wait for the holidays. Oddly enough, Bishop Cotton as a boy had been at my old school in England – Marlborough – where one of the houses, not mine, was named after him.

The only story Sheila ever told me about her year at the Punjab University was the occasion when an exceptionally ill-disciplined pupil made Sheila lose her temper, so that she seized her by her unruly hair and slapped her firmly on the cheeks. Sheila was severely ticked off by the university authorities.

The only record of her teenage years that I have is from a distinguished Cornishman. In 1932 'Toots' Williams was a subaltern in the Devon and Cornwall Light Infantry; he was posted to his regiment in Lahore in 1939. I'm doing an unconventional thing by including in this story a letter he wrote to me in February 2003. The only mistake he made in this letter was to promote Des Raj to the exalted position of a judge.

21.2.03

Dear Wilfrid

I arrived in Lahore in early October 1939 – fresh from Sandhurst. I was put in charge of 10 Platoon, and found Prince Hissam Mahmoud el Effendi commanding No 11 Platoon. We became firm friends, and it was through him that I was introduced to the Sawhny family. They were pretty well the only Indians I met socially. We were kept busy as young officers "at war" – Lahore had a large British population, and with Delhi the largest number of "fishing fleet" girls – despatched to India to find a husband, but stuck there for the war.

Fairly early in 1940 Hissam took me to the Sawhny household, and I remember both father and mother. I was very impressed that he was a judge, and Hissam said he thought they had met at Cambridge. Her brothers were great friends of Hissam, Reggie, in the Indian navy and Leslie, in the 16th Light Cavalry. Over the next 18 months it was

Reggie that we saw most of, as he used to come up from Bombay recruiting for the Indian Navy. He was most entertaining, and could tell a cockney story better than anyone I knew. I met his wife once, who was strikingly good looking. Hissam said he thought she was Goanese. But these days she would be ranked with the top models.

It struck me that the Sawhny family were very sensible in being thoroughly "Indian". I never saw Sheila in anything but a sari – and very attractive she was. Every Saturday evening there was a good party in Falletti's hotel, and there would be about 6 or 12 of us – young officers and local girls. The band was good, the food was good and the general set up of Falletti's was excellent. When that ended we often spilt over into Stiffles, a couple of 100 yards away, but rather down-market after Falletti's.

Sheila was the only Indian girl who was in our normal party; there were plenty of other girls who came in on this. No one had any particular attachment to any particular girl; the whole thing was very great fun. Life was very much work hard and play hard and Saturday night at Falletti's very much looked forward to. I think Hissam, like Sheila, probably preferred the wild "young officer parties" to more formal family parties, which the judge and his wife would have had. At any rate she was a good and very welcome member of our party whenever she came with us, and danced away with the rest.

I don't remember that she played tennis amongst the other girls, but I may be wrong. One or two hunted with us, but I don't know that she rode. In fact my memories of her were as an attractive girl who was nice enough to come out with a rather wild bunch of young officers, and look as if she enjoyed it!!

I left Lahore in November 1941 for the Iraq Rebellion, and next saw Mrs Sheila Russell in Rock, Cornwall!!

With best wishes
Toots

17

Sheila's closest girlfriends at the end of her brief university career were both younger than she was: Babli Gupta, a Bengali and daughter of the Principal of the Mayo School of Art, and Kikuk Dalip Singh. They were both highly intelligent; they were both Hindus and remained her closest Indian friends until her death. Babli's father occupied the same post, in Lahore, as Kipling's father, Lockhart, had done sixty years before, in Bombay. Babli's second husband, much later, of course, Brij Bhagat, was a contemporary of Duggie's, in the Indian Army. His eldest brother, Prem, was to be India's first VC as a second lieutenant in the Bombay Sappers and Miners, fighting the Italians in Eritrea where he defused a large number of landmines under fire and by himself, thereby contributing considerably to the final defeat of the Italians. Kikuk was the daughter of a ravishing Bengali mother, Reva, whom Sheila adored for the rest of her life. Kikuk's father, Sir Dalip Singh, was the Attorney General of Kapurthala State, one of the five Indian States in the British Indian Province of the Punjab. Among her men friends was Sleem, a Muslim and an international tennis player. He had been a familiar sight for many years at Wimbledon.

By another extraordinary coincidence, already mentioned as "my best friend at Cambridge" of the Government House cocktail party, was Muzaffar Ali Qizilibash. I never thought that Muz, as we used to call him, was much of a mathematician but he was certainly a marvellous hockey player. We used to play full back together in the college hockey team. He wielded his stick like an Afghan sword and scared the daylights out of the opposition forwards. We got to the finals of the University Hockey tournament in 1932. Thirty years on he was a Knight of the British Empire as well as being a Nawab (Leader) of his family's original country, Afghanistan. More amazing still, he became Finance Minister of a new country – Pakistan.

6

A Narrow Escape

"I never saw a man who looked
With such a wistful eye
Upon that little tent of blue
Which prisoners call the sky,
And at every drifting cloud that went
With sails of silver by…"

Oscar Wilde

In January 1942 I was taken completely by surprise like many other people considerably more important than I was, notably and unfortunately (among others) General Percival, who was in command of Singapore. I had been badgering personnel at AHQ in Delhi for some time to give me a flying job. To my surprise, a signal came with their agreement almost immediately. I was to take command of another Coastal Reconnaissance Flight, No 5 IAFVR, at Cochin, 2,000 miles to the south and considerably nearer to the enemy, whose armies by that time had reached the new frontier of India in the North East.

Sheila and I, with the approval of Duggie, Sonny and Mrs Sawhny (in that order) decided to get married and chose Bombay as the place and 16th May as the date. True to her nature, Sheila took the minimum of time to look 2,000 miles forward to Cochin rather than four miles backwards to her comfortable home in Lahore.

There were six poor decrepit old Wapitis housed in decrepit old canvas hangars when I landed on the island airfield of Cochin. Later, I took one of them to Bombay with one of the two other Englishmen in the Flight. Derek Wood was my navigator. At Juhu, I learned in the space of a long afternoon how to fly a four-engined civil airliner, a DH 86, which had been commandeered by AHQ, from Tata Air Lines Ltd. This splendid aircraft cruised at thirty m.p.h. faster than the Wapitis, had been refitted to carry two 250lb bombs under its lower wing but could not match the Wapiti for defensive armament. It had no machine guns but, rather understandably, it did have a radio, which was more comfortable for its operator than the open air unit carried by the Wapiti and, of course, there were no carrier pigeons, which we had to take out to sea with us in a wicker basket on the frequent occasions when our radios were unserviceable.

When we landed the DH 86 for the first time at Cochin our half-dozen splendid British NCO ground crews immediately dubbed it "The Monster". For the next two months, while Sheila was choosing a glittering trousseau of saris in the Lahore bazaars, I got to know the one hundred and fifty ground crews of my new command; most of them IORs, Indian Other Ranks, led by a formidable member of the old regular RAF, Warrant Officer "Screwy" Driver.

Later, in 1943, I got to know him well, in 194 Squadron, the Friendly Firm, a Dakota Squadron, which supported Brigadier Orde Wingate and his Chindits in Burma. Until Sheila joined me in Bombay from Lahore in May (accompanied by Duggie and Sonny), where she was to stay with Rashid and Tara Baig (Muslim Cavalry friends), I flew patrols and convoy escorts with Five Flight. But before 16th May our peaceful world was turned upside down by the Japanese Battle Fleet.

Before we could meet again to continue our marital programme, I feel I must outline the narrow escape that India (and Ceylon) experienced while Sheila was fingering the gold- and silver-brocaded borders of those beautiful saris in Lahore, and I was flying the Monster, 200 miles out into the Indian Ocean from the charming, yet utterly defenceless harbour of Cochin.

"Don't look now, Bill, but I think they have fired a broadside at us." This sentence, half light-hearted, half deadly serious, was spoken into his microphone by Flight Lieutenant Charles Gardner from the right hand, the second pilot's seat, of a Catalina flying boat, to his Captain, Flight Sergeant Bill Bradshaw. Charles Gardner had been an outside broadcaster for the

BBC before the war. He belonged to the well-known team of Richard Dimbleby and Freddie Grisewood; mad on flying, he had joined the RAF – I think just after the Battle of Britain. After his training, he had been posted to 240 Squadron of Coastal Command where he had hunted U-boats in the North Atlantic, often from Northern Ireland as far as thirty degrees west. His captain at this time was Bill Bradshaw, one of the most experienced flying boat Captains in 240 Squadron, itself one of the best known squadrons in Coastal Command. Their flying boat, *L for Leather*, was the so-called Bismarck boat, which in 1941 had searched for and found the most powerful battleship in the world, after a long search. The German pocket battle ship had, of course, disappeared into the Atlantic overcast, having sunk the *Hood* in the Denmark Strait and badly wounded the Prince of Wales.

Barely a week before, they had flown from a lake in Northern Ireland to Lake Kogala at the southern tip of Ceylon. The Admiralty had news from inside the fallen Singapore that the Japanese fleet had left that apparently invincible fortress on a north-westerly course, which could only mean one thing – India.

A minute later eight fourteen-inch shells plunged into the sea making an almighty splash and hurling them 500 feet into the air. But they and their flying boat were unscathed, as were Ceylon and India. Charles Gardner got off their sighting report, the course and speed of the enemy, to Admiral Drayton in Colombo, 350 miles astern; and so it reached the Admiralty and Winston Churchill; thus, in my opinion, it was *L for Leather* that saved India.

They had been on patrol, flying at fifty feet above the sea to avoid enemy radar when Charles Gardner to his amazement had seen, breaking the horizon, the outline of so many ships he could scarcely count them – four battleships, five aircraft carriers, with cruisers and destroyers to protect them.

L for Leather had been the third flying boat in 240 Squadron to leave Ceylon that morning. The first two did not come back. *L for Leather* retired but kept the enemy in sight all that day, 5th April 1942, (Easter Sunday). Towards evening they poked their heads around Cape Comerin and in the fading light made out the shape of a battleship, the *Nagato*; Bill recognised it from the outline in their copy of *Jane's Fighting Ships*. Its course was ominous – 280 degrees west – heading up the west coast of India where many allied ships were sheltering en route from Calcutta to Bombay. Just before dark Charles Gardner made out the *Nagato*. She was signalling to an invisible companion by Aldis lamp.

In the middle of the night I duly received a coded signal from my boss in Bombay, Wing Commander John Ker. "Take off due west at dawn – STOP – intercept Japanese battleship *Nagato*." Escorted by a Fleet Air Arm Fulmar Fighter flown by Lt Val Bailey RN, Derek Wood and I took off at dawn and flew as far as our fuel permitted, five hundred miles there and back. We found only the empty wastes of the Indian Ocean and retired with relief to our island base in the middle of Cochin harbour.

What about Sheila and the 16th May?

7

The Tide Turns

*"We've fought with many men acrost the seas
An' some of 'em was brave an' some was not..."*

                                        Rudyard Kipling

The one thing we certainly could not do was to use the Indian long-distance trunk telephone service to speak to each other across the 3,000 miles of petrified, hysterical India that separated us. All we could do was to wait and pray, which I think we both must have done together with Rudi von Leyden ("mein bester Freund") an exiled German who was to be our best man. He, of course, was in Bombay, almost exactly halfway between us.

The next stage in the impending battle between the Japanese fleet and the RAF was described by Squadron Leader Peacock-Edwards two years later on the deck of a British troop ship bound for England. Sheila and I looked down on the smooth waters of the Suez Canal. He gave us a blow-by-blow account of the part played in what was to be the most important battle of war in the East by his Hurricane Squadron, No 30. There were fifteen of them under his command. All fifteen had been flown off the aircraft carrier *Indomitable*, which was lying off Ceylon. Peacock-Edwards was given the rather confusing order to land on the Colombo Race Course.

"You can't miss it, it's quite close to the harbour."

It had been possible to give this order because the only airstrip in Ceylon, of which the Japs knew nothing, had been constructed a few days earlier by an enterprising Group Captain on the staff of Air Headquarters, Colombo. He must have had some fun, I imagine, in telling the English Chief Justice that he had better move out of his official residence as he, the RAF Group Captain, proposed to blow his official house up within twenty-four hours. It was sited within a few yards of the race course and, unfortunately for the Chief Justice, lay directly in the path of the prevailing wind and so of any theoretical fighter aircraft, which might find it necessary to land in the middle of the course. He did not bother to consult the stewards before ripping up the gleaming white railings of the race course to make way for his bulldozers.

About eleven a.m. on the morning of the same day, just as Charles Gardner in *L for Leather* had nearly been destroyed by the Japanese fleet, Peacock-Edwards and several of his pilots were lounging (probably on deckchairs) below the Grand Stand. The previous night they had concealed their aircraft under the trees, which sheltered the Paddock.

Suddenly his No 2 looked up and stared into the sky. He turned to his CO and asked him sharply, "Surely, sir, we haven't got that number of aircraft in Ceylon, have we?" Peacock-Edwards grabbed a pair of binoculars, which he turned on to a large number of aircraft flying in a stately formation at 5,000 feet above them. Peacock-Edwards counted them quickly as they wheeled to port in the direction of the harbour.

"Christ, they're Japs." There were fifty-seven of them, fighters (Zeros) and bombers (Oscars). Only one word was spoken, and that was by the CO. "Scramble!" Led by Peacock-Edwards, as he continued his story on the troop ship; "We got above them easily and it was rather like the Battle of Britain, though much easier." Peacock-Edwards crashed through the Jap formation, the first knowledge the Nips had of the Hurricane's presence. He shot two down in his dive, received a number of hits himself and force landed, wheels up, in a paddy field. His fourteen pilots had similar success. They shot down twenty-seven of them for the loss of nine Hurricanes. Winston Churchill wrote in the fourth volume of his memoirs of the Second World War, "It was the first time since Pearl Harbour that the Japs had tasted bone."

During the next ten days the Japanese fleet cruised off the coast of Ceylon and eastern India (never, thank heavens, the West Coast). They sank one British Aircraft carrier (the *Hermes*) and two cruisers, of which one was HMS *Cornwall*. The Jap fleet then divided itself up, one part steering north-east in the direction of Calcutta. What came next I could tell Peacock-

Edwards myself since it happened to one of my own Wapitis, flown by David Small, an ex-boxwallah of Pierce, Leslie & Co, appropriately enough of Cochin. Sheila, of course, had been in Lahore at the time and knew nothing of what had been going on in these far-off days. She listened with interest, leaning on the rails of the troop ship, somewhere near the Bitter Lakes. She was still wearing a sari.

8

Taking a Taxi into Battle

"In September 1914 General Joffre sent several thousand French soldiers in taxis from Paris to the front on the River Marne. They held the advancing Germans and saved Paris. The great capital of France never fell into the hands of the Germans throughout the First World War."

op. cit. Wilfrid Russell

The most spectacular operation carried out by the tired old Wapitis of 5 Flight sprang from another signal despatched in code from Bombay by Wing Commander John Ker. This one came on about 8th April ordering me to send an aircraft to the insignificant almost unknown port, halfway up the East Coast of India – Vizagapatam. It had been known to the Nizam of Hyderabad at the beginning of the nineteenth century. In April 1942, even its name was scarcely known to the Air Officer Commanding the RAF, in far-off New Delhi. I looked it up in our atlas and sent for Flight Lieutenant David Small. He took off at dawn next day with a young Indian pilot, called Barker. They flew 450 miles from Cochin to the other side of India. David took half a dozen five-gallon drums of aviation fuel, stuffed into the empty space near the rudder.

They had to land in a field – there was no airstrip. Before creeping into their sleeping bags that night they refuelled the Wapiti. At dawn the next morning they took off – David in the rear seat, Barker flying the aircraft. They took off into some pre-monsoon clouds and flew due east; thirty miles past the last buoy of the Swept Channel, David saw gunfire on the horizon,

26

then came upon an extraordinary sight – an aircraft carrier, a cruiser, and two destroyers (obviously Japanese) cruising in a circle around an unfortunate allied merchant ship, which they were pounding to pieces. David hid behind a handy cloud and did a pencil drawing (on the back of an envelope, of course) of the cruiser and the carrier. He then told his pilot to return to base (the empty field) where he jumped out on to the ground and by amazing luck was able to commandeer a passing taxi which took him into the minuscule harbour where he found the British Naval HQ (one room on the quayside) occupied by the XDO (extended defence officer) – a tall Ian-Fleming-type of four-ring Captain, who was surprised, to say the least, by David's news. "Thank you very much," he said, and picked up an antique public telephone, which, equally surprisingly, put him in touch with the Royal Navy Commodore in Calcutta. He, too, must have been surprised but he was equally helpless.

David, who had kept his taxi waiting on the quayside, returned to his companion in the field. They refuelled the Wapiti and returned to observe the one-sided operation. The merchantman had sunk. On the return flight to his field David had seen three Jap aircraft in formation, flying back to their base, the aircraft carrier. They were two thousand feet below him. They never saw him.

I put David Small up for an immediate DFC. He never got it. A week later he was a passenger in a Hudson, which crashed. He was killed together with all on board.

Suddenly, as quickly as it had arrived, the black cloud of doom which had enclosed Sheila and myself for a miserable week acquired a silver lining. John Ker sent me a third signal, in code. "Japanese fleet has returned to Singapore." I never found out how he knew but he was right. Rudi von Leyden was able to contact Sheila, 3,000 miles to the north, in Lahore. Our marital programme was set in motion once more.

9

All Saints, Malabar Hill

"Come live with me, and be my love
And we will some new pleasures prove…"

John Donne

On 14th April 1942, I had a fourth signal from John Ker. It was more than welcome. It was in clear and read: "THREE DAYS SPECIAL LEAVE GRANTED IN BOMBAY MAY 13th TO MAY 16th INCLUSIVE – STOP – ALSO ONE WEEK FOR HONEYMOON – STOP – CONGRATULATIONS."

The news was sent to Sheila and her family in Lahore, also, of course, to Rudi in Bombay. I was flown by one of my chaps in a Wapiti to Bombay. Sheila duly arrived in the Frontier Mail (the Bombay to Peshawar express) escorted by Duggie and Sonny. She was met by me, her fiancé; I was accompanied by Rashid and Tara Baig, her Bombay host and hostess; they were Muslims. The wedding, in All Saints Church, Malabar Hill, was like many others that had been celebrated in that tiny church except that the bridegroom was in Air Force uniform and the bride in a white silk sari, which looked from a distance quite like an English wedding dress.

John Tanner, the naval chaplain, took the marriage service. Duggie and Sonny were in uniform as were the ushers (pilots and navigators of my old Bombay Flight). They provided an archway of borrowed swords. Mendelssohn provided the music. The partners of Killick, Nixon & Co, with their wives, backed us up gallantly. They looked a little surprised and yet relieved at the familiar ceremony.

We had a cheerful reception at the Willingdon Club, the beautiful mixed country club established shortly after the First World War by that charming and far-sighted English aristocrat, Lord Willingdon, when he was Governor of Bombay.

We flew to Poona in a civil aircraft where an old Parsee contemporary of mine at Cambridge, JJ, (Sir Jamsetjee Jejeebhoy, Bart) had lent us his large upcountry bungalow for our first night. This minute and remarkable Parsee community, of which he was the head, was staunchly pro-British and staunchly Victorian. The drawing room of Fountain Hall was full of easels holding pictures of Queen Victoria, antimacassars galore and plenty of Monarchs of the Glen on the walls.

In the main bedroom, which was part and parcel of the drawing room there was an enormous and uncomfortable four-poster, complete with mosquito net. Sheila was a bit taken aback but with her usual calm took the unusual situation in her stride.

Next day we flew to Madras in a small single-engined three-seater Tata Air Lines Waco, stuffed to the roof with Sheila's trousseau. It was a change from the Wapitis. Our last leg was by train from Madras to Cochin on the other side of India, where we sank into a comfortable suite in the Malabar Hotel, our rooms overlooking the airfield to the east and the Indian Ocean to the west.

John Ker's gift of a whole week's honeymoon leave was spent at 3,000 feet in the Western Ghats (hills) among the cheerful, hospitable Scottish tea-planters of the Kanan Devan Hills Produce Co Ltd. It was very different to the turmoil of the first half of that momentous month of April 1942.

IO

The Naked Fakir

In 1940 when Hitler's hosts poured into France
With a few young Englishmen and many young Indians, too,
With a few clapped-out old Wapitis I flew
Through the gap in the palm trees,
Floating down to the tiny field we called Juhu

When a strange unlikely, happening took place—
It was India's poet, Sarojini Naidu,
Who took me to meet the leader of her race,
A wizened, half-naked little brown man
Sitting cross-legged beneath a bending coconut-bearing tree,
He was staring out to the Indian sea.
No bellowing, ranting Adolf Hitler he
But he truly wanted his India to be free.
"I know, dear boy, that England will be saved
As long as Mr Churchill guards the White Cliffs of Dover.

Do you know I once wore a Wig and a Bowler Hat?
And I will be your friend after
This war is over, even tho'
Your prisons here are no beds of clover.

For peace is in your country's soul
And mine, but not in Hitler's
Land beyond the Rhine.

So I will go on teaching satyagra
And you must teach our Indian boys to fly
And save the world for peace, up in the sky.
I thank you now, dear boy, "
He said with an understanding look and a tender sigh.

I I

South West Monsoon

*"Il pleut dans mon coeur
Comme il pleut sur la ville,
Quelle est cette langueur
Qui pénêtre mon coeur."*

Paul Verlaine

For the next four months I had to contend with an enemy very different from the Japanese – the south-west monsoon. The permanent dampness and humidity were made more uncomfortable by the fierce, heavy downfalls of rain. For Sheila it was an unexpected and uncomfortable change from the dry, invigorating climate of the hot summer months and cold winters of the Punjab, made even healthier by the glorious summer holidays in Kashmir. The people of the south were different too, slower and less energetic than the Punjabis; and so many of them suffered, poor people, with heavy swollen legs from that dreadful disease, elephantiasis.

Every morning I disappeared into my office – the airfield and the empty wastes of the Indian Ocean. I knew that Sheila missed her family badly. But she never complained and gradually moved into a new and unexpected family, the young Indian pilots and navigators whom she soon realised were as homesick as she was. They came from all parts of India, from Bengal and the United Provinces, from the Punjab and Assam. Soon she was able, tactfully and successfully, to mother them.

It was, I think, in July that Air Headquarters in Delhi signalled that Flight Lieutenant Charles Gardner would be reporting to me for a month's leave, while the famous Catalina Flying boat *L for Leather* was having an overhaul by the lake at Bangalore, two hundred miles west of Cochin. He would undertake to give a course of coastal reconnaissance navigation to our then less experienced air crews (compared to the regulars of the RAF). After a month with us he had formed a friendship with Sheila and myself that was to last for a lifetime. He got on so well with Sheila that in 1944, by which time he had become a Wing Commander in charge of all RAF Public Relations inside the Ministry of Information in London, he somehow or other wangled her into his office as his secretary. His incandescent humour was as good as her brother Sonny's. During that first visit I used to take Charles on patrols in the Indian Ocean in the *Monster*. It was then that he told me of the adventures of *L for Leather* in the days of the Japanese sorties from Singapore to Ceylon, also of his long patrols in the Atlantic with 240 Squadron. Sheila had found a stimulating companion who matched her for intelligence and humour and it was at this time that she took out her water-colour paint box and began to develop the hobby that was to engage her for the rest of her life.

Had we but known it our old Wapitis were nearing their end. Gradually they were falling apart; two of them disappeared on the same day into the monsoon. They took off into blinding rain and low cloud; that was the last we ever saw of them and their gallant Indian crews. A third, flown by an excellent young Indian Christian pilot called Sequeira, simply disappeared straight into the sea when he was practising machine gun firing through his propeller into a sea-borne target from about 500 feet.

I had to make one further short visit to John Ker in Bombay. So Derek Woods (my No 2) took over the Flight. Sheila was picked up, while I was away, by one of our tea-planter friends in the western ghats (hills) where the air was fresh and the monsoon spent.

When I reached Bombay, I was enjoying a gin and tonic with friends in the Bombay Gymkhana (a sports club). I was suddenly clapped on the back by a passing Wing Commander. Roger Falk (after the war, Sir Roger Falk) had just arrived from England where the Air Ministry had instructed him to make a rapid tour of India. He was to find a British officer with some knowledge of the country who would head up a public relations organisation at Air Headquarters in Delhi.

Roger lost no time in telling me, "Things are going to change, old boy; how would you like the job?" It was obvious he would have to take it on himself if I did not. Roger was yet another ex-Bombay boxwallah. He had owned and run a successful family advertising agency, D J Keymer & Sons and he was quite frank. "I'm in the Org (organisation) branch of my Group at home and I want to stay in it."

Over another round of g & ts he told me about the changes that were about to take place. They were drastic. Air Chief-Marshal Sir Richard Peirse, formerly Commander-in-Chief of Bomber Command in England, had arrived in India from Indonesia, just ahead of the Japs. He was to take over command of the RAF in India as well as of the single squadron, which was all that India possessed by way of an air force. Roger was evidently in his confidence.

"He plans to make the Indian Air Force a proper Air Force with ten squadrons and to re-equip them with Lysanders. Their Commanding Officers will be all the Indians who had been trained at Cranwell. Your Coast Defence Wing will no longer exist."

My value as a pilot aged thirty-one was on a par with the Wapitis. I could scarcely object. In addition Air Headquarters was situated in Delhi; Sheila would only be 250 miles from her home. Delhi was hot in the summer, but it was a dry heat.

"Yes, old boy," I said, "of course, I would like it, very much."

We had a third g & t to celebrate.

12

Gabardine Swine

"Long years of battle, bitterness and waste
Dry years of sun and dust and Eastern skies
Hard years of ceaseless struggle, endless haste
Fighting 'gainst greed for power and hate and lies."
                                    Field Marshal Lord Wavell

On the negative side of the first great change in our married life – the change
from Cochin to Delhi – was the fact that we had to move several times
before we could settle down into anything like a permanent home. I realised
only too well how disturbing this must be for Sheila. After several weeks of
moving from one temporary home to another, we eventually found a
comfortable flat, near Connaught Circus, next to the Imperial Hotel, also it
was conveniently close to my office. On the positive side were several
advantages, the first of which was the weather; the second, undoubtedly,
that her eldest brother, Reggie, and Reggie's wife, Phyllis, had a super flat
bang opposite Saftar Jang, the last and the finest of the Moghul tombs in
Delhi, although the experts grumbled that it already showed signs of
architectural decadence. Sonny – I shall always call him by this from now
on – was by now a Lieutenant Commander and was able to get ashore quite
often.

His flat was always full of people and laughter, lots of the latter. Sheila
had friends in Delhi, too. I think her closest was Hoochie, her Boston Bull
Terrier. We had not settled down for long before my boss, Ivor Jehu,
promoted overnight from being a Trooper in the Bombay Light Horse, to

being a Brigadier in the Indian Army – pre-war he had been editor of *The Times of India* in Bombay (after the *Statesman of Calcutta* the leading English language paper of India) – invited us to a tea party for the staff of the inter-services Public Relations Directorate, of which he was the director. He invited the Commander-in-Chief of the Indian Army to be the guest of honour; he asked Sheila to sit next to him. I had flown down to the front to get a feeling of the object of the exercise, PR, so I was not at the tea party.

Sir Archibald Wavell was one of the best generals England had in the Second World War. There was only one weakness as there was with the King – he was terribly shy and rarely opened his mouth on social occasion. His ADCs found this embarrassing.

Ivor Jehu told me this story when I got back from Calcutta. To everyone's surprise Sheila had opened the conversation. As his first cup of tea was being poured out by a bearer, General Wavell suddenly seemed to relax; he actually started talking and hardly stopped before the party broke up. I never asked her what she had talked about, but I think it must have been about that book, the collection of his favourite poems, *Other Men's Flowers*.

We had a copy, which had survived many journeys. Reluctant himself to show it to a publisher, it was Peter Fleming, brother of the creator of James Bond, who had pressed really hard to hand it to Jonathan Cape. The collection of so many utterly diverse poems had been an enormous success. Whether it was that or something else, he clearly enjoyed meeting the attractive young Indian in a white sari, whom he unexpectedly found sitting next to him; Ivor's tea party was evidently a great success.

The first job I was given by my RAF boss was almost as surprising. It was to draft his very first despatch to his own boss, Sir Archibald Sinclair, Secretary of State for Air. It took me a weekend and a good deal of archive research to complete. After he had read it he sent for me and pushed it across his desk. Firmly written in the margin in the brief staccato of men in important positions without time to spare, were the words, "Good – should be published."

Life for Sheila during that second summer of marriage might well have been dull had it not been for the proximity of her family and the fact that I only had to cycle about a mile from our flat every morning to Air Headquarters, which was on the ground floor of Lutyens' enormous pink and white sandstone building, rather than flying out to sea in an antique aeroplane to get to my work. And I came home for lunch, too.

Sheila made life-long friends with several of the Gulmarg fishing fleet who had been lucky enough to land a husband in wartime; and there were even dinner parties. I remember one at which I disgraced both my wife and myself. The hosts were her uncle and his rather orthodox Hindu wife. Ram Lall Sawhny, Chief Justice of Kashmir State, had a house in Delhi, not often used. The dinner, I suppose in deference to us, was "European style". I used to find that "flying a desk" in those days was more tiring than flying a Wapiti. I had been seated on the right-hand side of our hostess, Sheila's aunt. I failed to keep my eyes open and my head fell with a crash into my soup.

Most of my work was guiding the half dozen well-known Fleet Street war correspondents round the senior RAF officers whom they wished to interview, plus an occasional flight to the front. Bob Cooper of *The Times* was, I thought, by far the best of them. We often played tennis on the well-kept grass courts of the Delhi Gymkhana. Charles Gardner had given up flying, too, and had joined my staff in Delhi as a highly professional number 2. Sheila used to take him for afternoon walks round Old Delhi showing him the well-known relics of the Moghul Empire, Humayun's tomb, the Red Fort, Saftar Jang and the ridge of Mutiny days.

They used to take Sheila's Hoochie with them. Once in the hot weather of 1943, the dog almost died of heat stroke. Charles, with considerable presence of mind, collected some jugs of water from a villager, which Sheila flung over his prostrate little body. She saved him that time only to lose him soon afterwards to a couple of dog-loving BORs (British Other Ranks).

In the doldrums of this pause between one world not yet dead and a new one waiting to be born, a few incidents stand out in the flat round of Delhi life.

Our Saturday afternoon football matches provided relief and exercise. Charles McNeill, the C in C's Doctor, played inside right to my outside right; we fancied ourselves no end. Charles had played a lot somewhere; I hadn't played since my prep school. Peter Fleming was a roving left-centre-half-back. His large black boots looked better suited to the Koko Nor than to Willingdon Crescent football ground. I wore tennis shoes, so kept out of his radius of action.

Charles scored most of our goals, but we nearly always lost: once we had to recruit some bare-foot Delhi urchins to make up for absentees. They were wildly enthusiastic and refused to stop playing when the last whistle blew. It was the time of the bombing of Rome. The referee blew his whistle without result.

"It's rather like telling the Italians they have lost the war," said Peter Fleming.

13

"Thank God"

*"Surely there was a time I might have too
The sunlit heights and from life's dissonance
Struck one clear chord to reach the ears of God."*

Jerry Speer

By the middle of June, the southwest Monsoon had reached Delhi from Cochin and had hit us so hard, together with northeast and eastern India, that the Japanese Army, which was looking greedily into Assam, stayed on the Indo-Burma frontier for four whole months; the truly astonishing thing was, that even in October when the rains stopped, they failed to take advantage of the dry weather and sat on their backsides for a further six months — a delay that was not unlike Hitler's three-day halt order to Guderian's tanks, when they were on the outskirts of Dunkirk in May 1940. It resulted for the Japs, short-term, in their failure to invade India and, long-term, in their losing the war. During this remarkable interval, Air Chief Marshal Sir Richard Peirse's brilliant second-in-command, Air Marshal Sir Conrad Collier, assisted by an equally brilliant staff, which included another Bombay ex-boxwallah, Reay Geddes, were able to build several hundred modern airfields all over India. Each one had runways 2,000 yards long, buildings for 75 Officers and 1,000 men and aircraft pens capable of sheltering the growing number of up-to-date aircraft, which poured into India from England and the Middle East during these vitally important, peaceful months. And the RAF flew all through the monsoon. The Japs did not.

One evening Sheila and I were having a drink with Sonny in his lovely flat. I asked him casually why he thought the Japs were so obviously losing this wonderful opportunity. He thought for a moment then said, "They've probably gone back to Rangoon in the bad weather to play darts and drink Saki."

In this rather dreary period of the war, when Delhi seemed to be more than usually exhausting and dull, one thing did seem to provide us with a cheerful background: this was Sheila's family. She took several opportunities to stay with her mother in Lahore – her favourite town in all India – and although Sonny who, despite being a sailor, seemed to spend much of his time in Delhi, it was her second eldest brother, Duggie, of whom she saw the most. He was her favourite. There was, in fact, a closer bond between them than I had ever seen in any brother and sister I had ever known.

Duggie had inherited his father's charm, also his good taste in clothes. There was always, of course, the attraction of a uniform, especially if it carried the cavalry insignia on the tunic, but he also had the gift, which I think he must have inherited from his father, of looking smarter in civilian clothes than most Englishmen. He had a natural love of horses, which the 16th Cavalry did more than simply encourage. Where his skill at polo came from I do not know. He was certainly not a natural ball player, yet he soon achieved a handicap of four at polo. It was the same case with golf. He might have been born with a miniature golf bag in his hands. For many years he played down to a handicap of five. Like his sister, he was extremely good-looking; and like her, possibly, his greatest asset was his strength of character. At the end of the war, leading the 16th Light Cavalry in Burma – it was by then armoured – he moved on to command the Deccan Horse, one of the best known Indian Regiments in the 14th Army.

Sonny was quite different; he exuded the personality and theatrical skills of a professional humorist. He could imitate the cockney accent of George Robey and Indian babu-speak far better than Peter Sellars. He had a natural, even a devoted audience wherever he went. His circle of friends and acquaintances was enormous and included Lord Louis Mountbatten. He was a perpetual worry to his parents for he was always getting into scrapes; so much so that they despatched him to England after he left school for a year's apprenticeship with Vickers-Armstrong at Brooklands in England;

there he acquired a passion for cars and motor bikes. He returned to India aged nineteen; and was met by his mother and Sheila at Bombay. He carried a bulldog puppy under his arm, which I have already mentioned.

At the risk of embarrassing readers I can't resist telling one of his most successful stories, to appreciate which, it is necessary to understand babu-English, the vernacular of the Bengali clerks of Calcutta. It is, in fact, the Franglo of the under-educated Indian who wants to communicate, mainly with his English employers, couched in the exaggerated accent of the Welsh.

"There were these two Bengali babus strolling together on a platform at Howrah station, the Paddington of Calcutta. They were passed, going the other way, by a particularly luscious Anglo-Indian girl. Babu A says to Babu B, "I say, man, what a bee-utiful girl"; Babu B turns round and is stunned by the girl's good looks. He says, "I say, man, you are right. She is making water in my mouth.""

Then all of a sudden, our backwater was stirred by an inrush of fresh water. The tide had turned at last. It was mid-June 1943. Our Reuter's machine clacked away. It announced that we were to have a new Command. South East Asia Command was to be formed; its Supreme Commander would be Admiral Lord Louis Mountbatten. Sir Archibald Wavell would be promoted to Viceroy, General Auchinleck would become Commander-in-Chief of the Indian Army.

I tore off the piece of buff paper from the ticker machine and tried to think out quickly what it meant. Looking back, I think I did know. I realised that somebody at last meant business in this part of the world; that we would be getting modern aircraft, masses of landing craft and aggressive planners; that we would cease to be "the forgotten front".

I went upstairs to Collier's office to show him the message.

"Thank God," he said.

A week later, at Palam Airport, the new leader stepped smartly down the ladder backwards from the belly of Marco Polo, his Liberator – which takes some doing on such an occasion when the whole of the western world is looking on. His smile was one of the most exhilarating things I have seen.

The next evening my boss, Ivor Jehu, gave a small intimate cocktail party for him on the lawn of his bungalow to meet a dozen of the American war correspondents. We had, with difficulty, scrounged some bottles of Scotch.

I made a rum cocktail, which I'm glad to say, the Supremo seemed to like.

As he said goodbye to Ivor Jehu and myself, Preston Grover of the *New York Times* admitted grudgingly, "Well, he certainly is a Somebody."

14

Tour Expired

"There's a magic in the distance,
Where the sea-line meets the sky..."
                        Alfred Noyes

I came out of all this whirlwind of change with a new boss – Air Marshal Joubert de la Ferte. He had once been in charge of Coastal Command, so there was no difficulty in prising Charles Gardner out of his desk job at AHQ Colombo. I had to leave Sheila again, this time for a longish trip to England in search of additional officers for my team; a trip which took me to Algiers and the Italian front.

When I returned to India, Sheila showed me some of her first watercolour sketches. They were mostly of Kashmir and were, of course, the work of a beginner who was painting from memory. I am no art critic, but they did seem to me to possess both taste and promise. Sitting as I am now, sixty years later, in the kitchen of our house in North Cornwall overlooking the Camel Estuary, my eyes are drawn to a particularly striking still life of flowers in a white vase, flowers from our garden. It shows the ground she had covered since those wartime days in New Delhi. It is a large picture, beautifully framed by Henry Grattan in limed wood.

Soon after my return to India there were other trips that involved leaving her. Wingate's trips into Burma deserved and received immense publicity. On the second operation in 1944, which landed a whole division of troops and mules 200 miles behind the Japanese lines, I was able to fly as a gabardine passenger with a pre-war friend, Alec Pearson, who commanded 194

Squadron, known to the army as "The Friendly Firm", one of the best known of the Dakota squadrons which were then supplying the Chindits by air. Alec usually took his bull terrier, Sue, with him in the Navigator's seat (she had sixty hours of operational flying in her own logbook). Fatty – his nickname – also kept Rupert, the squadron bear, who was kept tied up to a tree in the middle of the open space in front of the officers' mess tent at Argartala.

When I returned from London to Delhi for the last time, after a series of flights with Fatty, it was time to start thinking of home. In RAF terms, I was "tour expired" or, if you prefer, "on the boat". My four years with the RAF were up in May 1944.

Would England, that distant country Sheila had never seen, extend to her, as well as to me, a welcoming hand?

15

A Troopship was Leaving Bombay

> "There is no promotion this side of the ocean
> For the long and the short and the tall
> And soon they'll be home – bless 'em all."
> > Traditional Song of the RAF Sergeants' Messes
> > in India in the 1920s

A long time ago, there used to be a haunting song, property of the Sergeants' Messes of the old regular RAF in India, which bore this title. It was charged with all the longing for home so many felt towards the end of their overseas tours. It was as haunting a melody as "Lillie Marlene" had been with their Luftwaffe opposite numbers in the Western desert.

For Sheila and for me, the troopship was uncomfortable and there was little sentiment. Wartime conditions meant overcrowded cabins and married couples were separated. I had a reasonable billet – six officers squashed into a four-berther. Sheila was going to a new life in a new country, she shared a six-berth cabin with five other women, all of the Memsahib variety. I was too exercised about her even to notice that she was already wearing western clothes. We sailed in an enormous convoy, escorted by half a dozen destroyers; once we reached the Mediterranean there was always the odd chance of a U-Boat attack, but we were lucky, for even in the Atlantic we never saw one. We knew nobody among the passengers and conditions were not favourable for socialising. There were many children.

Sheila, as usual, was calm and understanding. We took three weeks to reach Liverpool. It was June yet the closer we got to England the worse the weather. We arrived at Liverpool on 5th June 1944, in the middle of the storm that caused General Eisenhower to postpone the D-Day landings by twenty-four hours.

We were bundled out of our overcrowded carriage in the troop train at a London station I had never heard of – Addison Road. The first thing Sheila saw on arrival in England was a tiny rooftop-skimming aircraft which was flying fast at 500 feet above the platform, making a strange, throbbing noise which seemed to come out of a tube where the rudder should have been. Suddenly its engine stopped and everyone – except Sheila and me – flung themselves head-first on to the station platform. There was a loud explosion as the buzz bomb hit a row of houses in South Kensington.

Sheila found London a strange place – "All those little houses stuck together and they are so small". My mother's house in Belgravia certainly answered to this description, also the flat in George Street, off Baker Street, which Roger Falk had discovered for us. The bath was under the kitchen table. The table part folded up against the wall, when you wanted a bath.

And then there was my mother who came from an old-fashioned Winchester ecclesiastical family; her father was a Canon of St Paul's Cathedral. She was a widow, my father having died of cancer when he was fifty-one. She tried hard, and so did Sheila, to understand each other but it never worked. On the other hand there was my mother's sister, Auntie Sophie, also a widow – her husband had been the organist of St Paul's Cathedral and a great player of Bach in his time. She had lived for several years with her sister in Lower Belgrave Street and she immediately took Sheila to her bosom. Her son, Alasdair, my first cousin and boyhood friend, was one of the outstanding intellects of his day. A fellow of Trinity, Cambridge, at twenty-five he had been offered the Chair of Theology, at McGill University in Canada. Alasdair and Duggie, much later, were the only members of the family to achieve an obituary in *The Times*. My brother, Dorrien, was killed on 23rd October 1942, the first day of the battle of El Alamein. Alasdair was due to sail to Montreal on 3rd September 1939. At once he tore up his ticket and joined the RAF as a Navigator. He was shot down and killed in a Blenheim over Holland on his first operation.

My problem as well as Sheila's was quite simply: where would the RAF post me and to what kind of a job? For instance to become Adjutant of a squadron in, say, Inverness would be hopeless. Happily the personnel officer in the Air Ministry, who went through my file, happened to notice that I had read modern languages at Cambridge and had spent six months in my gap year at Munich University. "Go and see this officer in Norfolk House, in St James Square. His name is McDonald, Group Captain DMT. He might want to use you."

Within an hour I had met "Mac" McDonald who in time was to become another family friend. He was frank with me. He had been given forty-eight hours notice to form a school in London, the object of which would be to lay on courses of a fortnight's duration each to instruct 200 RAF officers at a time, as much German history and psychology as he could in order effectively to disarm the Luftwaffe whenever the defeat of Germany should take place. It was expected within months. He looked me in the face: "I know nothing about Germany," he said. "I've been given a block of flats just north of Regents Park to house these chaps. I can lay my hands on a dozen officers and NCOs who will help me but I need a Chief Instructor who knows about Germany. Would you take it on?"

I thought for a couple of minutes and then said, "Yes, sir, I certainly would but my wife is Indian and has never been to England before; we have only just landed."

The Group Captain interrupted me. He said, "You can have a week's leave while I get Viceroy Court up and running, then you must get hold of the best German scholars you can find in the country to lecture to these types. Can you do it?"

I had no hesitation in saying yes. Viceroy Court was ten minutes from George Street in a 74 bus.

I had spotted a Pet Shop in Baker Street and had bought a Pekinese puppy for Sheila, the first of our dynasty of Pekes. Sheila seemed delighted.

Then Roger Falk had said, "You must see Skye and the Coughlins. There's a wonderful hotel at the Kyle of Lochalsh. I'll book you in." So we took "Pekie" to Skye and for four wonderful days he chased sheep in the heather and we drank in the Highland air and quite a lot of Scotch whisky.

Then it was the turn of the number 74 bus and the search for German scholars. My first, I'm happy to say, was Harold Nicolson.

Suddenly Sheila was happy in her new country.

16

"Deutschland, Deutschland über Alles"

"Deutschland, über Alles"

German National Anthem

For the next thirteen months I lived, breathed and dreamt Germany, past, present and to come. Charles Gardner came once more into our lives; Sheila found being his secretary both stimulating and rewarding. She was earning money and there was Pekie to come back to when I was late home from the office. We had only one excitement, in September; one of the first V2s landed 100 yards from the flat. All the windows were blown in and the nearby pub on the corner of Baker Street simply disappeared, leaving behind a large hole. By this time Sheila had mastered rationing with all of its bumph.

One unexpected reward for Sheila was meeting her old girlfriend, Babli Gupta (now Babli Bhagat), who turned up at a drinks party which Group Captain MacDonald threw at Viceroy Court. She was the guest of a British Naval Officer and looked smashing in a blue and white uniform-like sari. She had become a WRIN (Women's Royal Indian Navy).

All this time Gilbert, my youngest brother, was a lieutenant in the Cheshire Regiment, fighting a punishing war in Malta.

Christmas 1944 came and went during the German offensive of the Ardennes; then, at last, in early May, the German Army collapsed in front of General Montgomery. Both Sheila and I (and Pekie) joined the crowd in front of Buckingham Palace where (with about half a million others) we cheered the King and Queen with Winston Churchill; all three were standing on the palace balcony.

For a few months in distant Norway, by differing methods devoted to disarmament than those used for disarming Saddam Hussein in 2003, I blew up umpteen JU88s and ME110s (plus a dozen or so one-man submarines) in a matter of minutes. Prince Olaf of Norway watched with interest and gratitude. A good-looking young Norwegian girl in national costume actually pressed the trigger.

17

Semi-Portly

"I have thrown away my de-mob suit..."

Alan Whicker

There were many perks attached to disarming the German Air Force. The most rewarding for me was the fact that my small part in it took place in that most beautiful of countries, Norway. Appropriately enough, considering Norway was the first European country to be invaded by Germany in April 1940; it was also the last to be cleansed of the Luftwaffe and the Wehrmacht, in the summer of 1945. I had the good fortune, having served my time with Group Captain MacDonald, to close down Viceroy Court in May of that year. I then saw the back of our last course of pupils and commanded three hundred-odd British experts on the Luftwaffe, who flew with me to the recently German owned complex of airfields at Stavanger on the west coast of Norway. Other perks were the many delightful Norwegian friends we made who were understandably happy to see us.

And then there was also the powerful and comfortable Luftwaffe Air Sea rescue launch complete with an obedient German crew. It was, in fact, its German radio operator who brought us the news of the Japanese surrender, while we were cruising up one of the steepest, deepest and most impressive fjords in the neighbourhood of Stavanger, glasses of Löwenbráu beer in our hands. A day or so later I flew from Oslo to Lowestoft in a Sunderland flying boat on my last flight in RAF uniform. I was on my way to Uxbridge and demobilisation. My de-mob number was 20, my size "semi-portly".

On that last flight I carried a five-pound salmon (smoked) back to London for Sheila. She had deserved much more.

18

"Ask Killicks about the Pomelos"

"If music be the food of love, play on."

Wm Shakespeare

By now, in mid-September 1945, Sheila had been on her own in London for four months. We had given up Roger Falk's flat in George Street and an RAF couple who lived in De Vere Gardens, near the Prince Albert memorial, kindly took her in. She still had her job and her Pekinese, also my mother and Aunt Sophie to whom, as I have already mentioned, she had become increasingly attached. By the time I emerged from Uxbridge, in my semi-portly dark suit, she had found a flat in the Kings Road where we stayed for two and a half months, waiting for the RAF to find us a berth back to Bombay. Killicks had been quite magnificent to the four or five of us Assistants whom they had allowed to join up at the outbreak of war. They paid our salaries for five years (including annual increases) and took us back when the Japs surrendered. Luckily we all survived intact.

It was during this brief space of about two months that, again by chance, Sheila and I were to hear some of the most delightful English dance music that has, in my view, ever been available to Londoners' ears. Sheila, as I have already mentioned, was not particularly interested in jazz, but the music to which we did listen on one enchanted evening was most definitely not like the jazz most of my contemporaries at school had played. I always had a penchant for the English type of jazz; in fact at Marlborough we formed a five-piece group which was not really approved of by Dr Ivemy, the school organist. I played the drums and doubled on the trombone. We had a good pianist, an indifferent tenor sax and a mellow kind of trumpet.

At Cambridge I played during one May week in the Footlights dance band. I remember playing on the stage of the New Theatre, while an Indian Prince, Jig Singh, danced an enormously energetic jazz solo, which confused me at the time since it did not seem right that the heir to an important Indian State should indulge in such disreputable antics.

Then in the autumn of 1945, an old chum from the German Air Force Disarmament School, Joe Radcliffe, got in touch with me and asked if Sheila and I would like to dine with him at the Savoy and listen to the Savoy Orpheans' Dance Band led at the piano by Carol Gibbons himself. I explained to Sheila where this remarkable dance band stood in the English dance band canon. Sheila said, "Yes, why not," and she wore her white sari. There were the three of us and there was no question of dancing.

For me the soft rhythmic dance music and the tuneful tones of the dozen or so tenor saxophones, bass sax, single clarinet and the gentle drums and even gentler bass section, all conducted by the immaculate Carol Gibbons playing a Steinway grand piano, was the best thing going on in the music world, almost as moving as *Figaro* at Glyndebourne.

Sheila, rather to my surprise, was moved by the music. Joe Radcliffe, who knew Carol Gibbons personally, had managed to book a table near the rostrum, where the Orpheans were playing and when their thirty minutes rest-time came along, Joe asked Carol Gibbons to join us at our table for a few minutes. He and Sheila got on immediately, so much so that for some reason or other, he told her that he was a practising Roman Catholic. Then he had to return to his Steinway when he played one of Noel Coward's current melodies and that beautifully soft rhythmic music came floating around our table like a magic mist. Sheila often used to ask me if we could somehow get a 45 r.p.m. record but I was never able to get one.

When Sheila and I went to the Mayfair, I would slip away to Ambrose's Band and listen to Max Bacon, the best drummer in England. Once, to my eternal shame, I asked Ambrose to play "Fish gotta swim and birds gotta fly, I gotta love one man til I die; can't help, lovin' dat man o' mine", in which I anticipated the modern craze for Karaoke. As usual Sheila did not turn a hair.

It was just before she and I returned to Bombay, in December 1945, with no idea where we could live and start a family, that, by another of those extraordinary chances, we came in touch with the name of Bates. When Mr Killick and Mr Nixon started their business in 1856, as importers of textiles from Lancashire to Bombay (piece goods as they were known), they were agents for an old Liverpool banking house, then Edward Bates and Sons, whose piece goods trade with Bombay flourished until the turn of the century, when it started to languish. In the intervening ninety-odd years, they had become the largest shareholders in and managers of a Liverpool shipping company called Cunard. They had then become a leading English shipping company, largely by carrying emigrants from Europe to America. But the Bates family always kept up their old connections with Killicks; and every Christmas the shipping department was instructed by the partner in charge to send Edward Bates & Sons a basket of Pomelos.

On our return to Bombay in December 1945, I was posted by the partners to the shipping department (we were agents in Bombay for other lines, including Ellermans).

A few days before we sailed for Bombay in a Polish ship (both of us this time in the same two berth cabin) Dick Lowndes, the shipping partner, asked me to go with him to Liverpool to pay our respects to Sir Percy Bates, then Chairman of Cunard.

Our appointment with Sir Percy was for three p.m. in his office in the Liver Building. When we reported to his secretary, she told us that Sir Percy had sent his apologies. He would be ten minutes late but would we go into his office – he had left a message on his desk. The message, actually it was to his secretary, was scrawled in huge handwriting on an impressive blotting pad. It read "Remind Killicks about the Pomelos".

As we went down in the lift, I asked my boss what a Pomelo was. Dick Lowndes said, "Except for the war years we've been sending them to Liverpool every year since 1856, but I'm not quite sure myself. I think it's like a gigantic grapefruit."

It was.

19

Bates Hill

"The hunter is home from the hill"

English Country Song

On the way back to London, in the train, Dick Lowndes said to me casually, "Have you any idea where you and your wife are going to live in Bombay, when you get back?"

I replied, "I've no idea. It was never a problem during the war, I expect we'll find somewhere."

He thought for a moment, then he said, "Have you ever heard of Bates Hill?"

"Yes, I have. Wasn't it built by Edward Bates & Sons, somewhere outside Bombay, Pali Hill, was it?"

Dick Lowndes then told me how the Bates family, at the height of their activities in Bombay, about the turn of the century, had sent several young members of their firm from Liverpool to Bombay and had built what sounded like an imposing Edwardian bungalow for their Assistants to live in. Before the First World War, England stopped exporting cotton piece goods from Liverpool to India, since the Bombay merchants had begun to build their own textile mills based on high quality Indian cotton. We had our own very prosperous Kohinoor Mill in Bombay.

Dick Lowndes went on, "We looked after Bates Hill (also the Pomelos) and during this Second World War we wondered what should be done with it. We decided, when we knew that you and the rest who had been fighting were coming back, that we would try to produce a home for at least two of you as soon as you got back — as a place to live in; that is, if you and Sheila like it. There's a marvellous view over the sea and we've divided the house into two fairly spacious flats on the ground and first floors. There's a nice garden too, which we have kept up. Would you like to have a look at it? You'll be getting a car anyway, I expect. The house is on top of Pali Hill, about ten miles north of Bombay."

I remembered Pali Hill well; it was only two miles south of Juhu airfield where I had flogged the old Wapitis in 1940 and 1941. I was touched, too, that he had called Sheila by her first name.

"It sounds marvellous. I know Sheila would love it," I said, "especially if there is a garden; could we see it?"

"Of course; you may have to stay at the Taj (Bombay's best hotel)) for a bit while Sheila gets it furnished. Ken and Olenka Milne will probably have the ground floor flat." (Olenka and her mother had made their way on foot through difficulties and dangers from Poland to Bombay during the war.)

Sheila and I were booked on a Polish ship for our return to Bombay. We made friends on board with Bobby Rumbold, a close friend of Sonny's, and his beautiful wife, Pam. His uncle, Sir Horace Rumbold, had been the British Ambassador in Berlin in Hitler's early days as German Chancellor.

Sheila could not have been happier at the thought of Bates Hill. Her mother, Duggie and Sonny were at Ballard Pier to meet us. Sheila had left Pekie behind in kennels until an Ellerman ship, for whose owners we were agents, would bring him safely to his mistress, in about three weeks time.

20

Love's Labour's Lost

> "Then for the place; where, I mean, I did encounter that
> obscene and most preposterous event, that draweth from
> my snow-white pen the ebon-coloured ink, which here thou
> viewest, beholdest, surveyest, or seest,
> But to the place where, — it standeth north-northeast and
> by east from the west corner of thy curious-knotted garden:
> there did I see that low-spirited swain, that base minnow
> of thy mirth…"
>
> *Wm Shakespeare*

Before we could move into Bates Hill we spent several months with an old friend, Sir John Greaves, who had earned himself a well-deserved knighthood controlling cotton textile movements for the Government of India during the war. He had an extremely comfortable air-conditioned house on Cumballa Hill, which rejoiced in the name of Sethna Cottage. I never saw a Mr Sethna anywhere and it was certainly no cottage.

Sheila and I had never talked about children. During the war it was clearly impractical. The whole business never crossed our minds, not even from the racial point of view. And then, inevitably, she was pregnant. In due course the baby was due to appear. The only hospital available for Europeans was an East India Company kind of place, which looked awful and was awful. All the other hospitals in Bombay were Indian and they were worse than awful. No Indians, of course, no matter how westernised, were admitted into St Georges.

The doctor we chose was recommended by Rudi von Leyden, my best friend, (der beste Freund), who had also been our Best Man. He recommended a recently arrived German doctor who was building up a successful practice among the rich Indian merchants of whom there were many at the end of the war. He was smooth and rather too well dressed, I thought, for a doctor. Neither Rudi nor I knew anything about doctors. Neither of us thought to ask him if he was in anyway a gynaecologist. I don't think either of us knew what the word meant.

My mother-in-law, dear Amy Sawhny, came down to Bombay from distant Lahore. Jack Greaves welcomed her into the air-conditioned cottage. The day came when Sheila's waters broke – I think that was the technical word announcing that she was under starters orders. We drove to the John Company Hospital and Sheila, obviously in pain, was put in a bed in a ward. I suppose it was a maternity ward. There was nobody else in it. The Herr Doktor So & So came in a shiny Mercedes. He had a gold watch in his waistcoat and was full of charm. No, there was nothing for us to worry about. We could go home and he would simply telephone.

My mother-in-law, dear Amy, said firmly she would stop in the hospital. "I'll sleep on the floor if necessary." I went back to Sethna Cottage; in those days husbands did not stay with their wives during childbirth.

Sheila raised a brave smile and I kissed her goodnight.

The next morning I returned to St Georges and was met by Amy Sawhny looking as miserable as the hospital.

"I'm afraid he's not breathing."

Rudi came with me – he drove his own car with the tiny coffin to a place in the poorer districts of Bombay, called Sewree. It was the cemetery for Europeans; Hindus were always burnt on a holy pyre. It was the worst car drive of my life. It turned out that the Herr Doktor had no experience of gynaecology. I think this is the place to record that in less than a year's time a Liverpool cotton broker, Chang Bramble, who had been a choir-boy at St Paul's Cathedral under the baton of my uncle, the organist, Dr Charles MacPherson, husband of Sheila's Aunt Sophie, would say to me, "There's an awful vacuum here, you know; Europeans simply haven't got a hospital and St George's will be abolished when independence comes. There is a European Hospital Trust Fund and we have collected about a quarter of a million pounds towards building a modern hospital especially for Europeans – Indians will be encouraged to use it, if they wish. Would you care to join our Committee?"

I said, "Of course."

Several years later the Breach Candy Hospital – fifty-five beds, air-conditioned, resident doctor, surgery, operating theatre, pharmaceutical department and dispensary – was finished. It was right on the sea front, below Malabar Hill. I was its first chairman and Sheila built a splendid little circular garden looking out over the Indian Ocean, with a sundial in the middle.

Robin was born there in 1954.

21

A New Land is Born

"Jahna, Ghanne, Mana"

India's National Anthem (1947)

It was to be a fateful year. 1947 was indeed a fateful year for India and for my firm, Killick Nixon and Company. Winston Churchill's title for the fourth volume of his memoirs of the Second World War – *The Hinge of Fate* – would be more appropriate. In this year Pakistan was born, India gained her Independence and the private partnership of Killick Nixon and Company became a public limited company, registered as Killick Industries Ltd. Many Indians (and not a few Pakistanis) bought the hundred-rupee shares, the issue price of which was a hundred and thirty rupees. The partners acted with their customary generosity (as I have already mentioned they paid all the Assistants who went to the war our full salaries, for five years), and gave us all free shares according to the number of years we had worked for them, also our jobs, if we wanted them.

Sheila and I moved into Bates Hill and Pekie duly turned up in the captain's cabin of an Ellerman boat. I think it was the *City of Venice*. Sheila was busy furnishing the top flat of the Edwardian house on Pali Hill, which overlooked the Indian Ocean. She had inherited her mother's skills and taste in creating drawing rooms and dining rooms, which could rank with anything that Surrey, Wiltshire or Kent could boast of. Then there was the garden with its cannas and salvias, frangipani and banana trees growing out of carpets of smooth green lawns, also the blood red bougainvillaea creepers, all of which took up much of her time. I went in our launch to the middle of

Bombay's beautiful harbour where the *City of Venice* was anchored, to collect Pekie. He showed little interest, either in me or in Bombay; but when we arrived at the front steps of Bates Hill there was the mother of all reunions.

Killicks had a quarter share with three large Indian firms in the ownership and management of one of India's largest industrial companies – the Associated Cement Companies Ltd. Each of the four partners had to produce one managing director. Since the ACC (as it was known) owned fourteen cement factories sited all over pre-Partition India from Peshawar in the north to Coimbatore near Cape Comorin in the south, it took four of us all our time to manage them. To my genuine surprise our partners sent me to its head office, Cement House on Queen's Road, as their Managing Director – my first peace-time job. No marks for guessing which Queen.

One of the first tasks I was set was to travel hundreds of miles on India's (and Pakistan's) railway networks to see how they could be unclogged so that the hundreds of thousands of tons of ACC cement could move faster than they did. The war had choked up the lines for the last five years.

During this work I soon came to realise how close to a civil war between Hindus and Muslims the country had come – and this included our own factories where most of the engineers, chemists and administrators were Hindus while the unskilled workers were mainly Muslims. I told the Killick partners of my fears and they sent me with a senior assistant, Terry Harrison, to London for the last half of July and the first half of August, to tell the tale to the most senior of partners, already retired (as all good Nabobs did) to England, Home and Glory. But this meant leaving Sheila alone once more. As ever, her mother came down from Lahore to live at Bates Hill. For Terry Harrison and myself it was an exhilarating time in London, which included meeting the Secretary of State for India, a talk on the BBC after the nine o'clock news, and sleeping in my old bedroom in my mother's little Georgian house in Lower Belgrave Street.

Back in India the best happening of all was the appointment of Lord Louis Mountbatten, by Mr Atlee's Government, as the last Viceroy of India. As a brilliant, dashing English sailor, Lord Louis Mountbatten replaced Lord Wavell in March and shook both the main Indian political parties, the Congress and the Muslim League, to their foundations by advancing the planned date of Independence from 15th August 1948 to 15th August 1947.

And before all that there was the Asian Relations Conference in Delhi, an overwhelming jamboree of most of the already independent Asian countries under the auspices of Pandit Jawaharlal Nehru, then already Prime Minister of India, assisted by Mahatma Gandhi, its Patron Saint. The Royal Institute of International Affairs (Chatham House) of which I had been a member since Cambridge days asked me to join Professor Mansergh as one of their two Observers of the Conference. Obviously and understandably they wanted to take advantage of my presence in India to save them the cost of a return airfare from London to Delhi. This book is supposed to be about Sheila and not about Indian politics but I can't help telling one story about this colourful gathering because, at least for me, it was hysterically funny. It also provided a moment of peace which we both needed badly before the horrors and the turmoil, which were to follow in less than six months time.

The Conference opened with a flourish in an enormous tent erected in front of the Purana Quila, one of Delhi's most ancient and most lovely ruins. Mrs Sarojini Naidu, the famous Indian poetess and leading Congress politician, who mothered the Mahatma on his frequent visits to British gaols, wound up the Conference with an oratorical flourish.

"The long night of India's darkness is coming to a close. We are fatalistic; we believed it was destined that we should be dependent, that we should be exploited, that we should be dominated. Alas! Alas! Alas! That period was ours, but no longer, my fellow Asians. My comrades and my kinsmen arise; remember our night of darkness is over; together men and women, let us march forward to the dawn."

My only contact with Tibet until then took place at this Conference. After Pandit Nehru's equally melodramatic overture was finished the delegates broke up into small study groups, which were held in a recently constructed Government building, "Constitution House". It was during the economic discussions in a small and crowded committee room in this rather dismal building that I made my first delightful contact with the delegation from Tibet. In its way this was quite an occasion, since apart from taking place in a crowded committee room, at a moment when Pandit Nehru himself was intervening and all ears were respectfully bent on hearing his views, it was, I believe, the first time any member of the dignified Tibetan team had gone so far as to speak to anybody outside their delegation. This is not to imply that they had been in any way stand-offish; far from it, they had indeed been signing their autographs from the first day more diligently than Sir Donald Bradman could have done and their smiling progress in Tibetan costume through the milling crowds lent an air of calm good humour which was as welcome as a mountain zephyr in the heat and bustle of Constitution House; but nobody had heard them speak.

On this occasion I was sitting in the second row not far from the Committee Chairman's table, from which the Prime Minister was speaking. Next to me sat the most dignified of all the Tibetans, his Homburg hat resting on his knees and his long jade earrings hanging down from a wrinkled, kindly face. Suddenly he turned to me and in measured terms, which could be heard all over the room, chose this embarrassing moment to speak.

"And where do you come from?"

Whether it was his slow and careful English or the fact that he had spoken at all which took me by surprise the most, I couldn't tell, but in any case there was more to come; I replied in a whisper, "I come from London."

The old gentleman's face lit up in a broad and leathery grin; and again in a stage whisper, which caused Pandit Nehru to look hard in our direction, he said, "Indeed, how interesting. I, myself, was educated at Rugby."

I began to feel hysterical, as the only possible reply, which I immediately gave, was that I had been to school at Marlborough, which in turn brought forth from this Ambassador of the Dalai Lama the observation that our two schools were in the habit of playing cricket against each other at Lords once a year. The old man was now well away and our Mad Hatters' conversation, which by now was on the verge of attracting disciplinary action from the chair, wound up with the discovery of a mutual friend, Mrs Weir, who was, I believe, the first English woman to visit Llasa and whose sketches of the Pothala are of striking beauty. As a matter of interest Mrs Weir was a good friend of Sheila's mother – she and her husband, Colonel Weir, owned a hut at Gulmarg. She also happened to be the grandmother of Joanna Lumley. She was a striking beauty and we often used to meet up in Gulmarg and later on in other parts of India. Colonel Weir was the British Resident at Llasa.

Happily the session was nearing the lunch interval and my Tibetan chum and I were able to cement our friendship over a sandwich at the canteen. After this remarkable introduction Professor Mansergh and I became firm friends with Mr Litsem Kyipup and the Tibetan delegation, although it turned out that he was the only one who actually spoke any English. The single occasion on which they made known their views on any of the burning topics of the day, which occupied the restless attention of the numerous delegates from less happy lands, was the never-to-be-forgotten moment in the economic discussion group when my friend from Rugby walked slowly up to the despatch box in his Tibetan costume, carrying his Homburg in one hand, to answer enquiries about the sordid matter of economic conditions in Tibet. After some desultory remarks he was asked,

"Who owns the land in Tibet?"

"The nobles, of course," was his reply. There was immediate activity among the Soviet interpreters, who felt that their trans-Caucasian employers would certainly want to know about this reactionary state of affairs; the young Indian professors jumped to their feet and clamoured for more information, which made matters far worse when it came, as Mr Kyipup's detached reply to the chairman's next question, "How do the tenants pay their taxes?" cast fuel on the flames. "Sometimes they pay in barley, sometimes in gold, depending on what is required by the nobles."

After delivering himself of this announcement, Mr Kyipup with great dignity declined to answer any of the numerous and indignant enquiries which were hurled at him from all sides of the room; picking up his Homburg he walked with cool, unhurried steps back to his seat.

The Conference at last came to an end and all the delegates departed to distant corners of the Asian Continent. As my memory of its beginning started with Mrs Sarojini Naidu, the great politician poetess, I feel it would be logical to end it with her and with one of her exquisite poems.

She had dragged it out of her memory as far back as 1937 when, as a raw recruit to business and politics in India, I had invited her to tea in my flat on Cumballa Hill with its breathtaking view over Bombay and its beautiful harbour. With my Parsee friend, JJ, (Sir Jamsetjee Jejeebhoy) we had founded a group of young Englishmen and Indians to which Mrs Naidu and other Congress leaders had given talks from time to time. Someone had told me she liked her food – she was by no means slim. My super Goanese bearer, Veraswamy, made a plateful of delicious cucumber sandwiches and I bought a Lyons iced cake from the Army and Navy Stores (all very English). Mrs Naidu was on her best Somerville behaviour – she was no longer exploited and certainly not dominated. She thought for a few minutes and then in her quiet Oxford accent she recited this short, but I think, exquisite poem, which she allowed me to type on to my ropey old Remington. It was called:

"Caprice"

You held a wild flower in your fingertips
Idly you pressed it to indifferent lips
Idly you tore its scarlet leaves apart.
Alas, it was my heart.

You held a wine glass in your fingertips
Idly you raised it to indifferent lips
Idly you drank and flung away the bowl.
Alas, it was my soul.

She signed it and wrote two dates below her signature, 1915 and 1938. What did they mean? I have no idea.

This friendly and unusual tea party actually took place on 28th December 1937, according to my old diaries.

In 1943, she was put in gaol together with Mahatma Gandhi, Nehru et al by Lord Wavell. Her daughter, Padmajee, became the first Governor of Bengal after India had become independent.

Before I was sent to London by the partners of Killicks, in the company of Terry Harrison, to explain the dangerous instability of India in April of 1947, Lord Louis Mountbatten had arrived as the last Viceroy, when he quickly decided that the original date for Indian Independence and the creation of Pakistan (15th August, 1948) must be put forward to 15th August, 1947. Mountbatten had arrived in Delhi in April 1947. His journey to England where he was incarcerated in London with Attlee for three whole days, during which he persuaded Attlee to agree with his advancement of D Day by one year, left only three and a half months for the British Government of India, which had lasted since the days of Clive in the seventeenth century, to clear out of India (and the new Pakistan) lock, stock and barrel.

Sheila's mother had gone up to her chalet in Gulmarg, as was her wont in May. Before I went off with Terry Harrison by air from Karachi for London, Sheila decided that we should spend a few days together in Gulmarg before I joined Harrison in Karachi for our sortie to London. Sheila would stay in Gulmarg while I was in London. On my return to a new subcontinent (Pakistan and India), I would go straight to Kashmir for my annual one month's holiday – this time with Sheila and my mother-in-law in Gulmarg. I could also call on the first-class Premier of Kashmir, Mr Kak, and endeavour to sell him a Vickers Viking aircraft for his employer, Harri Singh, the Maharajah. So Sheila and I went by train and bus to join her mother in the beautiful Meadow of Roses. I played golf for a week, then left Sheila, as I had done so often before, to find my way from the Himalayas to the mouth of the great Indus river at Karachi, in order to join Harrison and fly with him to London to meet with the partners of Killicks in the City of London. What happened there, I have described elsewhere.

22

Partition

*"It was a mutual affair, propelled largely by fear.
The minority communities on each side fearing the majority..."*
                                                    Colonel Leslie Sawhny

Before catching the flying boat to Poole Harbour I was able to snatch a
week with Sheila and her mother in Kashmir. It was not easy to get there
and would prove even harder to get out. By now 15th August was history.
Pakistan was born and I was in the midst of a milling crowd of Delhi Muslims
at Willingdon Airport with my golf clubs, holdall and air ticket to Srinagar
(capital of the as yet neutral Kashmir); catching my flight seemed an
impossibility.

Just as I was beginning to curse myself for having sent the office car
away I ran into Vaisca Stubbs, an old friend from Bombay and, as luck
would have it, a pilot of the very airline by which I was hoping to fly into
Kashmir. He was trying to prise his manifest from the hand of a harassed
traffic clerk near the baggage-weighing machine. He was surrounded by a
crowd of Muslims, each waving thousand rupee notes (£70 at the 1947
exchange rate) in front of his nose in the hope that he would take them
away from Delhi.

"Are you going to Kashmir?" I shouted across the heads of the mob.

"Yes, if I can find my way through all the chaps squatting on the runway,"
he shouted back. "Do you want a lift?"

In this informal way I was bundled into the back of his Dakota and within
three hours was miraculously deposited on the little plateau overlooking

Srinagar, having crossed the Himalayan foothills at 15,000 feet. It was certainly going to be much more difficult to get out. Gulmarg, the famous Meadow of Roses, one of the most secluded and perfect retreats in the British Empire, seemed scarcely to have changed since that day in July 1940 when I had first met Sheila in her white silk sari. I doubt if it can ever have been more peaceful than in this last summer of British rule. The weather was benign and the troubles down in the plains seemed to keep all but a handful of Gulmarg's oldest devotees away from its Alpine solitude. And, of course, Sheila and my mother-in-law were there to meet me and my hill pony, which had carried me up from the vale of Kashmir, 2,000 feet below.

Nestling snugly on this upland shelf beneath the 13,000 foot range of Apherwat, this village of chalets and gardens with its hotel, club, two golf courses and its English church, was a dreamland mixture of Swiss hamlet, English golf resort and Indian Cantonment – Mürren, with a dash of Peshawar and Westward Ho! set down in the Himalayas. Amy Sawnhy's little chalet was in the woods and she had been a regular visitor for thirty years. Sheila had spent every summer there except when she was at school. Her paint box was more in evidence during this last year of all. The only dog was Duggie's enormous imitation Rotweiler, which she was looking after for him. Bennibobo was the best cake snatcher north of the River Jhelum. I shall not forget her beating his enormous backside with the wooden handle of her Number 2 iron.

Gulmarg for all its seclusion behind the great barrier of the Himalayan foothills was still much affected by events in the plains. On my first evening in the club, eating one of the secretary's famous "lamb eggs", I met a friend of the family, a young Indian Colonel, whose regiment had found itself on D-Day in one of the most isolated outposts of the North-West frontier. He had not yet heard to which part of India he was to move but in any event he, his family and his regiment would have a long and sticky journey through a hostile Pakistan to reach their new posting in the Indian Dominion.

He had decided to see his family for a few days, also Sheila and her mother. He had come by jeep with an armed escort from his regiment through the 200 miles of mountain road, which passes over Muslim tribal areas. This road had been safe for half a century until ten days ago. Now this young

Hindu Colonel told us there were mobs of tribesmen all along the route and they were killing any Hindu or Sikh who should pass that way.

In the evenings we used to sit by the fireside listening to the radio, which was our only contact with the troubled world outside the valley. It was from these news bulletins that we first began to realise the appalling nature of the catastrophe, which had overtaken the Punjab as a result of its partition. Every night there were more horrifying reports of massacres and killings on both sides of the new border and of the increasing numbers of refugees who were trekking in panic from their ancestral homes on one side to an unknown future on the other. Before long I was to hear at first hand from my brother-in-law, Duggie, some of the astonishing tales of that mass migration of confused and panic-stricken humanity – probably the largest in the memory of man.

In fact, it was only a day or two after my arrival in Gulmarg that we heard on the radio that General Rees's Boundary Force had been disbanded into its component parts of Hindu and Muslim units. Pete Rees was a gallant, much decorated Welsh General of World War Two. It was clear that the non-communal character of the Indian Army had not been able to withstand the emotional pressures exerted by the fearful sights these boys were being forced to witness, which had made them turn against their own long-serving comrades.

The same bulletin announced that each Dominion would henceforth use its own troops to look after refugee movement within its borders. The 4th Indian Division, famous for its battles in the western desert during the war, went more or less intact to India. Duggie became its General Staff Officer under Major General Thimayya who was responsible for all refugee movement in the East Punjab until the end of the year. Duggie had served under Timmy Thimayya when he had commanded the 16th Light Cavalry.

Into September and the beautiful colours of autumn painted the Alpine meadows of Gulmarg in ever more glorious tints, a chill began to settle over the dwindling population of visitors who seemed to be trying desperately to hold on with both hands to the happiness of a place they had loved, a happiness already almost a memory. And so the handful of visitors began to thin out. Some managed to hire cars at exorbitant rates to take them down to Rawalpindi and, invariably, when they had gone there were stories that they had been murdered on the way.

As September wore on and even the most stalwart visitors melted away from Gulmarg I thought it was time for us to move, at least down to Srinagar in the valley. I was supposed to be back in Bombay, over 1,500 miles away, on the other side of the mountains and the Punjab Civil War, by the beginning of October. It was not easy to get a car even to cover the forty miles that lay between Gulmarg and Srinagar. Happily I had an old Muslim bazaar friend in Srinagar, a carpet dealer who turned up trumps by sending a station wagon up the hill which took Sheila, myself, my mother-in-law and two dogs, with our belongings to the capital of the State.

We hired a houseboat down the river among the meadows and the poplar trees. When the family were settled in I set off to call on my Muslim chum in the bazaar. The houseboats on the Jhelum River on the banks of the Dal Lake will be familiar to anyone who has seen that remarkable film on TV, *The Jewel in the Crown*. They were lakeside homes, moored to the riverbank and so beautiful in their setting that they are almost impossible to describe. Ahmed Bhabar, the carpet dealer, was gloomy. He assured me the Maharajah had entered into a secret agreement with Pandit Nehru to accede to India as soon as an opportunity should offer. His subjects, of course, were mostly Muslims. He told me that a mutual friend, Ali Currimbhoy, one of our sales managers in the Cement Combine, a Muslim of considerable standing in Bombay, had been brutally murdered in our office car on his way from the company's house in Delhi to Willingdon Airport. It was time for us to clear out, although the splendour of the approaching autumn and the idyllic comfort of our houseboat made this decision painful.

By now it was not easy to get transport down the road from Srinagar to Rawalpindi, 200 miles away through the mountains to the plains. Pakistan had cut off all supplies of petrol. Once more Ali Bahbar came to our rescue. Yet another station wagon was produced into which we piled. As usual there were rumours of mobs lying in wait along the road, who would go for anyone regardless of nationality, provided they looked lootworthy.

In fact, the journey to Rawalpindi was uneventful. We reached the plains just as the sun went down.

Sitting in the confusion of our room that night in a second-class hotel in

Rawalpindi, we held a family counsel of war. This famous cantonment town was as confused and chaotic as every other town in Northern India at the time. Sheila and her mother were splendid. I had to leave them to find a telephone in order to get in touch with our factory at Wah, which fortunately for us was only twenty-seven miles away on the Grand Trunk Road so we decided to take refuge there with our old friend, Frank Hennessey, the Irish Manager, until the situation cleared. Frank sent a car for us, and a lorry for our luggage but before we could get through the factory gates we had to drive through many thousands of unfortunate refugee Hindus and Sikhs, to reach the quiet lawns and bungalows of the factory's senior staff. The noise and the smells of this camp, which we learned later, contained thirty thousand refugees, penetrated into the quiet seclusion of the factory's gardens and bungalows.

The relief at finding a temporary haven for Sheila and Amy and our two dogs in the midst of all this confusion was tempered by our arrival at an empty house and a more or less empty factory. Frank had gone off to Lahore to find money to pay the staff and workers. I had to take over the running of the factory where there was considerable tension and unease, since most of the unskilled labour were tough Muslim tribesmen and the skilled workers were Hindus and Sikhs who naturally went in fear of their lives. On the third day of this peculiar existence, Frank Hennessy returned from Lahore with stories of the new frontier.

He had managed to get some money to prevent the possibility of an outbreak in the works where the temperature was steadily rising and where the unfortunate Hindus and Sikhs were daily becoming more terrified. It was at this point that we decided I should, somehow or other, have to get down to Bombay, to arrange an evacuation by air, since the trains were a death trap at this stage in the civil war, more and more of them being ambushed and attacked by organised gangs before they could cross the respective frontiers.

As there were no trains I decided to take the works car as far as Lahore, a distance of 200 miles, then try to get down to Karachi or Bombay, from Lahore by air or train. As good luck would have it Sardar Bharkat Hyat Khan, the squire of Wah and leading member of the Wah family whose limestone hill was turned into our cement, said he would come along with me, as he wanted to find out what was going on in Lahore where his nephew, Shaukhat Hyat Khan, was Revenue Minister of the West Punjab Government. He had served with Duggie as 2nd Lieutenant in the 16th Light Cavalry.

At one place we were turned back by floods and had to spend the night with a charming Muslim from the old ICS, the Indian Civil Service, a Mr Mahmoud, who was the newly installed Deputy Commissioner at a place called Gujranwalla, forty miles short of Lahore. He made us as comfortable as he could for the night in his official residence, which contained two chairs, one sofa and three string beds. He had left Bombay on 12th August, three days before Independence, where he had held a responsible government post. All his considerable belongings had been despatched by train in a goods wagon on the same day – he had elected to serve Pakistan and had been posted to this town.

His goods wagon had been looted the day after it had passed through Delhi station and his family had barely escaped with their lives. Almost the only possession left to him, a bottle of Scotch whisky, he shared with Bharkat and myself that night. There was no question then of the Koran overcoming the White Horse Whisky. Bharkat and I turned back the next morning for Wah when I played my last card by calling on the tiny contingent of RAF still left behind at Rawalpindi; fortunately I knew the Group Captain at the airfield who put me on a VIP Dakota which was leaving that afternoon for Delhi. It was with considerable misgiving that I left Sheila and her mother at Wah but I was determined to be back as soon as possible with our own aircraft to carry out our own evacuation and bring them, hopefully, to safety in Bombay.

23

Operation Exodus
(November 1947)

" 'Ye have robbed,' said he, 'Ye have
slaughtered and made an end,
Take your ill-got plunder, and bury the dead;
What will ye more of your guest and sometime friend?'
'Blood for our blood,' they said..."

Sir Henry Newbolt

Once again I found myself sitting in the senior partner's office trying to explain some of the things I had seen and to describe as dispassionately as possible the chaos and the misery of Northern India. That it was difficult to do was not entirely the fault of Bombay and its continued insulation by geography and good fortune from the troubles besetting the North. Lord Louis Mountbatten, who stayed on for six months at Nehru's request, was clearly exercising an effective press censorship. It would have been unreasonable, under the circumstances, to expect people in more fortunate parts of India to appreciate the extent of the disaster which was overtaking all that stretch of country, between Delhi and the North West Frontier. Yet watching people play bridge for high stakes in the air-conditioned card room of the Willingdon Club, I could not help but reflect that Bombay was too comfortable, too untouched by misery and too rich. Until men and women find their daily lives disrupted, food hard to find, that servants are running away and disease is breaking out all round, they are seldom shifted from the complacency of everyday routine.

The first quarrel between India and Pakistan broke out soon after my return to Bombay. It took place over the small princely state of Junagad, which lay along the west coast of India, north of Bombay, and which was chiefly famous as the last refuge in India of the lion. The Government of India had been making quite a fuss during the previous weeks over the accession of the Muslim Ruler to Pakistan, since his subjects were all Hindus. A small combined force of air and infantry was despatched to blockade this tiny, maritime State; in a short while the ruler capitulated. Because it was a maritime state they sent a destroyer, which only stayed there for a day or two. It was commanded by Sonny, of all people! So Sheila found her two brothers at one and the same time trying to keep Hindus and Muslims apart.

It was a far cry from the cholera-ridden refugee camps of northern India, with their crowds of diseased and fear-ridden humanity, to the cathedral-like tranquillity of the Cement Combine's board room. A few days after my return to Bombay, at my first board meeting as a director, I sat with seven others, all Indian businessmen, at the immense oval table, which stretched the whole length of the imposing boardroom.

It was not easy in an atmosphere attuned to finance, industrial policy and business, to paint a picture of the horrors and miseries of so many of the company's own workmen, who lived and worked well over a thousand miles away. In fact, had it not been for the arrival in Bombay, at this very moment of the Danish manager of a factory in the East Punjab, with his account of the massacre of over a hundred of our workers and their families by the employees of another community, I doubt if it would have been possible to put across my plea for air evacuation without being accused of exaggeration. I was also only too conscious of the danger, because Sheila and her mother were up there sheltering at Wah in the shadow of the Khyber Pass over 1,500 miles away.

Sorenson, who spoke little English, confirmed the tale of the old Muslim gardener who, a month before, had turned up at Wah from the factory in Patiala State and had first told us about this multiple crime. Without being invited to sit down the Dane, shabby and exhausted, then told us, in moving phrases, of his attempt to take a party of his Muslim workers with their families from the factory to the refugee camp at Kalka, some eight miles away, from where they were to be escorted in refugee trains across the border into Pakistan.

It appeared from his tale that no sooner had he led his column of lorries through the factory gates, accompanied by a handful of Sikh troopers assigned to him as his personal bodyguards by the Patiala State authorities, than he ran into a road block and the whole party was set upon by a crowd of Sikh workers from the factory, men who had lived and laboured with them for years on terms of friendship and tolerance, whom they now proceeded to butcher.

Sorenson himself had miraculously been spared while the old gardener, to whom I have already referred, was the only survivor of the convoy. Sorenson, on his way back to the factory, stopped further lorries from coming out of the main gates and was fired at for his trouble by the State troopers who had been posted to protect him.

The plea to my fellow directors that the Hindu and Sikh employees in our Pakistan factories should be evacuated at once by air before a similar fate should overtake them was accepted, if grudgingly. I also asked that such Muslims as worked in the twelve factories situated in the rest of India and who wished to go to Pakistan should be flown in the other direction; permission was granted by the directors at this my first board meeting.

I asked, too, that I should be allowed to fly with the aircraft during the operation. I could take quick decisions on behalf of the board. My wanderings were thus not yet completed and this final trip into the troubled area of the new frontier was to bring me in touch both with the beginnings of the war in Kashmir and with my army brother-in-law, Leslie Sawhny. From him I was to learn much at first hand about the catastrophe of Partition.

Bill Burbery, who had commanded 31 Squadron of the RAF during the first Wingate campaign in 1943, was now General Manager of the airline, which employed my pilot friend, Vaisca Stubbs. Burbery was fortunately able to charter us his single freight-carrying Dakota for the necessary week which we would require to exchange the Muslim and non-Muslim employees, together with their families from the wrong side to the right side of the new border.

On the Indian side of the border we selected the factory at Gwalior, about three hundred miles south of Delhi, as being the most convenient point at which to gather all the Muslim workers from the twelve plants situated in the Indian Dominion. Gwalior also enjoyed the advantage of an excellent airfield built for the RAF during the recent war.

As luck would have it there was also a small RAF strip within two miles of the factory at Wah, which was to become the Pakistan terminal for "Operation Exodus". It was unlikely that we should have been able to transport the non-Muslims from the factory to the nearest airport at Rawalpindi, thirty miles distant, without risking attack by the tribesmen.

On 20th October we took off from Gwalior airfield at dawn with a full load of Muslims. I reckoned the Dak would hold about 250 Asian bodies with their luggage and children. There would be no seating; they would sit on the floor. I sat in front with the crew for most of the journey and when we came to the Pakistan-India frontier I went back to tell the Muslim menfolk that their troubles were over. The smiles of relief which greeted this news was proof of the anxiety they had all felt, although they had been in no immediate danger in the parts of India from which they had come. I could not help comparing their fortunate lot with the many unhappy people struggling along the roads ten thousand feet below who had no idea of what fate awaited them, even if they should be lucky enough to reach their goal alive. These men in the aircraft had jobs and houses and a big organisation waiting for them at their destination.

They had lost one home but they would soon find another. In a sense they were the elite among the refugees – some of them were fitters in the workshops earning comparatively low wages. As I looked down on the flat plain of the Punjab, across which Sir Cyril Radcliffe had been forced to draw his line, I could not help feeling that it would be very difficult to defend from a military point of view since the real frontiers of India and Pakistan were still in the passes and mountains of the north-west and to a lesser extent the north-east. In the end the two governments would simply have to get together and work out a common defence and foreign policy.

After four hours of steady flying we reached Rawalpindi, and memories of those far-off days at the beginning of the war when I had learnt to fly at Risalpur crowded in on my mind as the old landmarks came up beneath our nose – John Nicholson's monument on the Grand Trunk Road, the ribbed and corrugated hills of that desolate area beneath which flowed the rich mysterious rivers of oil, and in the distance the two chimneys of our factory. In a few minutes we were levelling off with flaps down and motoring in to the small strip by the Grand Trunk Road. At the far end of the runway I could make out a small party of cars and people including, to my relief and delight, Sheila and her mother. Around the perimeter were groups of Indian Army soldiers with rifles and sten guns.

Mrs Hennessey, wife of Frank Hennessey the manager, took the crew off for a well-deserved breakfast while Frank and I, with Sheila and her mother helping, supervised the loading up of the luggage and the refugees for the return trip. It was during this operation that we noticed a column of country buses approaching us along the Grand Trunk Road from the north-east in the direction of Rawalpindi. There must have been nearly fifty of them and they appeared to be crammed with people, both inside and clinging to the roofs.

We would have paid little attention to this sight in ordinary times but just then it was distinctly unusual to see a single bus during a whole day. We stopped our loading operations and watched them carefully as they passed the strip, which at the northern end of the runway abutted directly onto the Grand Trunk Road.

"Pathans," said Frank, as the first bus rumbled by with its cargo of unmistakable tribesmen. "We had better find out what they are up to."

With these words he motioned me into his car and ordered the Muslim driver to wait for the tail of the convoy then to pass them and follow them into the village of Hassan Abdal, where they would probably stop under the shady avenue of trees. Sheila and her mother stayed behind with the aircraft, both of them still helping the Hindus and Sikhs with their families to be loaded onto the aircraft.

We followed the last bus and saw at close range the arsenal of rifles and ammunition which each man was carrying and the streaming green banners with the crescent and star of Pakistan which they were brandishing from the roofs of the lorries. The village of Hassan Abdal was only two miles from the strip and its long shady avenue of trees had tempted the tribesmen to halt for refreshment. In the village, Frank dropped off our Muslim driver with instructions to mingle with the boys and find out where they were going. It was pretty obvious that their most likely destination would be Kashmir.

1 The Wedding of Wilfrid and Sheila in May 1942,
at All Saints, Malabar Hill, Bombay

2   Top: the author's father, Francis Henry Russell (1872-1924).

3   Middle: the author's mother, Henrietta Elizabeth Newbolt (1880-1957).

4 Bottom: Aunt Sophie, Sophia Menella Newbolt (1883-1982).

5 *El Oezleh, Ghezirah Island on the Nile; the house in which the author was born. A watercolour by Wilfrid W Ball RA (1910), the author's godfather.*

6 *Waterfront of Bombay with the Taj Mahal Hotel and the Gateway of India.*

7 *Amy Sawhny with Reggie, Leslie and Sheila (1922).*

8 *Sheila Sawhny* (right)*: bridesmaid at a wedding in Rawalpindi.*

9 The Sawhny Family in 1936.

Back Row: *Reggie, Sheila , Leslie;* Front Row: *Des Raj, Phyllis, Amy Sawhny.*

11 *Reggie (known as Sonny),*
Lieutenant in the Royal Indian Navy.

10 *Leslie (known as Duggie),*
Full Colonel 16th Cavalry Indian Army.

12   *The Wedding of Wilfrid and Sheila (1942):*
Leslie, Phyllis, Wilfrid, Sheila, Reggie.

13   *Guests at the Wedding Reception at the Willingdon Club, Bombay.*
From left to right: *Phyllis, Family Friend, Rudi von Leyden (Best Man), Bride and groom:*
Wilfrid and Sheila, Reggie (Lt RIN), Rashid Baig (High Sheriff of Bombay), Leslie (Capt
Indian Cavalry), Tara Baig.

14 *Wedding of Leslie Sawhny to Rodabeh Tata in Petit Hall:*

Back Row: *Friend of Rodabeh, Capt Reggie Sawhny, Hugh Milne (Chairman Killick Nixon & Co), Duncan Shephard (Chairman of Killick Industries Ltd), J R D Tata, Safrides, Wilfrid Russell, Sir Dinshaw Petit Bart.*

Front Row: *Friend's wife, Amy Sawhny, Leslie , Rodabeh, Mrs J R D Tata, Sheila, Secretary.*

15 *Family Portrait at Bates Hill, from an original painting by Walter Langhammer.*
From left clockwise: Kneeling on floor: *Moneesha*   Seated: *Amy Sawhny* Standing:
Reggie On Sofa: *Wilfrid with Sheila holding Robin* Behind: *Rodabeh   Phyllis*   Seated:
Leslie On floor: *Venetia with dogs Albert and Victoria.*

16 *Chalet in Gulmarg, from a watercolour by Miss Gregson (Greggy) a friend of Sheila's*
mother to whom the chalet (Hut 119) belonged (1946).

17 Venice: an oil painting by Walter Langhammer (1936).

18 Rudi von Leyden (Wilfrid and Sheila's Best Man), on the River Camel in Pickereel.

19 Killick, Nixon & Co Building in Bombay.

20 Breach Candy Hospital, Bombay, from a watercolour by K K Hebbar.

21 *Painting on Black Silk: Artist Unknown.*
Given to Wilfrid and Sheila by Reggie.

22 *Moghul Miniature: probably eighteenth century.*

23 Elephant Gate, Bundi City: from a watercolour by K K Hebbar.

24 Sheila with Françoise Gaston-Breton on an elephant, at Jaipur on the way up to the Amber Palace.

25 Portrait of Sheila Russell by Françoise Gaston-Breton, painted in Paris in 1980.

26 *Robin Russell aged fourteen.*

27 *Venetia Russell aged sixteen.*

28 *Clare College, Cambridge.*

29 *Dr Charles Macpherson & son Alasdair (Binks), fencing at Amen Court.*

It seemed that only part of the column had stopped in the village, since we drove on in the direction of Peshawar and soon caught up with a number of buses just as they were turning north off the main road in the direction of Abbottabad, one of the few roads leading north into Kashmir; it was the only one in fact in that particular part of the country. The traffic policeman was waving them on with gusto.

We turned back to the village and picked up our driver, who was grinning all over.

"Kashmir, Sahib," he said, grinning.

The tribesmen had evidently taken the bit between their teeth, having heard rumours that the Hindu Maharajah was intending to accede to India, and having also become aware, probably to their amazement, that the rigid control exercised by the British of the mountainous areas in which they lived, had come to an end. These unruly men, whose main interest in life was loot, had evidently descended from their hills to see what they could find in Kashmir. During the hundred years preceding 15th August 1947, they would never have contemplated such an excursion from their own territory, which would involve passing through the plains for some distance from their own mountains in the north-west and to those of Kashmir in the east. Under the old regime they would have been blasted off the road by artillery or aircraft before they had gone ten miles.

Back in the bungalow, after our Dakota had taken off for Gwalior with its first load of Hindus and Sikhs, Frank and I naturally speculated on the extent to which Pakistan was privy to this astonishing development. Frank thought it was more than likely that some officials, probably at a low level, of the new government of Pakistan had something to do with the organisation of the transport, since the improvident Pathans were unlikely to dispose of the necessary lorries and petrol. He was equally certain that the government of Pakistan had not deliberately connived at such a foolhardy act since they were up to their eyes in the refugee business and would hardly court serious trouble with India at a moment when most of their troops were escorting refugees or were still stuck on the other side of the border trying to get to Pakistan. From what I could see at the time and from what I have learned later, I think that it was another example of the policy of a government being sabotaged by its own servants at the bottom of the ladder.

Certainly the incursion of the tribesmen into Kashmir did no good either to Pakistan or to India and nearly brought them to a state of war. In any case, once they had crossed the open plains into the Himalayas there was nothing Pakistan could do to stop them and any overt move by the Dominion Government to send them back or block their reinforcements might well have resulted in the north-west frontier province and part of the Punjab breaking away from the new Dominion with possibly fatal results to its future stability.

Within twenty-four hours we heard some of the early results achieved by the columns of tribesmen, who had passed through Hassan Abdal on the day of our first landing. They had stopped and wounded two Englishmen motoring down through the mountains from Srinagar, capital of Kashmir, to Rawalpindi; they had destroyed the power-house, which provided the Kashmir valley with its tenuous supply of electric light, plunging the capital into darkness; they sacked the small town of Baramulla, which stands at the entrance to the beautiful valley of Kashmir itself, where the slow-winding Jhelum river slips from the flat meadows into the turbulent gorge below.

At this little town they had entered the Roman Catholic convent, killed the Mother Superior, all the nuns, and an English family who were taking refuge in the convent.

It was at this moment that Harri Singh, the Maharajah, at last made up his mind and appealed to the Indian Union for help, at the same time begging for permission to accede to that Dominion. As far as we could see the tribesmen with their uncontrolled craving for loot had given this unloved ruler just the opportunity for which he had been waiting since 15th August.

The Indian Government could only bring succour to the ruler in his ineffective resistance to the tribesmen by commandeering every single civil transport aircraft in India to carry troops over the mountains into the Kashmir valley — the three existing roads all led into Pakistan. The killings and lootings in which the tribesmen now indulged not only deflected them from their purpose which was presumably the capture and the sacking of Srinagar, the capital, but also placed Pakistan whose case over Kashmir was not altogether a weak one, in a false position. When we learned that my mother-in-law's chalet in Gulmarg had been looted, together with many others, and that the communion plate had been taken from the little Anglican Church in Srinagar,

I began to feel that Pakistan had been criminally slack in allowing these wild men to get so terribly out of hand. Happily the tiny airfield was held by the incoming Indian troops and so gradually the raiders, as they came to be known, were driven back and out of the valley. Frank and I wondered whether they would look in at Wah on their way back, if they should be routed. It was not a pleasant thought, particularly when I reminded myself that Sheila and her mother were still there.

While the aircraft was droning back and forth over the six hundred miles which separated Wah from Gwalior, completing one round trip every day, I took the works car and drove to Lahore in order to call on some of the ministers of the West Punjab Government. I wanted to discover whether there was any prospect of law and order being maintained in the district round our factory. By chance, one of the first people I ran into in Lahore was my army brother-in-law, Leslie Sawhny, who was up from the Indian side of the border for a conference with some of his old friends now serving in the Pakistan Army. I learnt from him that if it had not been for the professional soldiers of the old undivided Indian Army, who refused to be carried away by the prevailing hysteria, it would have been quite impossible for even a fraction of the ten million people who moved to have arrived safely at their destination.

We sat on the lawn of Falettis Hotel in Lahore the evening we met, and I heard some of his experiences as G1 of the Fourth Indian Division. It seemed that the flight of the refugees had only began after the announcement of the Radcliffe Boundary Award and that it was a mutual affair prompted largely by fear – the minority communities on each side fearing retribution from the majority for having shouted their extravagant claims so loudly before the award was announced.

"Once this movement started," said Leslie, "there was no stopping it, particularly as it was the leaders of the minorities who had shouted the loudest for Partition who were the first to leave. I'm sorry to have to say so," he went on, "but it was the wealthy landowners and the merchants who began the stampede. They put the wind up the sturdy peasantry, who followed their example."

"I suppose there would have been a certain amount of disturbance anyway, even if the rich people had not cleared out?" I asked.

"There would undoubtedly have been pillage, arson and murder, but I am positive that if the leaders had stuck to their posts on both sides, the refugee movement would never have started."

It seemed that once this rush of population from East to West and from West to East got under way the functions and resources of the Punjab Government had broken down completely. No police force could cope with the gigantic problems that arose at one and the same time and in widely separated districts. No Deputy-Commissioner administering his District could begin to compete with the problems that confronted him. The snowball grew into an avalanche until it finally had to be recognised by the Indian and Pakistan Governments that the only practical thing they could do was to see that as many as possible of those, who wished to leave, should get to the other side in safety. In the end ten million people moved, of whom it was estimated that over a million succumbed.

"The point I want to emphasise," said Leslie, "is that this movement of terrified, frenzied, and in some cases vicious people was one which no government could foresee or control."

"What about the Boundary Force?" I asked him.

"I'm afraid General Rees had an impossible task," he replied. "Once the movement of refugees and the panic and killing began in earnest only a military force, which could maintain a minimum of a platoon in every village and a brigade in every city, could have hoped to stop the rot."

As the sun went down and the cold evening air of the approaching Punjab winter sent us indoors to his room, he went on to tell me of the misfortunes of the ill-fated Punjab Boundary Force, surely the unhappiest command that has ever been given to a soldier so successful in war and so beloved by his Indian troops as Pete Rees. His headquarters, to which were attached one senior officer from each Dominion, had been set up in Lahore. Soon the Force was being criticised by both sides and lost the support of both governments. Worse still the virus of communal hatred soon spread to the troops in the Force itself.

This development might well have been foreseen by the British authorities, who in the last analysis were responsible for the establishment of the Force and its composition. Later, towards the end of this story, I shall tell how first-class military advice regarding the solution of this problem was turned down for reasons which appeared to me to be based on emotional and political considerations rather than on logic and facts. In those days, individual battalions of the Indian Army were made up of both Muslims and non-Muslims; quite often each battalion was made up half of one community, half of another; it was not logical or reasonable to expect that a Sikh or a Muslim, each of whom had heard that his own family had been butchered by the kinsmen of the other, should continue working in harmony and comradeship. As soon as it became a question of preventing strife between the troops of the Boundary Force itself, its fate was sealed.

"We have read so little in the papers after the disbandment of the Boundary Force that I have been wondering what is happening now?" I asked.

"Each Dominion is responsible for the safe movement of the other Dominion's refugees through its own territory, and we are slowly developing very successful close escort of columns by the troops of the same community as the refugees. This could only be done, of course, because of the solidarity of the soldiers of both sides. Once the mixed units of the Boundary Force had been thrown overboard all was well and the basic unity and discipline of the old undivided army saved the situation."

"I suppose you are doing this now?" I asked.

"Yes, we are. My General has a number of brigades, which he is using for Area Defence, for patrolling the roads and railways and for providing close escorts for columns. We never seem to have enough troops – some of the refugee columns are a hundred-thousand strong and stretch for twenty miles. We try to protect these columns with a battalion of infantry and occasionally an Auster (a light aircraft) is available – they have often spotted gangs of attackers lying up in the crops for the columns of refugees. Anyway now that we have got these close escorts from the same community as the refugees, attacks are less frequent. This could not have been organised without magnificent co-operation between my General – Thimayya – on our side and General Key of the Pakistan Army. This military co-operation, I can tell you, was like a breath of fresh air."

Over dinner I asked him what he thought of the Radcliffe Award.

"It's a just and fair one, without any doubt. From a political point of view both sides criticise it, but apart from some anomalies, which were not

Sir Cyril's fault, it's as good a line as could have been drawn. He took the old tehsil boundaries, many of which were years out of date; and some of the canals are cut off from their head works; but to have put them together would probably have created worse trouble. From a military point of view it's absolutely indefensible – but then he wasn't doing a Staff College Exercise!"

"Perhaps that will be a good thing in the long run," I said.

"Yes, perhaps it will. I should like to see it left undefended like the American-Canadian frontier. One thing I do know and that is it's quite impossible for either side to patrol the border by day or night, which is an admirable arrangement for the smuggler boys."

I know that Kashmir was just as much in the forefront of his mind as it was in mine but we did not speak about this subject, probably because it was clear to both of us that sooner or later India and Pakistan must work out a common defence and foreign policy. If a foreign power should choose to invade the subcontinent through the mountains of the north-west, this was the obvious place to stop him. He would meet one smallish army in a strong position, backed up by another somewhat larger force three hundred and fifty miles further back holding an indefensible line in the plains. It would be like forcing your wicket keeper to stand up to Lindwall, discarding all your slips and placing one fielder at longstop.

"When are you going back to India?" I asked, as I had to leave for Wah the next morning in order to catch the last flight back to India of our Dakota for the final contingent of Hindu and Sikh employees. I was also planning with some anxiety to get my mother-in-law and Sheila safely away to Bombay with this last plane.

Leslie replied, "I've got to leave early tomorrow morning down near the Grand Trunk Road. You've no idea what fearful sights one has to witness on that road. I suppose I'm getting used to them now but I think you'd have to go a long way to see anything more gruesome or pathetic. A drive along this road from here to Amballa (in India) leaves an impression of dirt and filth and misery. There's not a blade of grass by the roadside nor a leaf left on a tree throughout the whole stretch of two hundred and fifty miles. Where the convoys have halted for the night the ground stinks to high heaven for miles around – the carcasses of dead animals and humans are all mixed up together. One night I happened to find an old man and his wife sobbing by the side of the road. They were unable to move any further and had been abandoned by their family to die. I was able to fly them over to Lahore and have them cared for until they met their children again, but there were thousands who just perished of fatigue because they couldn't move another step."

It was hearing these stories from my brother-in-law, who was in the midst of this great tragedy, that made me realise more clearly than before the utter senselessness of this enormous exchange of peasantry from one side of an imaginary line to the other. The futility of it all was nowhere more tragically illustrated than in the story of the meeting of two convoys of refugees travelling in opposite directions on the same road, which I listened to that night in Lahore.

The army authorities on both sides had rightly allotted separate routes for refugees in order to avoid clashes, which might have developed into pitched battles with thousands of men taking part on either side. During the floods of September it was reported to the army that two such convoys had in fact met face to face on the same road going in opposite directions; instead of falling on one another they spent the night peacefully camping side by side. The women cooked the food together and shared their milk with each other's children, while the men gathered round a common fire and gossiped. It was reported that the elders exchanged information about the crops and holdings they had left behind. They even agreed to take over the villages each had abandoned; then the Muslim leader is said to have scratched his head and asked the non-Muslim elders: "But if it is as simple as all that, why then are we moving at all?"

The non-Muslim leaders thought this one over for some time, then one of them said slowly and solemnly:-

"It is by order of the government."

By now it was nearly midnight and as we both had to be away early in the morning I suggested we go to bed. Before we said goodnight Leslie told me two stories of great gallantry by young British officers, which for courage and steadfastness must be hard to beat even among the many valiant deeds of World War Two. There were comparatively few British officers left in the Indian Army after 15th August, although some had been asked to stay and some had volunteered.

This story is of a young subaltern who was Escort Commander of a train carrying refugees from one side to the other. By this time lack of discipline among the troops was prevalent on both sides. The train was brought to a sudden halt as the result of a plot between a station master and his pointsman, who knew that a gang of ruffians was waiting in the corn to attack the train. As soon as it had stopped, the train was rushed by the waiting killers and panic seized the refugees. The subaltern ordered his troops to fire on the approaching mob; they were co-religionists of the attackers and refused. He exhorted them to do their duty; they still refused. He then stepped out on the line – a lone figure with his sten gun. He advanced on the infuriated mob alone. He emptied his gun into the foremost ranks of the crowd, who fell back.

Then seeing that his ammunition was gone, that he was defenceless and alone, they surged forward and engulfed him. Leslie did not know the name of this boy. Somehow it has always seemed to me that bravery of this kind in a foreign land, surrounded by frenzied people and strange hysterical emotions, far from the horrible yet familiar battlefields and friendly comradeship of a war such as we had all known, is something altogether special and magnificent. I wondered if anybody would ever know his name.

The second story concerned a young Sapper subaltern, who with a few others was responsible for the maintenance of a portion of the road and railway line near the Beas River and railway station. One night a refugee train pulled into the Beas Railway Station and was at once attacked. The subaltern heard the cries of the refugees, collected half a dozen of his men and rushed to the scene of the attack. Within fifteen minutes he had cleared a mob of several hundred times the number of his small force and had saved the refugees from slaughter. This in itself was a deed showing the highest order of devotion to duty. The next day the rivers of the Punjab spated and a whole column of refugees, which had camped on a tongue of land in the middle of the broad Beas River, was swept away – most of its members were drowned.

This young officer, accompanied by some of his men, spent the whole day and most of the night at the bridge, rescuing people from drowning. He had braced his body against the stonework of the bridge and, surrounded by the swirling waters of this mile wide river, had spent a day and a night pulling men, women and children out of the floodwaters. Finally, exhausted, he was prevailed upon to go to a nearby hospital where he died of exposure the following day.

Next morning we each went our separate ways and I for one was convinced that, had it not been for the armies of the two dominions, which had both been cast in the same mould and been tested in the battles of the Western Desert, of Italy and Burma, the situation in the north of India would already have been a hopeless one and, in all probability, the germs of hatred and fear might well have spread over the whole subcontinent. We were still in the middle of the Punjab migration and in Kashmir heaven alone knew what was going to happen, but I had the feeling after this talk with my brother-in-law that in the end all would be well; I only hoped that the politicians would realise at last how much they had to thank not only the ordinary sepoy of the Pakistan and Indian armies but India's own officers who had suddenly been thrust into positions of great responsibility far beyond their years by the virtual disappearance overnight of that devoted and efficient band of British Officers, who themselves had served India and its army with such loyalty and ability through three hundred years of history.

I reached Wah after lunch and was told that the last flight to India would leave the following morning. This was important to me for apart from anything else I knew I should be taking Sheila and her mother out with me.

During the afternoon Frank Hennessey invited me to the works clubhouse for a tea party, which was to be given by the Muslims to the departing Sikh and Hindu employees. It was a remarkable affair and probably unique in the whole subcontinent at that time. Now that they had all seen the effectiveness of the air evacuation scheme all fear among the Hindus and Sikhs had vanished. But what amazed me even more was that the Muslims now seemed genuinely sorry to see them go. This was in itself certainly a natural emotion, since they had all lived and worked together for many years; but this was true of the Punjab generally where everywhere such natural instincts of human friendship had been quickly overwhelmed by the raging torrent of fear and hatred that had engulfed them. But somehow here in Wah there seemed to be an oasis of goodwill between all communities, even at this late hour. This was due, I think, to the leadership of Frank Hennessey, the manager, and to the character of our old friend Bharkat

Hyat Khan, who always threw his considerable influence for good into the scales, if things looked bad. When the Muslims had garlanded the Sikhs and Hindus at the end of the tea party, I had to rub my eyes, so narrow is the dividing line in India between life and death, hatred and love; that the scales came down on the right side was largely due to an Irishman's ability to crack a joke with his men.

He had also been supported by the efficient influence and gallant courage of an Irish woman, an English woman Amy and my own wife, Sheila Sawhny, themselves surrounded as they were by some of the wildest men in the world.

The next day we roared over the strip by the Grand Trunk Road and waved goodbye to that brave Irish couple, who were staying behind in the midst of turmoil and uncertainty. I was naturally overjoyed to see Sheila and her mother climb into the aircraft. The sprawling refugee camp was still crammed full with suffering humanity. I felt sure that tribesmen were sitting up in the hills watching for any chance to pounce on an unguarded convoy. As we climbed, I could see over the foothills in the direction of Kashmir where Indian troops were fighting Muslim tribesmen. Soon the factory chimneys with their cheerful plumes of smoke streaming away to the west had disappeared from view.

We set course for Gwalior. On the way there was only one incident of note when my mother-in-law who, at the age of sixty, was sitting up front with the crew, mildly reprimanded the captain for leaving the aircraft to fly itself while he buried himself in *The Times* crossword puzzle.

As we approached the new frontier our Indian passengers couldn't have cared less if there had been no crew at all. At a rough estimate the operation had saved three thousand five hundred lives.

24

Pali Hill

*"They marched to the top of the hill
And then they marched back down again."*

At last — and really it was at last this time — we settled down at Bates Hill. Sheila occupied herself with completing the furnishing of the house. The most effective thing she did was to see that our large bedroom and my small study (the snuggery) were air-conditioned. It wasn't so much the high temperatures in Bombay that were uncomfortable as the humidity. Air-conditioning made a big difference.

However, a much bigger change faced Sheila's mother. She could no longer live in Lahore which was now a Muslim city in a Muslim state. Although Amy Sawhny was English, her surname was Hindu and the people among whom she and her children had lived for so many years had been Hindu. Now the Muslims and Hindus were busy killing each other, ever since 15th August.

By this time, 30th November, Duggie was living at Wellington in the far south of India (not far from Cochin) where he was a full Colonel and Deputy Commandant of the brand new Indian Army Staff College. The famous all-India Staff College, which for the last hundred years had been at Quetta, was now in Pakistan, and so had fallen on 15th August to the new Muslim Dominion. Wellington was about 2,500 feet up in the Nilgiri Hills. It was in fact a miniature Gulmarg, complete with golf course. The neighbouring and much larger hill station, Ootacamund (Ooty for short) boasted its own hunt (it hunted jackal) with huntsman, hounds and horn.

Amy stayed with Duggie until she was able to rent, on a long lease, the well-known and delightful bungalow, just below the Ooty Club where she soon recreated the atmosphere of the hut in Gulmarg. So Duggie could still play golf and Sheila could develop her painting. Macaulay, who gave English to the Indian people, wrote his historic Minute to Lord William Bentinck in the building just above the bungalow.

The people living on Pali Hill were nearly all English businessmen and their wives. They were very different from the cosmopolitan, intelligent men and women among whom they had lived in the Punjab. It is not being unfair to this group of Europeans I think, to classify them as being both dull and, underneath a rather tough skin, suspicious of well educated, upper-class Indians. Sheila at this time didn't drive a car, so once more she was alone all day. And then came our daughter, Venetia.

The new hospital at Breach Candy was not yet in operation so our daughter was born in a nursing home where a Scottish doctor, Mac MacKenzie, gave Sheila the maximum of help and later the maximum of his and his wife's friendship for the rest of our time in India. Venetia, Guineth (in Welsh, the Blessed) was a Newbolt family name. I had known great happiness since 2nd July 1940 but had never experienced anything like the euphoria of 14th July 1951, the National Day of France, "le quatorze Juillet".

There was a second dose of happiness – this time it was for Duggie. To the family's surprise he had married Rodabeh Tata only a few weeks before, about whom I shall write later. Dabeh, as she was known, was just forty. She was Jehangir Tata's youngest sister, so she was half Parsee and half French. Duggie had left the army and had joined Killicks where he took my place in the great cement combine. When Venetia was born he and Dabeh were enjoying their honeymoon in France. Their telegram of congratulations was in French and it begged Sheila and myself to choose a second name, which they hoped would be Marianne, the heroine of the French revolutionary epoch. I shall write of this remarkable event and its consequences later on.

We found it hard to take in at a time when so much else was happening, not least, in 1948, the assassination of Mahatma Gandhi in Mr Birla's house in Delhi, by a fanatical young Hindu. Our team of servants was headed by Ram Dayal, our Head Bearer. Then came Cookie, the Goanese expert at

European and Indian dishes who presided over the kitchen and then Gunia, from the great province of Maharashtra, a gardener of whom the Royal Horticultural Society would have been proud. I knew nothing about flowers but one day in the garden I ran into Gunia and I could just recognise my faded Cambridge Ski Club sweater which somehow or other had come with our luggage in the Polish troop ship from Liverpool. You could hardly fail to recognise the light-blue crossed skis across the chest of our gardener. When curiosity made me ask him how he had come by this ancient trophy of my past, he simply grinned and said in Hindi, "Memsahib give me." So it was no surprise when a few days later I recognised my down-at-heel cable stitch Hawks Club sweater in the same place. I remembered Freddy Brown, the great slow bowler who had captained England against the Aussies and had proposed me for the Hawks Club in far off 1931. Then there was our Goanese nanny, complete with perambulator and nurseries; the christening of Venetia, who was baptised in the small church on Pali Hill, was handled by the Protestant Bishop of Bombay. He subsequently became a good friend a few years later when he was Suffragan Bishop of Truro in Cornwall. The whole team of servants truly adored Sheila, who looked after them and understood their ways so well.

25

The Land of the Free
(A Digression in Time)

"The Star-Spangled Banner"

American National Anthem

Before Sheila set foot for the first time in America she had settled into a reasonably happy social life based on Bates Hill. This was about 1953. Like me she found little stimulus in our rather suburban European (read English) neighbours. Unlike me she never showed it. Every now and again we gave a largish cocktail party – the house and its garden were ideal for that sort of thing. The one I remember best was in February 1953 when most of the Everest climbing team landed in Bombay from a P & O ship. They stayed two nights in the Taj Mahal Hotel before continuing their journey to Nepal, by train. John Hunt and I had been friends and contemporaries at Marlborough. He had tried hard in those days to persuade me to take up mountaineering. I had found skiing more pleasant and less frightening.

John flew out to Katmandu from England; Hilary, also – from New Zealand. Tenzing, of course, was there already. The remaining members of our most famous group of climbers, ever, were a delightful lot and they were more than ready to listen to Sonny's catalogue of stories and jokes. I can remember across the years, Lowe – George was his first name I think; he was a New Zealander and he had friends on Pali Hill with whom he stayed. He played tennis with Sheila most mornings for a week at the Pali Hill Gymkhana. It was Lowe who pioneered the route from the western

90

Cym, to the south Col, which made the attempt at the summit possible. Sonny brought about six American naval officers in smart white uniforms from off the cruiser, *Boisy*, which was anchored in Bombay harbour; other climbers were George Band, the geologist, and Major Whiley, a Gurkha officer, who was the administrator. They will always stay in my memory.

Back in London, Sheila and I were due in April for my summer leave from Killicks, and I had reserved a balcony on the first floor of Grosvenor House, from which to watch the Queen and her Coronation procession pass by in Park Lane. It was then that we learned that Everest had been climbed – a new Elizabethan age had dawned – or had it? The rain came down in torrents as it had done in Cochin ten years ago. However, the Queen of Tonga was marvellous and raised our spirits as high as Everest; but our own Queen's smile was the best of them all.

By this time I had left the Indian cement world forever and had been posted to our Mining Department, which meant numerous visits to America.

My first visit to the land of the free had been in the Cambridge long vac of 1932 with Fat Mac McLenaghan, who, in the following year, was to become the first Clare College Mellon scholar at Yale University. Paul Mellon, the scholarship's founder, will appear often from now on in this story. Apart from becoming a lifelong and beneficial friend of Clare – it was said that in his lifetime he gifted £57 million to his old college and its university – he was to become a good friend of Sheila and myself. I had met Virginia Hobart (later to be Mrs Ginnie Fairbank), my first American girlfriend in 1929 – my gap year – in Munich where my mother, God bless her, had sent me – via Gabbitas and Thring – for six months to Munich University, where I was a paying guest in the flat of a Baronin von Shreck, who lived near the English Garden.

My second visit to the United States was to Winnetka, Illinois, in the summer of 1939, a year before I was to meet Sheila in Gulmarg.

Ginnie knew something of my activities in Bombay through our occasional exchange of letters. Without telling me, she had arranged with the Rotarians of Oak Park in the adjacent Chicago suburb to hers, the birthplace of Ernest Hemmingway, for me to address their rotary club about India. Bravely she took me to an enormous hall where she was seated in a place of honour while I was led away to a stage where I was to make my speech. I think it was about the Moghul Empire. The embarrassingly large audience was clearly bored with what I had to say until I told them that the Taj Mahal, apart from being the most beautiful building in the world, had been especially built by the then Emperor, Shah Jahan, as a tomb for Mumtaz Mahal, the most beautiful of his wives – I think, in 1638. I had told them also that the architect of the Taj Mahal had been an Italian. There were immediate cheers from the Italian lobby. At the end they gave me a thoroughly undeserved ovation and the Rotary Chairman introduced me, to all and sundry, as the husband of our good friend "Mrs Virginia Russell" from Winnetka! I scarcely knew what to do, having only just accepted an invitation to Ginnie's wedding for the following week. She was to marry Ben Fairbank, also of Chicago, whose mother, among other exalted positions, was chairman of the America First League.

"Lucky they didn't call you a maharajah," was Ginnie's whispered comment, as I climbed into her Oldsmobile.

As soon as I heard about the Ribbentrop-Molotov pact, I quickly took my leave of Ginnie and Chicago, found a tourist berth in the cheapest part of the *Mauretania*, abandoned a clutch of opera tickets at Salzburg, said goodbye to my mother in London and took a City Line ship to Bombay – once again it was the *City of Venice* – where I reported to the Noble House of Killick, Nixon & Co and swiftly joined the RAF.

Post Script

I think, perhaps, this is the moment in the story to describe what my godson, Toby Fairbank, wrote to me later about this period in Sheila's life, when we were staying with them in their house in Cambridge, Massachusetts. Toby wrote,

> *"The only other thing I remember from that visit (or another earlier one) is my mother telling me that one night before dinner she knocked on Sheila's door to ask her a question and Sheila invited her in. She was dressing for dinner and while they chatted Sheila showed Ma how to put on a sari, folding the front part through her fingers so that the pleats were uniform."*

And here is an extract from a letter written by Sheila to Ginnie, which was sent to me, a long time after, by my Godson. In fact it's the only letter I have, written by Sheila to somebody else.

Dear Ginnie,

This is just a line to tell you that Wilf arrived in England today, only sailing for New York on the 28th of this month and will arrive on the 3rd November. The boat he's going by is the Mauretania and his departure date from America is the 28th of November. I do hope this trip is not going to be all business, though I'm rather afraid it will be. And anyway I thought I'd better warn you just in case he arrives unannounced! I have a horrid feeling that the last letter that I wrote to you perhaps never reached you. I enclosed some Indian stamps for Heddy (Toby's sister) and as a result the envelope was rather a queer shape and no doubt the Indian Post Office thought that something illegal was going on... . So I've sent more via Wilf. I only hope that he doesn't lose them en route. I do, do wish that I could have accompanied Wilf on this trip but it would have been frightfully expensive and it would have meant leaving the babe (Venetia) again; I think that we're renting a house at Henley for our leave in England next summer and it would be such fun it you and Ben and the elder children came over... . I'm hoping that my mother will come over next year and I gather there is a cook of sorts in this house, so I'm sure we'd manage to have some fun...

Do think about it.

How are you all and your delightful house? I shall be so jealous of Wilf when he's up in Boston with you all but I suppose one can't have everything... . Do give all my love to the kids and I hope Janet's eyes are all right now. You must have had a very worrying time when she was operated on.

Bless you all and much love from

Sheila

26

Marianne — 1953

"We would like Venetia to carry the name Marianne.
It is the symbol of France."
> Cable sent to Sheila and Wilfrid by Rodabeh Tata and Leslie
> Sawhny who were spending their honeymoon in France when
> Venetia was born.

The next five or six years of Sheila's life were spent mostly looking after Venetia, and later, Robin, with the help of our nanny. Occasionally there was a social event such as the Everest party, and some of her time was taken up with the family portrait. Painted by Walter Langhammer, this immense picture showed three generations of grown-ups (known as The Groanies by my American godson) as well as numerous Pekes. At six feet by four feet it was almost too large to find a lodging. However, these few years really did introduce Sheila to France and French culture, especially to Paris, where her taste in western clothes caught up with and even passed her Indian wardrobe.

There were many influences at work led, I suppose, by Dabeh Tata, her sister-in-law and, of course, the overwhelming attraction for any young woman who likes and appreciates painting as well as clothes; somehow she had already made several close and chic-looking women friends, whose friendship overflowed onto me. Like many civilised people she came to France via Italy. Dabeh and Duggie never lived together in France, but Dabeh's closest friend, Mimé Sauvin, had a smart apartment on the Champs de Mars. Every morning she woke up in the shadow of the Eiffel Tower and through her other window she could see the resting place of Napoleon Bonaparte.

A young Indian artist who really taught her how to paint (in Bombay) was K K Hebbar, a young Maharashtrian, later to become the first President of India's new Academy. He had said we ought to spend our 1953 summer leave at a place he knew well on Lake Como. It was called Bellagio and he introduced us to a wonderful hotel overlooking the lake. Sheila spent many happy hours at her easel while I tried my hand but gave it up quickly in favour of map reading and organising car drives in that wonderfully beautiful land of lakes and hills and Victorian paddle steamers. The only historical shadow was the village opposite Bellagio where Benito Mussolini had been executed in 1945 prior to being hung upside down from a petrol pump in Milan.

We drove to Paris and stayed in the Hotel St James and Albany in the Rue du Faubourg St Honoré, where my father used to stay on his way from London to Cairo via Marseilles. His chartered accountancy business in the Levant made the Paris stopover as important in the first decade of the twentieth century as it became for his son en route from Bombay to London in the 1950s and '60s. We went out of curiosity to one Dior show where I nearly fainted at the price tags; Sheila brought me round by falling for a dress at a less alarming house where she bought it for the equivalent of £80 which in these days is quite a modest sum but in 1953 was pretty startling, at least for me. But her great discovery was, I think, almost her very first boutique; she found it under her very nose at the St James and Albany. Hermès became Sheila's second home in Paris. It was a small, beautifully furnished salon where the clothes were smart and cheap, the service friendly and efficient and the owner kept her poodle in the shop.

Sheila soon became a friend of the Patronne, and our visits to the Louvre became less frequent as a result. Hermès was so close and fortunately so economical. We met Françoise Gaston-Breton and her friend Vivienne Worms through an introduction by Joanie Clive, an English friend. Françoise became another of those close women friends whom Sheila had a genius for collecting. She was a well-known artist who later painted the best ever portrait of Sheila that was ever created by anyone. Her Norman husband, Jean, spoke Franglo as fluently as Sonny talked Babuspeak. My favourite Anglo-

French sentence of Jean's described Abrahams, our champion miler at that time, as "le record man du mile du monde".

Years later Sheila took Françoise and Jean with Françoise's sister on an inspiring tour of Rajasthan and the Agra-Delhi circuit with its centrepiece, the Taj Mahal (by moonlight as it turned out). In May 1940, Jean had flown his French Air Force fighter Squadron from under Hitler's nose, across the Mediterranean to Algiers. In those distant days he had been "le record man de l'Armée de l'Air Française". Jean and Françoise had a flat in the Avenue Bugeaud near the Arc de Triomphe. Sheila often stayed there and was not as loyal as I was to the St James and Albany; who can blame her for that?

We returned to the house near Henley which we had rented and where the gardener's good wife had taken care of Venetia. Robin, of course, had not yet arrived.

We flew home to Bombay in a Tata Air Lines Constellation (business class).

Venetia was born in the comparative discomfort of a Bombay nursing home which was cosy and cheerful compared to the Victorian greyness of Saint George's Hospital where Sheila had lost her first-born through an arrogant over-confident smooth German medico with his gold watch and his conceited incompetence. Beside him the modest yet solid skill of the Highlander, Mac MacKenzie, was manna from Scotland, carrying with it as it did his character and the humour to hold her hand and bring her through what must be for every woman the most painful and most challenging experience of her life.

Robin appeared – again it was in our lucky month of May – at the same time of year that critical battle had been between the Royal Air Force and the Indian Air Force against the Japanese Battle fleet in 1942. Robin's appearance, aided once more by Mac MacKenzie was even smoother and happier than Venetia's. It was amid the air-conditioned comfort of Bombay's most up-to-date hospital at Breach Candy overlooking the Indian Ocean where Sheila had created a charming circular garden, its centre a sundial, its beds cheerful with cannas and salvias on the south-western corner of the gleaming modern building, next to the famous Breach Candy Swimming Pool.

The nurses had been recruited from all over the Commonwealth and her husband was its first chairman.

I was in my office when Sister Needle telephoned to tell me I was the proud father of a seven-pound son. For a fortnight he was known as Champagne Charlie. Later in life, he scarcely ever touched the stuff in contrast to his father who, as was the custom in those days among both Indian and European communities did nothing to help their wives and occasionally paid an embarrassed visit to the hospital.

They had been some time coming, due largely to those turbulent years we had lived through. But when they did come they brought their parents great happiness. Venetia (the blessed) was a Newbolt name and Robin could be a cheerful air traveller or a defender of the dispossessed. Robin was to do both when he grew up, particularly of the former with his almost weekly hops across the Atlantic pond.

27

Little Oak Spring

> *"I will remember Carquinez Straits,*
> *Little French Lick and Lundy's Lane*
> *The Yankee ships and the Yankee dates*
> *And the bullet-towns of Calamity Jane.*
> *I will remember Skunktown Plain*
> *I shall not rest quiet in Montparnasse*
> *I shall not lie easy at Winchelsea*
> *You may bury my body in Sussex Grass*
> *You may bury my tongue at Champmedy*
> *I shall not be there. I shall rise and pass*
> *Bury my heart at Wounded Knee."*
>
> *Stephen Vincent Benet*

John Masters, the best-selling author, who, if he had pursued his Indian Army career would have ended up as a Lieutenant-General, came into our lives through Sonny, who in his own brief career as a second-hand car salesman in Bombay had off loaded an early Morris Cowley onto 2nd Lieutenant Masters of the 4th Gurkhas.

Sheila had much to do with the creation of one of John Masters' best-known characters, Victoria Jones in *Bhowani Junction*. She was the Anglo-Indian heroine whose part in the movie was played by Ava Gardner. Originally Masters had some difficulty in getting her personality right and letters would fly between Centenary, the Masters' home town (fifteen miles west of Washington Bridge, New York), and Bates Hill (ten miles north of Bombay).

The story of John Masters' transformation, from a Gurkha officer in the Indian Army, into a job-hunting English civilian in 1948, has been told by himself in *Pilgrim Son*, the third of his autobiographical stories. It is a fabulous tale of guts and imagination for he was down to his last hundred bucks in New York when he wrote and sold to the Viking Press his first novel about the Indian Mutiny, *The Night Runners of Bengal*.

It was Book of the Month in New York and in London. His second book, *The Deceivers* about the thugs, the holy stranglers of Central India, followed his first with a right and left, as the American and English books of the month. The manuscript of the third, to be called *Bhowani Junction*, landed on our doorstep at Bates Hill with a thud some time in 1952 with a letter asking Sheila if she would study as carefully as she could every aspect of Victoria Jones, as also the houses, clubs, clothes and general behaviour not only of the Anglo-Indians five years after Independence, but also of full-blooded Indians too. He only asked me one question, which I couldn't answer.

I shall always remember during one of my Killicks business trips to New York the occasion when I was walking unsteadily with John Masters down 49th Street after an unashamedly vinous lunch at the Pierre Hotel when he said to me,

"You see, Wilf, I want to describe the whole of the historical, emotional and political connection between England and India through the eyes of one English family, the Savages. The French couldn't do it because we had thrown them out of India in the eighteenth century but we, the English can and I intend that we shall."

Sheila worked hard on Victoria Jones and his other questions. When the book came out in 1954, it was a far bigger hit than the other two. He wrote inside the cover of our copy:

Sheila and Wilfrid

Here it is at last. I ought perhaps to have made a printed acknowledgement of the help you gave me but I didn't because I would rather take the brickbats myself, if there are any, and there will be, but if it is true and moving, a large part of the credit is yours. Come

over here and I'll show you my gratitude in more potable form.

Love and best wishes

Jack

Centenary March 7th 1954

In the summer of 1954 we went together to Cambridge, Mass, for a happy week with Ginnie and Ben Fairbank. They laid on one uproarious dinner party at which we met their closest American friends, John and Barbara Cross. Ben produced a large bowlful of lobsters, which he cooked and which were assisted on their way with bottles of Vouvray. After several of these Ben slipped into his conjuring mode. He was a long-standing member of the Magic Circle. All good things come to an end and those especially happy weeks in Cambridge, Mass. simply flew.

Our next call was three-quarters of the way across the continent to Sun Valley, where we looked up Min and Barny Beresford. Barny had the distinction of winning a DFC before the war on the North West Frontier of India in 20 Squadron, flying a Hawker Hart which was only slightly younger than my old Wapiti. He also won a DSO in the Battle of Britain. He had risen to the rank of Air Commodore by 1945 and would have achieved at least an Air Marshal's baton had he been able to be polite to senior officers. Min had become one of Sheila's wartime buddies in Delhi during the war. Barny's independent personality resulted in his early retirement from the RAF and, like John Masters, he sought a new life in the New World.

They settled in Sun Valley, bought a ranch at a village called Ketchum where they ran a small DIY business called the Busy Bee – "go anywhere; fix anything". I got to know Ernest Hemmingway's fourth wife who was their next-door neighbour. It was there too that Hemmingway, like his father before him, had shot himself in Oak Park, Illinois.

Min and Sheila drove to Yellowstone Park where they spent a few nights in a small bungalow. On the second night Sheila heard an ominous noise outside her bedroom window. She took a torch, unlocked the kitchen door and opened it, only to face one very large bear. The bear was evidently annoyed that he couldn't find any full jars of honey in the trash can. Sheila outstared him, switched off her torch and went back to bed.

I said goodbye to Barny and flew south to Santa Fé, New Mexico where I joined the Masters Walking Club. Jack always managed to inspire successful American stockbrokers and lawyers into exchanging tennis courts and golf courses at weekends for hill walking of the most energetic kind. He and Barbara always left the townies miles behind. Yet the Wall Street millionaires always came back for more. By this time he was, of course, one of America's best-selling novelists. Sheila by now had grown more independent than she had been in various Anglo-Saxon environments and went on her own to stay in Virginia with Paul and Bunny Mellon. We had arranged to finish our fairly breakneck tour of America in Cambridge, Mass, with Ben and Ginny. While she was staying at Upperville, Virginia she had the most unusual experience of an artistic life.

By this time she was a good friend of both Paul and Bunny Mellon; with Paul because of her interest in and growing talent for painting; with Bunny for her undoubted skills at gardening and embroidery. In both spheres she learnt a lot from Paul's second wife who was exceptionally good in both disciplines. During the brief space of an afternoon in the Mellon drawing room she soared high into the stratospheres of art. The story as she told it to me later went like this:

"We were halfway through a very English session of afternoon tea, just the three of us. Suddenly the butler came in looking disturbed. He spoke to his boss reporting the arrival at the front gate at the Oak Spring Farm of a large truck driven by a strong man who had a parcel, so he said, which he would only hand over personally to Mr Mellon.

"The truck driver was duly ushered into the drawing room carrying a large parcel protectively packed in layers of tough cardboard and brown wrapping paper. Paul, who had evidently been expecting it, asked Sheila and his wife if they minded him opening it there and then.

"They nodded their assent. The butler and the truck driver withdrew. Sheila's host then pulled a formidable folding knife out of his trouser pocket and proceeded to rip off the protective layers of packing from the parcel."

Sheila took a deep breath as she finished the story, "And do you know, Wilf, he slowly and very carefully pulled out a framed picture. It was a Van Gogh!"

Before leaving Upperville, Bunny Mellon told Sheila that she had, at Jackie Kennedy's request, designed and created the Rose Garden at the White House.

28

The Setting Sun over the Estuary

"I know so well this turfy mile
These clumps of sea-pink withered brown…"

John Betjeman

It was about this time, 1955, halfway through our last decade in India that I began to hear faint sounds of distant music, like the whispers of the bagpipes heard by the prisoners in the Residency at Lucknow after months spent in the dungeons — not that our life together remotely resembled that of those unhappy predecessors. Sheila never showed any sign of wanting to give up our happy life in India; but I did occasionally mention to her the question of how and where our children should be educated. Venetia was four and Robin one year old. No sooner had this particular note floated across the Indian Ocean and, like one of Harold Acton's moths, flown through the open balcony into Sheila's lovely drawing room, than it disappeared through the dining room and into Cookie's kingdom. There was no question that they would go to boarding school in England; so we had taken it for granted and had scarcely ever talked about it again; but the sound of the distant bagpipes drew ever nearer.

What then, were those sad yet happy sounds, and the soldiers whom they led, going to do to us when they finally arrived? The answer, of course, although we were scarcely conscious of it, was the creation of two civilised citizens of the world.

Before the romantic music grew too loud it is, I think, time to draw a few sketches of our life in Bombay, which might appear inappropriate or unconnected to the main thread of the story – Sheila Russell – née Sawhny. Yet they are threads in both the skirt and the sari of her wardrobe.

I have scarcely touched on the vexed subject of prohibition, which the orthodox Hindu Premier of our Province – no more the Bombay Presidency – had forced upon us. If Hickey, a typical eighteenth-century nabob of Calcutta, had learned that, across the two intervening centuries, English men and women were being forced by law (to say nothing of Indian women who had married English men) to eschew alcohol, he would have had a heart attack. As it was Morarji Desai was persuaded to allow, as a concession to Europeans, that they be issued with a ration book (of considerable size, paper-wise, but not drink-wise), which led to uncomfortable unfolding and rubber stamping in clubs, restaurants and bars. Yet no prohibition police, thank heavens, ever invaded our hearth and home.

I used to have my "chota peg" (small whisky) every night before dinner, as did almost every other Englishman in the subcontinent; this was almost invariably followed by a "burra peg" (a large whisky) and was often followed in turn by one, sometimes even two, pink gins (a small or large gin tinted with a touch of angostura bitters).

Until she married Sheila never touched alcohol. The Duke (her father) had always taken his peg nightly – sometimes two but never more. Sheila did the same, as the sun went down, but never more and never gin. Years later, I always felt that her conversion to a whisky before dinner was, in my imagination, like that of Margaret Thatcher. There is little doubt that all over the world whisky is considered to be the best medicine of all for energetic women, and Sheila was nothing if not energetic, so it became a regular custom.

So every evening before dinner, Ram Dayal, dressed in his best white uniform and *pugree* (turban) would present himself in a most dignified way, in the drawing room to receive our orders. This comfortable ceremony ended with the final instruction, usually from me, "Panch minute" – (dinner in five minutes time). Of course none of this elaborate ceremony applied to wine, but at this time there was hardly any good wine available in the whole of India.

One morning at Bates Hill, three weeks before we were due to leave India for good, Sheila took a phone call. A voice came ringing round the top floor of Bates Hill.

"It's Dabeh, she has had a call from Kikuk, whose sister has just rung her from Delhi about some English chap called Cheshire who is in Bombay. Apparently he's in some trouble with the Customs about importing a jeep and a bus. It all sounds a bit odd but he used to be in the RAF. She thought you might be able to help – the RAF and all that."

Sheila was sitting at the telephone, which lived on a small table at the top of our staircase. I was in my study (the snuggery); I shouted back, "I'll take the call."

I remembered having seen a small photograph in *The Times of India* about an Englishman called Cheshire who apparently had just arrived in India on some 'do-gooding' operation. Apparently he had won the VC in the RAF during the war. I had been mildly interested but as we were due to sail for good in three weeks time, I paid no particular attention. But why should he want to see me? I telephoned Dabeh. I knew, of course, that Kikuk Thadani was Sheila's oldest friend. I also knew that Kikuk's sister, Rajkumari Amrit Kaur, was an important politician; in fact she was Pandit Nehru's first ever Minister of Health. I rang Dabeh and asked her what it was all about. She asked me to call round at Petit Hall on my way to the office.

Once more, looking across her brother-in-law's beautiful lawn over to the Indian Ocean, I found her as usual very business-like, sitting at her desk. She was active with many charities and had an office on the ground floor of Petit Hall. She then told me what it was all about.

"This chap Cheshire – apparently he was a highly decorated Bomber Pilot in the RAF – had started several homes for disabled people in England and now he has come to India to get one going in Bombay. He has some helpers with him, also a broken-down bus, but he has no money and no papers for the import of his transport, which the Collector of Customs has impounded. He must have some influence because Nan Pandit (Nehru's sister) had contacted Rajkumari Amrit Kaur, the Minister of Health, who knew about my charity work and I, of course, knew that you had been in the RAF, so I rang Sheila. And there we are!"

She asked, "What's to be done?"

I asked Dabeh where Cheshire was, as I felt at least I had better try and meet him. "Apparently," Dabeh said, "he's somewhere in the jungle north of the airport. He seems to have a secretary, a girl called Margot Mason. She is living at the YWCA but she has never been outside England before in her life. I think you had better contact her. Here's her phone number."

Dabeh then gave me a piece of paper. Because I knew that Kikuk Thadani was Sheila's oldest friend I moved into top gear and Margot Mason had lunch with me that day at the Taj Mahal Hotel in the air-conditioned dining room.

Margot Mason — (I didn't know whom or what to look for) — apparently was the Group Captain's Secretary; the Group Captain had a VC, a jeep, a broken-down bus and he had disappeared into the jungle to the north of Bombay's international airport. He was said to have no money and yet he had a secretary who had never been out of England before.

She should get on well with Sheila, I thought, who had never been out of India when I had first met her. In fact they did get on with each other well when they met a few days later. After Kikuk, she was to become one of Sheila's best friends. I had asked her if we could meet at the reception desk of the Taj Hotel. When I advanced on the imposing reception desk there was no difficulty in recognising her — short and athletic-looking with a warm smile and complete self-confidence or, perhaps, was it courage? She wore a simple dress, and looked fit and healthy. There was absolutely no side to her whatsoever. Upstairs, in the air-conditioned dining room, we sat at a table on the small stage at the western end of that large impressive room, a sort of East of Suez Savoy Grill.

The first thing she said was, "Gosh, I hope I don't put up a black. I'm terribly hungry. They are so good to me at the YWCA but I can't take this hot food, I'm afraid." She ordered a conventional English lunch, which she ate with gusto. There was something aristocratic about her manner and there was a lot to talk about — enough to fill several books. Several years later it almost filled one of my own. By the end of lunch I knew quite a lot about Group Captain Leonard Cheshire VC, DSO and two bars, DFC, late Commander of 617 Squadron RAF, the Dam Busters.

Margot had been, for a number of years, secretary to Earl Ferrers, whose sixteenth-century seat in Leicestershire, Staunton Harold, had been almost demolished during the war, whilst serving as a German prisoner of war camp. Robin Ferrers who had inherited this noble ruin from his father in

1953, was about to sell it, together with a lot of valuable land to a developer; just then Cheshire had turned up with £10,000, which a friend had given him and so had been able to buy off the developer.

Robin Ferrers agreed with enthusiasm to serve as a Trustee under Lord Denning, who was Chairman of Cheshire's recently formed Foundation. He sold the beautiful house with its Cromwellian Chapel, for £10,000 which he immediately gave back to the Cheshire Foundation. The whole of Leicestershire then poured into Staunton Harold every weekend to restore the place. They were helped in this task by Rolls Royce.

Long before it was habitable, in the conventional sense of that word, thirty disabled men and women were living happily, if not comfortably, in this wonderful old house. Lady Ferrers, Robin's mother, the dowager, had put in much time and knee-work scrubbing the tiled floor of the immense entrance hall. Margot then became Leonard Cheshire's Secretary and Staunton Harold his fourth Home in England.

And now he had answered a letter from an English businessman in South India and was about to start his first home outside England, in Bombay. Margot also told me about the bus and the jeep. "The demurrage is more than £1000 already. I have about £90, in my purse, that's all we've got. Can you possibly help?"

I must say she looked one hundred per cent better after lunch.

"First of all," I said, "hadn't I better meet him?"

"Of course; he's got one hut up already near a place called Santa Cruz. It's near Bombay Airport."

The English head of the new Shell oil refinery had given the hut to him.

"There are three old Indians in it already with more to come."

I was beginning to feel as wobbly and almost as hysterical as I had done with my Tibetan chum, Mr Kyipup.

"When can you take me to meet him?" I said.

Margot replied, "Have you got a car?"

"Yes, it's in front of the hotel."

"Why don't we go now? I can show you the way."

"Why not?" I said.

It proved to be the most serious commitment I had made since I had married Sheila in Bombay on 16th May 1942.

The drive from the Taj to the airport at Santa Cruz – about fifteen miles – was easy. I must have done it a hundred times. We went straight on past the turn off to the airport and had to slow down when pushing our way through the crowded village of Andheri. Margot told me a lot more about Cheshire's strange new career – after he had left the Air Force.

Margot went on: "His father, a marvellous man, was Vinerian Professor of Law at Oxford, where Sir Alfred Denning (as he then was) was one of his pupils." Names such as Sir Archibald Jamieson, Chairman of Vickers-Armstrong, Lady St Levan, châtelaine of St Michael's Mount in Cornwall, and, of course, Earl Ferrers of Staunton Harold dropped from her lips quite naturally; they and others of that ilk had helped him start his new career. On the far side of Andheri we speeded, and suddenly she placed a hand on my left arm and said, "This is our first turning, next on the right."

I had no idea until that moment that the jungle was so close to this enormous town of ours. Bombay, (with a population in 1955 of nine million) was indeed huge. We had driven a mile or so down this side road when she pointed to a tiny signpost six inches off the ground on the left-hand side of the road. It read simply "Bethlehem House".

"He gave it that name ten days ago when we first arrived. I've no idea who, if anyone, gave him the land; He's about three miles down that track."

I turned left into the jungle and we drove at about ten miles an hour over many pot-holes in a rough country lane through thick trees, past several stagnant tanks (Indian ponds) until suddenly we broke out into an open space, lit up by the afternoon sun. It seemed to be quite empty until a cheerful voice called out from somewhere, "Hello, Dopey, we hadn't seen you for so long we thought you had gone home."

A slight young Englishman in grey flannels, gym shoes and an open shirt appeared from inside a small asbestos hut. He came up to me, looked me in the eyes and said, as he shook my hand, "It's good of you to come out here. Excuse me a minute, will you? I've just got to wash old Pop, then I'll be with you."

He disappeared into the hut where I could just make out a broken-down old Indian squatting on the floor. Margot dumped some letters on a desk outside the hut. She then drew up a kitchen chair and got to work on the mail. In a few minutes Cheshire came out onto the veranda followed by Pop, who was easing himself along the floor on folded legs.

He proceeded to kiss Cheshire's feet and then started eating some curried stuff with his fingers from a bowl. Cheshire beckoned me into a kind of office at the end of the veranda. It reminded me vaguely of a Flight Commander's office in an RAF operational squadron — orderly disorder; nothing very much was there but everything that was there was practical and useful. Across the open space, underneath a palm tree was a camp bed covered by a mosquito net and an upturned cardboard box, which served as a bedside table. There was a prayer book on it.

"I'm glad we've met; it's good of you to come out here."

The blue eyes and the serious look suddenly gave way to an infectious smile; it was a combination I had never come across before.

"I expect you're busy. The things I really want are the jeep and the bus — we can't move without them. Can you prise them loose from the customs?"

"I'll try."

"Good."

I drove Margot back to town. On the way I said, "Why Dopey?"

"You must have seen the seven dwarfs film. The Ferrers family called me that; they thought I was small and, somehow, walked like Dopey in the film. I hope you'll call me Margot."

I said, "Of course I will. You must come to tea with us now. Our house is quite near here on the way back to Bombay; then you can meet Sheila; she's my wife."

"I would love to."

It all seemed a long way from the Möhne and the Eeder Dams.

Just before we left I said to Cheshire, "I'm not sure about getting your bus out of the Customs. I have to deal in business with the man who runs them. He's a tough egg but I'll do my best. Is there anything else I can do to help?"

He thought for a moment. "Well there's this rough track. The monsoon is due soon and when that comes we'll be out of business for several months. Could you do anything there?"

I said I would get Margot Mason to let him know as we were going to have tea with Sheila, my wife, on the way back.

Again the smile and the one word, "Thanks." He went back to Pop. Margot met Sheila; they got on at once. I had known they would.

Over tea Sheila said to me, "Sobruto Muckerjee is trying to get hold of you. He just rang. He's inspecting a squadron of the IAF and wanted to talk to you. Here's his phone number."

Air Vice Marshal Sobruto Muckerjee commanded the new 10 Squadron Indian Air Force. He had been trained at Cranwell. We had known each other during the war.

I dumped Margot back at the YWCA and said I would contact her if there was anything to report about the bus and the jeep.

Back in my office I had an idea. I rang Sobruto and asked him if we could have a drink that evening. We met at the Harbour Bar at the Taj.

He looked smart in his Air Marshal's uniform. I didn't waste any time.

"Did you know that Group Captain Cheshire is here?"

"Do you mean *the* Cheshire of 617 Squadron?"

"Yes," I said.

Then I told him about the bus and the jeep and the demurrage and the Collector of Customs. Sobruto said, "But that's absurd, can I meet this Collector chap?"

Next morning the Collector, a grumpy unaccommodating bureaucrat, received us in his large office in the docks. He was clearly surprised at meeting a smartly dressed senior officer of the Indian Air Force. He obviously didn't know such a thing as an Indian Air Force existed, especially not one commanded by an Indian officer. After I had explained the situation he said to me, "Have you got the money? It's the equivalent of £1500. No money, no bus."

It was at this point that Sobruto rose out of his chair and said curtly, "Will a Government of India guarantee be all right?"

The Collector was taken aback. "Yes, but I would have to have it in writing."

Sobruto didn't even bother to be polite. "Give me a piece of your own stationery and a pen."

The astonished senior civil servant handed the glowering Air Marshal a piece of paper. Sobruto sat down and wrote out five words: "The Air Force will pay."

"I propose to push them through the Red Gate myself with the help of Mr Russell, here. Please order one of your officers to show us where the vehicles are and to give us every assistance." He then said a formal goodbye and we left the office. The vehicles were duly pushed out into the street. Sobruto came home to Bates Hill for a whisky and soda with Sheila.

Next morning I rang the Secretary of the Premier of Bombay State, Morarji Desai, and asked her if the PM could receive Group Captain Cheshire the next day. I felt sure he would like to meet someone who had actually watched the atom bomb being dropped on Hiroshima, an event, which later Cheshire told the PM had changed him from being a man of war to a man of peace.

Next morning Cheshire and I were ushered into the Prime Minister's imposing office. There they were, the Brahmin and the Kshartrya – Morarji Desai was wearing his white dhoti (a sort of cotton skirt). Cheshire had on a thin well-cut tropical suit. The politician was serious, the warrior deferential but light-hearted. Morarji just wanted to know about the atom bomb. Then he remembered his brief.

"Tell me, how do you get your food and helpers up into those thick jungles? There's no road, is there?"

"It's all right now, sir, in the dry season. I'm not sure how we'll do it in the monsoon."

I noticed that Morarji was writing something on a small notepad. Then he rose and made a Namasthe, the Indian greeting made by raising the two hands placed together and then raising them from face to forehead.

"Thank you, it has been a pleasure to meet you. I wish you success in your endeavours."

Cheshire gave the politician a dazzling smile. "It has been nice to have met you."

Cheshire and I walked to the lift.

Suddenly he said, "Bet I can beat you to the ground floor down the stairs."

I charged down from the third floor to the hall, three stairs at a time. At the bottom there was Leonard Cheshire, wreathed in smiles. The lift doors were just closing.

"Good thing I didn't put any money on it," was the only thing I could think of to say.

29

The Decision

"How happy is he born and taught,
That serveth not another's will
Whose armour is his honest thought,
And simple truth his utmost skill!"

Sir Henry Wotton

The time had come at last, the time to decide where we stood. In fact, there were two decisions to be made. We were both agreed, on what they should be.

One evening Sheila and I stayed at home together; there were no pegs, burra or chota, to influence our choice.

The first concerned the firm, the House of Killick Nixon. Would it always remain British or would it become an Indian Company?

The second, a more fundamental question; was the environment in which we had lived up till now, inspired by the Christian ethic, by Hinduism or by Islam?

We tried to keep our questions and our answers as brief and as uncomplicated as we could. Hence this chapter will be a short one. We took the material questions first and then the spiritual one.

After exactly a century of trading Killicks had shown that ultimately it must become wholly Indian in money matters and in outlook. The arguments in favour of this line of thought were clear enough both in logic and in sentiment. Ever since India had become independent politically and Pakistan had come into existence, in 1947, a growing fault line in the shape of a split between the senior British and the senior Indian employees had become only too evident. As time passed recruitment from "home" – that is, England – would slowly die.

Victor Noel-Paton, now retired and a life peer (Lord Ferrier) was sent out from London to Bombay by the older generation of partners to knock our silly young heads together. He failed completely as anyone could have told him he would if he had cared to ask anyone. The Marwaris (Hindu millionaires) were hiding round every corner, their pockets bulging with the rupees they had made during the war – a conflict which had saved their own lives together with their fortunes.

On the spiritual and intellectual side, India would always dominate Pakistan by its financial power. A fighting faith like Islam could never conquer the world, neither the Eastern nor the Western half of it. But there was little doubt that it would have a good try.

And why was this? I put this question emphatically to Sheila.

Her reply was equally emphatic. "There's one main reason," she said, "indeed, it is possibly the only one."

There was a pause. I waited for her to go on.

"The pressure exerted by the Mullahs (the priests), the pressure in fact of the whole Islamic system is against their women."

She then recited in all its miserable details – how women were given no proper education, as a matter of course, neither in the arts, nor in sexual nor domestic matters; they were not allowed to tempt Muslim men by dressing well, by attracting them in any way either intellectually or physically, as all women have done since Adam and Eve in the Garden of Eden. In fact, their women were hidden behind the burquah (the covering of their face by a stifling sort of fishing net). It was a "men only" way of life.

Sheila had enjoyed a number of happy Muslim friendships in her youth. Nevertheless she knew the truth. She only mentioned this subject to me.

"Our children are going to be brought up in the West," she said; and that was that.

So we made our decision. This meant goodbye to Mother, Duggie and Sonny. I booked our passage for 16th May 1956 from Bombay to Tilbury on the P & O liner, *Himalaya*. We could never say goodbye to the Family until that last farewell of all.

There were any number of farewell parties; too many of them were just pretend goodbyes. The only non-pretend one wasn't a party. They all collected around our mango tree, which stood in front of the steps leading up to the front hall of Bates Hill – Ram Dayal, Cookie, Francis (the young Goanese driver), Nanny, two Jacks-of-all-Trades (the Hamals) – and finally my fellow member of the Cambridge Hawks and Ski Club – old Gunia, the gardener. There was no pretending there.

We all blubbed a bit and I saw a tear or two on the White Sari.

30

Birth of a Bestseller

> *"There is an art of reading, as well as an art of thinking,*
> *and an art of writing."*
>
> Isaac D'Israeli

John Masters, the well-known English novelist became a friend of our family, especially of Sheila, in Bombay just after the war ended in 1945. He then had two careers, both of which were hugely successful. He was really an Indian for he was the fifth generation of his family to serve in the Indian Army in which his father had won the DSO. He had been at Wellington and Sandhurst. He joined the Gurkhas and won his DSO as a Column Commander in Wingate's second penetration of Burma in 1944. He had met Sonny, Sheila's elder brother before WW2 on landing at Bombay when he bought a second-hand car from him (Sonny's first job on his return to India from his apprenticeship with Vickers). They had a cheerful lunch to celebrate the car purchase. "How come you are Indian?" Masters had asked him. "I fell into the Black Sea on the way home," was Sonny's quick reply.

Masters joined the 4th Gurkhas (plus the second-hand car) in 1935, direct from Sandhurst. Sonny introduced Jack, as he was called by his many friends, to Sheila in Lahore. He joined his regiment at its base on the North West frontier, fought regular skirmishes against the tribesmen and went to Iraq when WW2 broke out in 1939. His regiment fought the Pétain French alongside the British Yeomanry and beat them. He became and was indeed a promising Subaltern and passed out top at the Quetta Staff College, was chosen by Orde Wingate to be second-in-command of a column in his first long-range penetration of Japanese occupied Burma in 1943.

He then met Duggie and later Sheila. They all clicked and he became a friend of the Sawhny family. When the war ended Jack was a full colonel with a DSO and an OBE, a wife, Barbara Rose, two children and a job at Sandhurst as a member of the directing staff. He disliked Labour England, left the British Army, went to America with only his army pension, there to make his fortune. In 1947, he was down to his last buck in New York. In 1948 he set about writing novels covering the three centuries of the Anglo-Indian connection. His first two were *Nightrunners of Bengal* and *The Deceivers*, each book was Book of the Month in London and New York.

In 1954 he wrote *Bhowani Junction*, about the Anglo-Indian community in Independent India. His heroine, Victoria Jones, was the daughter of an Anglo-Indian engine driver. He asked Sheila to help him bring Victoria Jones to life, which she did. The book *Bhowani Junction* was the most successful of about twenty-five which he was to write. Needless to say, in 1954, it was Book of the Month in London and New York. Ava Gardner played the part of Victoria Jones in the film; Stewart Granger was the hero, a portrait of Masters himself.

The rest of this chapter records the correspondence that followed between Masters and myself in which I acted as a conduit for Sheila's bringing Masters' heroine to life. Masters recorded his gratitude in his hand-written 'thank you' in the flyleaf of the book (printed in Chapter Twenty-seven).

13th February 1953

AIR MAIL

My dear Jack,

I am sending you herewith my own comments on Bhowani Junction *as you would probably like to have them as quickly as possible. Sheila has read the book but unfortunately she has just gone to bed with 'flu' and I think it may be a few days before she can put her thoughts on paper. I will naturally encourage the process as much as I can!*

I enjoyed the book very much and am sure that it can be developed into the same excellent production as the Nightrunners. *If you would like any further comments from me or if you would like to ask Sheila any particular questions or direct her criticism into specific channels in the light of my comments please write to me by return.*

I will send the manuscript back to you by Air Mail when Sheila has finished her comments.

All the best

Signed WWR

John Masters, Esq.,
Centenary,
New City,
New York, U.S.A.

Centenary
New City, N.Y.
Tel: New City 4-2720

Feb 24, 1953

My dear Wilfrid,

Very many thanks to Sheila for her comments which have just arrived. Before I forget, let me note one question which has been exercising me and which might take a hell of a long time to get sorted out here. When was the AF(I) (Auxiliary Force India) disbanded? If you know anyone who was in it you might be able to get the answer by a telephone call — but don't go to any great trouble over it. It will affect me if they were already gone or going; it would affect Patrick of course and might make my later chapters easier and more effective. As far as I can recall it was in 1946, but when, I can't recall.

Do not think too hardly of my publishers here! They are very good and sympathetic people. They obviously cannot concern themselves over the accuracy of a portrait especially of Anglo Indians 7 years ago. The accuracy or otherwise of Portraits, situations etc, is my business. But they can and do concern themselves with the effect of my words on the readers of the book — Americans. They say, 'This is the impression we get — do you mean that?' In this case the impression I have given is one of unpleasantness, and a kind of squalidity for which they cannot feel sympathy. That is not what I mean to give — sullenness certainly, and squalidity, and frustration etc; but the reader must feel sympathy. Therefore it is up to me to re-write in such a way that the reader gets the right impression. Wait till you read the new version and I think you will agree I have been able to do a good deal both to improve the 'feel' and give a truer impression.

I suggest, with modesty, that the average Indian Army officer was too polite to speak openly anywhere near Sheila — or even any stranger of whatever sex. Rodney is meant to be rather a tough egg and becoming increasingly bitter as the affair with Victoria leads to its inevitable conclusion and India starts sliding out of his reach. Furthermore, he speaks deliberately in that way to Victoria (and only to her, you will note), because he has been trying to show himself exactly as he is. The language is not, as a matter of fact, at all overstressed for a wartime officer though only in special cases would it be on display. I'll be careful to try and give the right impression this time.

It now appears likely that I shall be in England during the early summer — bidden by Korda. We are arguing about terms at the moment. Will write again when the MS arrives.

All the best

Jack

Centenary
New City, N.Y.

April 27, 1954

My dear Wilfrid,

I was relieved to hear that your copy of BJ rolled up, because the first letter we opened in the mail today was one from Betty Cole (a mutual friend in Bombay), in which she said you were expecting to get a copy, but hadn't then had it. You mustn't blame the poor publishers for the multiple first person approach, except to the extent that they, or rather the editors, Keith and Helen, pointed out to me that Patrick Taylor was an unsympathetic boor, and was this what I meant him to be. You had said the same thing, if you remember. Of course I did not mean that at all – but the desired effect could not be achieved by making him more efficient because then the whole tragedy of the situation would have been watered down. What to do? It was I who decided that the only solution was to present the characters from the inside, thus allowing the reader to understand a great deal which he could not otherwise have done. Pritchett didn't think it came off, and so did a few others; I think the general consensus would be about 2:1 the other way; but luckily I don't read any reviews unless they are forced under my nose by excitable publishers and agents. If I refuse to consider the bad ones, on the legitimate grounds that they don't know what they are talking about, I must and do refuse to consider the good ones, on the same grounds.

Your book sounds interesting, and please do send the MS along here when done, and I will put it in to Viking at once. I think it is at least as likely to appeal to the public here as anywhere else – this public is very large and has a praiseworthy passion to be informed. It depends – brace yourself for a cliché – on who it is done by. Rachel Carson got a hatful of prizes and pounds and pounds of the folding stuff for THE SEA AROUND US, which was a treatise on the waves and fishes and tides of the sea; it happened to be beautifully done, and most interesting.

Viking don't get away with a cent of the movie money — I got a new and extremely tough agent just before signing the original contracts for BJ, and she cut the publishers out of all participation, and somehow made them agree. Uncle Samuel, of course, is going to share heavily, but I don't mind that, considering what the old gentleman has done for me. It is just possible that MGM may ask my opinion about technical advice for the film, and I will tell them to hire Sheila, if they do. It's worth trying, and she can always say No. The by-products of notoriety are beginning to appear now — my travel agent has asked me to sponsor a tour to India next winter. This turns out to mean a free passage with a bunch of tourists, plus a bonus of some size, and the outlines of the tour to be dictated by me. I am thinking about it; we both want to come very much, but I'm not sure that the free passage is worth being saddled with a mixed bunch of rubbernecks for; and in 1957 we definitely have India on the agenda because I intend to be present at the centenary celebrations of my regiment. However, we may do it if work permits. Coromandel [his next planned novel] *ought to be finished by then but the publishers are beginning to make noises as though they now wanted me to brush up and produce the first volume of my autobiography, BRUTAL AND LICENTIOUS, which was the first thing I wrote — it was turned down freely on all sides in 1948. I am torn between two wishes, one, to improve it, as it is fairly amateurish, and two, to make the bastards publish it with acclamation exactly as they refused it 6 years ago. I shall probably re-write it in the end, because Viking didn't turn it down; they never saw it.*

We are beginning to knock hell out of this poor old house, of course, now that Hollywood has spoken — making a study above the barn, giving the kids a decent playroom etc. The garden looks quite lovely now — peach and apple blossom everywhere, pink almond blossom, yellow forsythia, tulips just over, daffodils and narcissus out and the grass green. Will see you in the spring — and will then make an earnest attempt to kidnap you so that you come and live here; but here in Rockland. If we find manganese in the orchard, I'll cable you.

Barbara joins in sending her love — thanks again for your help — and good wishes.

Jack

BHOWANI JUNCTION
Notes by Wilfrid

These remarks are quite independent of Sheila's. We have naturally discussed the book a lot together but will make separate observations as hers are likely to be more valuable than mine.

Generally speaking I think you have dealt with this very difficult subject successfully and I would not be inclined to write the three parts separately, as you have suggested. By doing so you might make the book psychologically more accurate but not more popular in its appeal. As, in my view, you have hit the nail pretty truly on the head, I would not be inclined to depart from convention to the extent you suggest.

I think you have made Victoria too intelligent and Patrick far too boorish. For the purposes of the book you will presumably have to leave Victoria as an exception to the run of her kind, which you have in any case depicted in Rose Mary. But could you not indicate that there might be a hereditary explanation of this by making her grandfather or great grandfather one of those adventurer Englishmen of good family who strayed from the beaten path in the 19ᵗʰ century — such as Sir William Rumbold of the Hyderabad firm of Palmer and Co whose wife (daughter of Lord William Bentinck) died in Ooty in about 1830 and was buried in the church there. He, I believe, was a bit of an adventurer and, I think, stayed on in the country. It might be difficult to weave this in to the Bhowani background but it would certainly explain her sensitiveness to her surroundings and in particular her sympathy with India and Indians which is not evident in most A-Is. Her sulkiness is quite typical and personally I don't find it at all unsympathetic, especially as it melts away as she comes under the spell of Rodney. If you or your publishers feel it is too thickly laid on for the G.A.P. (Great American Public), why not try to make her more gay and uninhibited in the later chapters, as Rodney awakes her basic instincts about India and her essential "englishness"? A corollary of this would be a gradual soft pedalling of the sex angle towards the end and by this token the elimination of the last physical episode on the railway embankment which should be cut out, which brings me to the next point — the fact that you have, I think, been too hard on the A-I community.

At the time of which you write — and, of course, before — they were at sixes and sevens in every situation. In 1946 they were completely bewildered and your story illustrates this state of mind well. Nevertheless they have in a curious way fitted into the new dispensation much better than many of us could have expected. This is a very broad generalisation, I realise, and some might challenge it. But I have seen a number of the admittedly younger ones do damn well in the Army, Navy and Air Force where they seem to have identified themselves with the new India and so are much happier. Of course it's easier for the young men to start afresh in (for the A-Is) new services. It's probably not so on the Railways. But the fact remains that they do, so that the outlook for some of them is not so tragic. In fact I think the A-I youth will, in a curious way, serve the new India in their armed forces in the same way as they did the old in the subordinate services, and will identify themselves with the go-ahead elements of the country which at the present moment find themselves in the armed forces — to the benefit of both. All this doesn't help you much except perhaps that you could indicate in some way that their future is not necessarily so tragic and hopeless as your picture presages — in the marriage of Victoria and Patrick.

Patrick is, I feel, altogether too beery and beastly. Obviously he must have the "wog" complex but could he not be slightly more promising and develop during the book under the impact of Rodney in the same way as Victoria does? The A-Is in our collieries, on whom my observations are based, are much as you have painted him but they do have other interests than their work and beer – it is usually shikar (shooting big or small game), at which ours are surprisingly good. Could this not be in some way Patrick's redeeming feature round which might be woven the promise of redemption? Couldn't he do something reasonably brave – as much a surprise to himself as to Rodney and Victoria – which would indicate that there may be a future for Victoria and for him, and so for their community in the new India? I realise this suggestion might upset "the death of Birkhe" incident. Could Patrick, perhaps, save Birkhe or catch K P Roy (by mistake, or both at once, of course)? As regards Patrick and his future I had in mind that you might perhaps indicate very lightly a different future for him in some other sphere, which is not impossible. How about, for instance, introducing our big cement factory at Kymore near Katni, which can't be so very far from your Bhowani Junction? Could not the President of the Education Society be a Director of the Factory and happen then to give in over closing the school (as I had to do) for which Patrick might, perhaps, get the credit – also there could be the promise of a job at the Factory in the hard times ahead – or perhaps the School would be sold anyhow after an effort on Patrick's part, however clumsy, to have the decision changed. I realise all this may be miles beyond your brief to me but you can probably see what I am driving at – an indication – it need be no more than that – that there is more in the future for Victoria and Patrick than brawls and beer and misery. After all even if Rodney is not her real answer – and I agree with you he is really married to the real India and to his regiment – the Anglo-Indians have produced at least one real Duchess and a leading film star, neither of whom I'm sure are as attractive as Victoria!

Regarding the lower middle class Indian home Sheila will be better on this than I. My impression is that it is difficult to describe because there is so little to describe. The rooms are usually devoid of furniture except in orthodox Hindu homes where you may still find the bolsters on the floor. Generally tho' I have the feeling that they are giving way to 'western' furniture which, in the home you have in mind, usually consists of an occasional rickety chair and a cheap table. The accent seems to be on cheapness and lack of what we would consider taste. There are usually brass pots or silver 'lotahs' about the place and execrable pictures either of Hindu Gods and Goddesses or of Gandhi and Nehru in bad frames and garish colours. You would see string beds in unexpected places and, of course, as you know, all the care, spit and polish lavished on the kitchen which is always the most important room in the house, full of shining, scoured aluminium 'dekhshies' of all shapes and a big curry stone somewhere. There would be a courtyard at the back with a high wall around it containing firewood and probably none too clean, plus a cow and/or goat contributing to the noise and general confusion. Coming to the middle class Hindu home the general atmosphere is one of constant coming and going to no plan, time being of no object, and everything being highly informal and friendly and dreadfully uncomfortable by our standards. There would also probably be an all pervading scent of what for lack of a better word I would call incense. Also bright lights, all over the kitchen, either electric bulbs without shades or probably in your case petromax lamps fizzing and attracting all manner of insects! There would be no mixed parties in your lower middle class Indian home, they would speak in Hindi in your part of the world, would do 'namasthi' (the Indian greeting with both hands pressed together below the chin) to each other when meeting – probably a bit exaggerated because of the national forms coming in during the changeover – the Hindi would be richly interspersed with English in the political circle you are writing of, they would eat on the floor from brass or silver saucers with tiny bowls on the silver tray each with its sample of a different type of food on it, and the rice heaped up in the middle somewhere. They would eat with their fingers, thumb, first and second finger bent back in a curve from years of finger-eating. There would be chapattis to mop up the liquid curry gravy, rather messy, which would probably upset Victoria if you get her at one of these meals (which I think you did not do?) but which would not, of course, worry Rodney in the least.

On points of detail Sheila has one or two notes. My only query concerns the date of the R.I.N. Mutiny which you put somewhere late in May. It actually started on Feb 24th 1946. I was wondering whether placing your story in the 'hot weather' has any significance. Heat usually has in most Indian novels and, of course, it had to in the 'Nightrunners' because of history. It seems to me that you could paint the Indian rural background with more lustre and freshness in the cold weather rather than the hot and at the same time remain accurate in your timing. It would still be terribly hot in the tunnel on the footplate. Patrick's surname doesn't seem right unless the G.A.P. requires something with a 'Cuban' ring about it. If he is to be an R.C. then De Mello would be more normal or DeSilva or, perhaps, Gonsalvo. More normal still, I think, would be something like Gilbert Leader, Warner or some such name.

Incidentally I don't know whether you want any local colour on the A-I home? I am an expert on this, as I have to spend some time in them on our colliery inspection visits! Bead curtains, the walls covered with stuffed bison of enormous size and depressing features, rather moth eaten tigers and panthers on the floor, over which one is always tripping; monsoon sunsets in black lugubrious frames on the walls with an occasional faded photo of Patrick in the school hockey eleven or A.F.(I) platoon with some pot in the middle – as for the food! I suppose that when alone they eat curry and rice, probably rather poor stuff, but when a European is visiting it's ghastly. The worst boarding house imaginable and all rather dolled up to strike an attitude, especially the puddings, soggy, solid and 'superior'.

April 27, 1954
AIR MAIL

My dear Jack,

Herewith Sheila's remarks about Bhowani Junction. I am afraid they are not as extensive as I had hoped but I think that this is largely due to the fact that, like myself, she found your portrayal of Victoria on the whole a very accurate one. I have just received your letter of the 13ᵗʰ instant from which it would seem that the accuracy of the picture is not basically important as your Publisher's ignorance of the type does not enable them to appreciate its interest and so its inherent attractiveness! If this is the case I suppose then there is nothing for it but to fall in with their wishes and re-write the book through the eyes of the three different characters, although I don't think I would enjoy the book so much written in this manner. Anyway here are Sheila's notes: -

Anglo-Indian girls are by and large very sulky as is to be expected from their general attitude towards life – but Victoria's intelligence, guts and sensitivity are well above average – there have been quite a few like her who have achieved success by their standards.

Patrick Gonzalvo is, I think, a bit too 'oafish' and stupid – I don't think Gonzalvo is a very suitable name, especially with the typical colouring of eyes, skin and hair that you have given him.

Ranjit's mother should not be called Begum – but her title should be "Sardarni" and when spoken to she should be addressed either as "Sardarni Sahiba" or "Beji" (My comment is that the latter would be the more likely form of address).

Would suggest that Govindaswami went either to Clifton, Cheltenham or Harrow – not Rugby. I would not stress the point that his grandfather was actually a sweeper – it would be sufficient to say that he sprang from that caste.

The Indian lower middle class home is very uncomfortable — a few solid Charpoys (string beds) with bedding rolled up in a 'Durrie' and tin trunks containing the family belongings. Towels are frequently used as Table Cloths, a few brass ornaments and a holy picture or two with a garland of small marigolds strung round them. They rarely give a "party" except on a big occasion but it is very frequent in Hindu or Sikh homes for the neighbours to call and for friends to drop in at odd times, and in many cases, little parties then spring up from this "calling". They are mixed in the sense that the sexes mix but not mixed in the racial sense. In other works it would be surprising to find a European in an Indian lower middle class home. It is usual for the men to gossip together and for the women to congregate separately.

Sheila, who knows the Indian Army officers, (both Indian and European) is of the opinion that Rodney's language is too harsh in places for a self-disciplined "gent" which is what he is presumably supposed to be. I rather agree with her on this point. I think Rodney is an excellent character but towards the end of the book he seems to coarsen, particularly in his language during the last chapters.

I am afraid this is not a very exhaustive or detailed commentary from Sheila but she has not been very well. I showed her my notes after she had written hers and she agreed with most of what I have written. I think the best plan would be for you to ask her a series of definitive questions requiring definite answers if there are any points over which we can help.

Thackers should have sent your manuscript by airmail yesterday. Please let me know when it arrives.

All the best	*John Masters, Esq.,*
Yours,	*Centenary,*
Signed WWR	*New City,*
	New York.
	U.S.A.

3 1

A Tribute to Indian Industry

*"In 1876 the late Mr L R H Forrest became a Partner in
Messrs Killick Nixon & Co. and it was largely due to his
initiative that the Firm, from the year 1896 decided to
strike out on entirely new lines of business in the direction
of floating and managing various companies, beginning with
Railway Companies and the Kohinoor Mills."*

*Small notebook issued by the Partners of Killick Nixon &
Co., East India Merchants, Bombay, to each new Assistant on joining.*

There are three of them, which concern this story. First of all come their
names, the House of Killick, then the House of Porbunder and finally the
great House of Tata. Starting with Porbunder because it was small and not
particularly important, yet most people in India would believe, quite rightly,
that it was the most important of all the states in India, for it was the birthplace
of Mahatma Gandhi. A small, princely territory a few hundred miles north
of Bombay in Gujarat, it lay on the sea and it was near here that the Mahatma
had set out on his famous salt march in the 1930s, in defiance of the British
Indian Government of those days.

Sheila knew the delightful Maharajah of this State because he owned a
house in Ootacamund in South India. She liked his charming personality
and felt drawn towards his wife, the Maharani, who was Welsh and who
wore saris almost as strikingly as she did. I liked him for one official reason,
he owned the land on which one of the cement factories, for which I was
responsible, reposed; and one altogether unofficial reason was that he once

had captained the Indian Test Match cricket team and had in fact led the first all-India team to play against England, in England.

The second unofficial reason for my admiration was that he was an excellent violinist, who, every Saturday evening, led his personal quartet of courtiers in the main square of his capital, also that his favourite composer was none other than Wolfgang Amadeus Mozart.

In pursuit of good relations, I once took the ACC (Cement Company) cricket team to play his State side. Porbunder won. Sheila came to support us and Porby (as we used to call him) gave a Hollywood-Victorian-style banquet, lit completely by wax-dropping candles wobbling on silver chandeliers, in honour of Sheila and myself and, of course, the whole team. It had covered a weekend and there was one free night. Despite my protests that I had never shot big game in my life, his son, the Raj Kumar, was ordered by his father to take me into the jungle on that single free night. They would guarantee me a real, live tiger. So the Crown Prince took me at dusk, complete with two beautiful looking Purdy shot guns and a dozen beaters, but not, as I had expected, to a tree for me to climb up. I expected that I would have to crawl out onto a branch with a goat staked out below where I would wait for the tiger who would probably arrive late for his dinner. As it was I found myself creeping into an insecure-looking square wattle-hedged piece of jungle in which there had been installed a comfortable-looking sofa. There was a largish hole in the sofa side of the wattle hedge, through which I could not even see the unfortunate goat. The Crown Prince loaded my Purdy, handed it to me and said, "When the tiger comes I will pass you the gun. You will then get up and shoot the tiger. I will be here in case anything goes wrong."

Within half an hour the goat screamed and by the time I had struggled out of the sofa, taken aim through the hedge and fired, all I could see was the tiger's tail and one dead goat, stretched out flat on the ground, tied to the stake. I was apologetic, His Highness was polite. I returned to Bombay having lost a cricket match and a tiger. "Bugles and a Game."

The next famous House was that of Killick, which I have mentioned before and which had enabled Sheila and myself to live comfortably as a Squadron Leader and his wife and better than most by paying my Killick Nixon salary all through the five years of war. On top of that they had thoughtfully provided a house and lovely garden when I was demobbed. Can anyone ask for more?

The third House was the House of Tata.

James Clavell, one of our finest novelists at the end of the twentieth century, who had spent most of the Second World War as a p.o.w. in Changi gaol in Singapore, wrote one of his best novels about Hong Kong into which he had woven the history of Jardine Matheson, a small merchant house in Hong Kong. He called this book *Noble House*. The company itself had started business about the time of the Opium Wars in 1840. Its success had been partly due to its ability to draw on the mercantile skills of Scottish workers together with the money it abstracted from the City of London, also the opium which it exported to India and the dyes it imported from India; it sent to India and to England a great deal of the excellent tea which grew in China in large quantities.

The House of Tata was created by one single family from the small community of Parsees, which counted only about 200,000 souls. They had fled from Persia in the ninth century as a result of religious persecution of their Zoroastrian faith at the hands of an early Shah. Having escaped from Persia, they settled in Karachi and Bombay. Because of their minute numbers, compared with the many millions of Hindus and Muslims in India, it was, in my view, little short of miraculous that they could have built up the wealth they had done in such a short time. They returned the protection which British rule had given them by staunch loyalty to the Government of India. They were more Victorian than the Victorians and more charitable both to each other and to the poor of the many foreigners living in India than any other community.

Long before I arrived in Bombay in 1935, Jamsetjee Tata – grandfather of Dabeh, who was to marry Sheila's brother, Duggie – had built the first steel works in India at Jamshedpur in Bihar, the Province nearest to Calcutta. By the turn of the century it was the largest steel works in the British Commonwealth, which it still remains today. Tata Sons soon became the largest and most powerful industrial group in India, with companies making almost everything from soap to firebricks. They built the famous Taj Mahal Hotel in Bombay (it was said that it had been built the wrong way round) and the Great Eastern in Calcutta. Jehangir Tata – JRD to his acquaintances,

Jeh to his friends – was, like Charles Gardner, mad on flying. In the mid-twenties he was the first Indian to fly solo from England to India, in a Puss Moth. He was Chairman of the family firm at the early age of thirty. One outcome of this situation was the formation of India's first civil airline, Tata Airlines Limited, now Air India (belonging, of course, to the Government of India).

Until the jet age he could pilot himself every type of aircraft flown by Tata Airlines. He had learned the groundings of business economics from a Scotsman.

Jamsetjee Tata was the great founder of the Tata Empire. He married a French woman and when the First World War was started in 1914, which resulted in the first of the two German defeats in the twentieth century by the French, the English and the Americans, Jehangir Tata actually did two years soldiering in the French army, starting with the Foreign Legion. He was to rule the Tata Empire for sixty years. These are described by his nephew as an addition to this story about the life of Sheila Sawhny who had lately become his sister-in-law.

For me it was not only a House but also a very Noble one. His grandfather had married a French woman so the House of Tata was inclined to lean in the direction of France and its culture, rather than towards the Anglo-Saxon world. Jeh Tata and his two sisters, Sylla and Dabeh, were educated in France; all three were bi-lingual in French, English and Gujarati. The girls wore saris as smartly as Sheila did; in Europe they dressed in 'haute couture'. They were patriotic Indians, as was Sheila. Our daughter Venetia's second name was Marianne, at the suggestion of the newly married Dabeh and Duggie Sawhny.

The actual wedding ceremony was, I think, very private indeed. Zoroastrian priests wore a simple white robe and a curious hat, shaped like a cow's hoof. I never saw one in Petit Hall, where the ceremony and the reception were held. I imagine Duggie and Dabeh took the ceremony in their stride. There was only about fifteen of us at the reception, held in the enormous Victorian, stately looking house by the sea at the bottom of Malabar Hill. Sir Dinshaw Petit, Bart, "Falli", as he was known to his friends, had many houses, the most beautiful of which and certainly the smartest was at the top of Èze village, about ten kilometres west of Monte Carlo. He was Dabeh's uncle. Jeh Tata's wife was a permanent invalid, so the Petits did the honours. Only two of my three Noble Houses were represented at the wedding. My violin and cricket playing Maharajah "Porby Porbunder" was an orthodox Hindu and had no connections of any kind with the millionaire Parsees. Falli Petit would certainly have captained India at bridge, if they had mounted an Indian national team in those days.

Killicks was well represented in the wedding photograph. Amy Sawhny of course qualified, being Duggie's mother, and so did Sheila.

I managed to claim a modest right to a place in the wedding photograph even if I did stand at the back of the group behind the stars who sat in a solemn row in the centre. Hugh Milne and Duncan Shepherd, both of them partners now in Killicks, had been invited. Duggie, the bridegroom, of course, had a foot in both camps. He was still just in Killicks but was later to cross over to Tata Industries Limited when he and Dabeh got back from their honeymoon. Amy wore a splendid hat, which was completely new to me. It would have been familiar, I feel sure, to the yeoman farmers of say, Dorset or Devonshire, in the first two decades of the twentieth century. After the photographer, with his ancient camera and tripod had left, the scene changed swiftly to Veuve Cliquot and caviar. Sheila told me later that Amy Edwardes came from a village, Hannay in Berkshire.

I found myself, after several flutes of the great French Widow, leaning over the balcony, with Sir Dinshaw Petit himself devouring his amazing view westward over the Indian Ocean, while he told me how he had beaten the Reserve Bank of India hollow in getting most of his considerable fortune out of India past every kind of exchange control and into France. It was very simple and had been very successful – not qualities which either Indian or British bureaucrats, for that matter, either enjoy or understand.

When Dabeh and Duggie came back to Bombay from their honeymoon in France, they moved into a comfortable modern flat near Kemps Corner.

Sheila and I gave them a portrait of Amy Sawhny, painted by the Viennese artist, Walter Langhammer, who had fled from Vienna in 1935. His wife was a Jewess. He was a first-class artist. Dabeh and Sheila had become close friends since well before Duggie had joined the Noble House of Tata.

Mr J R D Tata, Chairman of the Tata Group of companies for over sixty years, led a colourful and interesting life. Throughout his business career, he was known for his charisma, his personal charm and his great human touch. He espoused several causes, which he believed to be right and worthy of his support.

Born to a Parsee father and French mother in 1904, Jeh or JRD, as he was popularly known, did most of his early schooling in France. He also spent some time during the First World War as a young boy in Japan. He then joined the French Foreign Legion in North Africa as a part of his French National Service.

Jeh possessed a truly adventurous spirit. He became India's first private pilot (with Licence No 1) in 1929. He participated in the Aga Khan Trophy Air Race between Karachi and London in an open-cockpit single-engine biplane. At Aboukir Bay, Alexandria, when Jeh landed, he found Aspi Engineer (who had also taken up the challenge from London to Karachi), in distress. Engineer said he had just been stranded for want of a spark plug! Jeh readily parted with his extra spark, and then took off for London via Naples while Aspi Engineer departed for Karachi. Naples was a military airport then and Jeh was not permitted to take off, as he would have liked to, at an early hour of the morning.

This resulted in Engineer getting a lead of a couple of hours and he landed at Karachi before Jeh could land in England, thus winning the Trophy. Recollecting the occasion later, Jeh had remarked, "I'm glad Aspi Engineer won the Aga Khan Trophy, it enabled him to get a position in the Royal Indian Air Force. I had my position in Tata's." After independence, Aspi Engineer became the second Chief of Staff of the Indian Air Force. This episode portrays Jeh's great adventurous spirit and human touch, for which he became known throughout his life.

The first airmail service from Karachi to Bombay in a Leopard Moth was flown by Jeh. He then went on to create Tata Airlines which grew to be the largest private airline in India up to 1953 when all airlines were nationalised.

He also created Air India International, which was, perhaps, the first government-private sector joint venture, as a national flag carrier, and was invited by the government to continue to be its chairman after nationalisation. Air India (as it was subsequently known after nationalisation) became an airline known for its impeccable service and Asian warmth. Many world airlines looked to Air India as a model for service and operating effectiveness. The airline truly gained a world stature, and his involvement in the company and passion for excellence continued to make Air India the airline of choice for many, until he was removed by a subsequent government in 1978.

Jeh had been appointed a Director of Tata Sons in 1926, on the death of his father, Mr R D Tata (who was a relative of the founder) and a partner in the parent company. He was appointed Chairman in 1938 at the age of thirty-four. During his long tenure, he achieved many 'firsts' within and outside the Tata Group. His passion for excellence spanned his dual role as Chairman of the Tata Group and as continuing Chairman of Air India. Under his leadership, the group entered the fields of commercial vehicles, saw a bold expansion in its steel plant, entered the basic chemical business, expanded its hotel activity to become the largest hotel chain in India, and pioneered India's entry into Information Technology through the creation of the nation's first software services company, TCS, which has now grown to be the largest IT services company in Asia.

All through this period, Jeh adhered to the highest ethical standards with unwavering values. There were several instances when Tatas were denied licences (in the post-independence 'Licence Raj'), entirely due to their unwillingness to compromise their ethical standards to meet the exigencies of the political demands. Despite these roadblocks, the group grew and retained its predominant position under his leadership.

Jeh's immediate family consisted of his brother, Dorab, who also served as a director in the Tata Group, his sister Sylla, who married Sir Dinshaw Petit (she lived most of her life in Europe). His sister, Dabeh, married Colonel Leslie Sawhny. Dabeh lived in Bombay and, perhaps, was therefore closest to him. Leslie Sawhny, or Duggie, as he was popularly known, joined Tatas in 1960. He came to Tatas from a British business house, where he occupied a senior management position, following his retirement from the Indian Army.

Duggie began his career in Tatas as an executive assistant to Jeh, following which Duggie very successfully headed the group's hotel, chemical, and oils and soap businesses. Duggie's greatest strengths were his ability to create meaningful business structures, his ability to identify and to motivate effective managers, and his ability to create 'teamwork' throughout the group. He was also a mentor for many young people with the group. He was broadly seen as a very effective 'man manager' and has been credited with identifying and rewarding managers in the companies which he led, who subsequently grew to be the chief executives and chairmen of their respective companies.

It was no secret that Jeh considered Duggie to be his likely successor, and Duggie would have fulfilled that role well and with panache. Unfortunately, Duggie suffered a massive heart attack during a game of golf in 1967 and died that same day. Duggie's death was an enormous blow for Jeh. His succession plans were upturned by destiny and for several years he continued as Group Chairman, giving up the chairmanship of each company to different people, thereby creating what later was often referred to as a set of 'fiefdoms'. Admittedly, each of these companies did exceedingly well in their own areas, but the identity and cohesiveness of the group was diminished somewhat. The group was often referred to in later years as "a loose confederation of companies".

Jeh played an important, patriarchal role in holding the group together in an informal manner – entirely through the respect he enjoyed and his standing in the eyes of his colleagues. However, it was obvious that it was only his personality and personal intervention that retained the bond between the companies, and not an institutionalised structure.

Jeh believed in physical fitness and an athletic life. He worked out at home in his own gym throughout his life, played low-handicap golf, and began skiing at the age of forty! Skiing became a passion with him and provided him with the excitement and adventure that he needed. He was always looking for the longest ski runs and the steepest slopes. The more exciting and the more dangerous they were, the more he hungered to conquer them. He continued skiing till almost two years before his death, unhindered by a broken hip and other lesser injuries. Almost all his skiing was done in Europe, for which he took time off from work in India each winter.

Jeh remained active in the Tata Group until 1991 when, arising out of a heart problem, he decided to step down and handed over the reins of the group to me. His decision was sudden and at that moment I was unprepared for the tremendous expression of faith and confidence which he reposed in me. During the two years that he lived following this change, he became my greatest mentor. He gave much of his time to me to provide the advice and counsel that I so often sought from him. During this period he had a wonderful knack of being there when I needed him and turned to him, but never imposing his view or presence on me. I often mentioned to him that I wished that this change had taken place ten years earlier, as we had become extremely close.

In October 1993, Jeh went to Europe for a holiday from which he regrettably never returned. He fell ill and was hospitalised in Geneva. He passed away in the hospital a few days later, at the age of eighty-nine, due to medical complications.

We had all come to believe that he was immortal. His passing away was certainly an incomprehensible loss to many of us personally, and to the Tata Group, but the spirit that he created lives on after him.

Part Two

32

To Find a Nanny and a House

"Its seasons are my seasons, for me winter
Is the sound of a muffin bell through the gathering dark,
And spring for me is neither a lamb nor a primrose,
But a crocus down by the lake in St James' Park."

Jan Struther

Sheila took her second arrival in London very much in her stride, compared to Addison Road and its V1 on that dreadful, stormy 5th June 1944 – the day before the landings on the Normandy beaches. The weather was not much better this time and we had our children with us, too – Venetia, aged five, Robin, two. Tilbury was about as depressing as Kensington High Street had been but I carried a bit more rank in 1956 than I had in 1944, so Killicks' London office had organised a large car, which took all of us and our luggage to a solid – oh, so solid – hotel in Kensington – near the High Street Tube Station – the Glendenning, whose only asset that we could see was an Indian restaurant immediately opposite its front door. In a few days we came to know the headwaiter, who also seemed to be the proprietor. He told us it was the finest Indian restaurant not only in London but also in the whole country – "Whole UK. Also General Auchinlech, he come here often." If this was true, it was really something, as the Auk knew his stuff about "desi khana" (Indian food).

The next morning I took the tube to Killicks London office, within spitting distance of Liverpool Street Station. It was only slightly less dingy than the one in which I had been hired twenty-one years before – the old one had been flattened in the blitz by the Luftwaffe. But the faded photographs of Mr Nixon's old metre gauge railway engines in the CP (Central Provinces), Gujarat and Bengal were still there on the walls – tough old characters as they had been.

Sheila said goodbye with relief to the memsahib-style nanny who had been wished upon us for the return voyage by a Pali Hill neighbour who had taken the opportunity to save the cost of her passage home by hiring her out to me to look after our children on the ship. Before the *Himalaya* had up-anchored at Ballard Pier, Sheila had discovered Robin in his tiny berth drowning in a bath of chocolate and I had discovered her in the bar, talking up a tea planter from Assam.

For some reason during our last month in India I had found myself writing poems instead of helping Sheila pack up Bates Hill. Feeling rather sad after my first lunch in our civilian troop ship that was just leaving Bombay, I retired to an empty public room, sat down at a writing table after lunch and said goodbye to the country that had brought me so much happiness through the years. "Flame of the Forest" had always been my favourite jungle tree.

> *Twisted and crooked like an ageing clerk,*
> *I saw you first in blue December's sun,*
> *A jagged tracery of rough grey bark,*
> *Naked of leaves retired your life's work done.*
>
> *But I was fresh to India's jungle way*
> *And you were laughing silently at me.*
> *When I returned soon after New Year's Day*
> *The worn out clerk had turned into a tree.*
>
> *But not a tree, for trees are green and quiet*
> *And all your greenery seemed but a fire*
> *Of pink, vermilion, orange and a riot*
> *Of flame pinned smokeless on a net of wire.*

30 *Lord Leonard Cheshire DCO OM VC.*

*31 Mill Reef: winner of the Derby, owned by
Paul Mellon.*

32 Paul Mellon.

33 Paul and Bunny Mellon on their farm
'Little Oak Spring' at Upperville, Virginia (1965).

34 Sheila relaxing by the pool at the Tata Hotel on the island on Udaipur Lake.

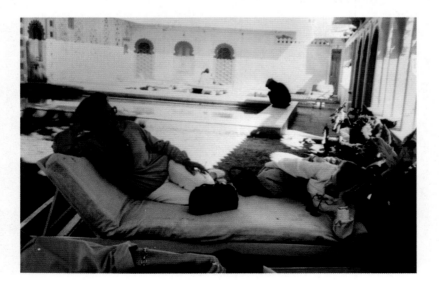

35 Juhu Beach near Bombay: *a watercolour by Sheila Russell.*

36 Wonders of the Seashore: *a tapestry by Sheila Russell (Bombay 1955).*

37 Still Life by Sheila Russell.

38 Jack Masters with the author in the Rocky Mountains.

40 *Rudyard Kipling (1865 – 1936).*

39 *Jack Masters.*

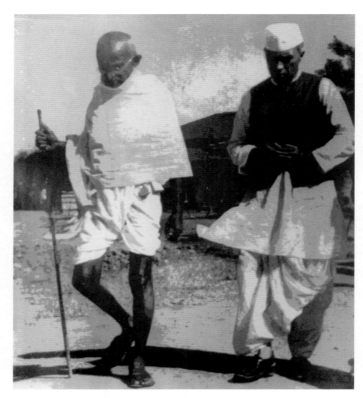

41 Gandhi and Nehru.

42 A sadhu contemplating by the Ganges.

43 Champaner Mosque: *a watercolour by the author (1954).*

44 Amy Sawhny with
   pet terrier.

45 Sheila's mother,
   Amy Sawhny.

47 Sheila's brother Leslie (Duggie).

46 Sheila's eldest brother Reggie (Sonny).

48 *A watercolour by Syed Haider Raza. Painted in France during his two-year sojourn. The author thought it might be the artist's sentimental reminder of Europe – notice the punts in the foreground (Cambridge) and the Sacré Coeur in the distant background.*

49 *Still Life by Sheila Russell.*

50 Still Life: Fruit on a Plate *by Sheila Russell (1980).*

51 Still Life: Fruit on a Table *by Sheila Russell.*

52 Lower Cole, Rock: detail from a watercolour by Rosemary Grattan.

53 Lower Cole, Rock: a photograph by Henry Grattan.

54 A Quiet Corner at Lower Cole: a photograph by Henry Grattan.

55 *The Poet Laureate Sir John Betjeman's resting place at St Enodoc Church:*
a photograph by Henry Grattan.
56 *St Enodoc Church with Stepper Point: a photograph by Henry Grattan.*

Cerulean blue, the sky is like a sea
And on it float your flowers, orange keels,
Vermilion boats bound for eternity
And many a sunbird through its rigging steels.

The purple sunbird knows your flames don't burn;
That in your galleon's hold lie nectars rare;
His slender bill probes in the deepest urn,
Stored in your velvet barques, as light as air.

Then suddenly the forest catches fire
In smouldering March; sailor pull for the shore
Your boats of gold float to the funeral pyre
That glows and crackles on the jungle's floor.

After arriving at the hotel our priority, obviously, was to find a nanny, then to show off Venetia and Robin to my mother and Auntie Sophie, then – and this was bound to be the most difficult part – to find a house in which to live. I had never advertised for anything in my life. I didn't even know where to start; but I remember sitting in the corridor of the Glendenning Hotel's third floor with the day's copy of the *Daily Telegraph* in one hand and my old Remington in the other. The outcome was a desperate plea to the world at large for the perfect nanny. The reply came from somewhere in Ireland, called Letterkenny from a person called Mona McTeague (no age given) who said she could be with us almost within the hour, for an interview.

Mona turned up in Kensington within a couple of days and stayed with us for the next seven years. She was a Roman Catholic and she was twenty-five, ready to go anywhere at any time. Best of all, Sheila and the children loved her very much.

✳

The meeting with my own mother was, as usual, more difficult but with Auntie Sophie it was instant understanding and love. Then came the house hunting; Sheila had always liked Georgian London, ever since we had lived in 90 George Street at the end of the war. We saw umpteen houses; one of them belonged to Randolph Churchill, an unforgettable experience for us both as we were able to study half a dozen of his father's pictures, which hung on the walls of the drawing room and dining room. But the price was way above my ceiling.

Then all of a sudden, the estate agent said, "We had a house come to us only this morning – 32 Chester Street."

"That'll be more expensive than the Churchill house, surely?" said Sheila.

"Not at all," the agent replied for me. "This one belongs to the Grosvenor Estate (the Duke of Westminster) and the sellers are willing to offload the twenty years still left of the lease for £5,000."

"Done," I said, without even asking Sheila what she thought. She said at once, "I know Chester Street and I know the house. It's on the corner of Chester Street, which opens on to Grosvenor Place."

Good going, I thought, for someone whose first visit to England had only been for about four months in 1944. We went round next day to see the house, which was to be ours for fifteen years. We met a nice couple, mother and daughter. The daughter, a Miss Golding was on the staff of *The Economist* which I used to read weekly. It was always her article to which I turned first.

Both mother and daughter were delighted that we wanted to take possession as soon as possible. The mother said, "I'm afraid there might be quite a lot of repairs that will need to be done." There were!

33

Pitts Head Mews

"But (when so sad thou canst not sadder)
Cry:- and upon thy so sore loss
Shall shine the traffic of Jacob's ladder
Pitched betwixt Heaven and Charing Cross.
Yea, in the night, my Soul, my daughter;
Cry, – clinging heaven by the hems
And low, Christ walking on the water
Not of Gennasereth, but Thames!"

Francis Thompson

It was a good thing that Killicks' London Office provided a minimum of
work at this time as Leonard Cheshire had asked me before we left Bombay
if I would help him when I got back to England. He always moved fast and
had already founded two homes in India – Bethlehem House – in Bombay
and a second one at Dehra Dun in the foothills of the Himalayas, by the
time Sheila had made 32 Chester Street habitable – all six stories of it.

Our schedule was a simple one. I bought a car and I would drop Venetia
at her day school near Sloane Square, drive to the city, go through the
Bombay mail then drive back west to Cheshire's tiny office in Pitts Head
Mews just off Park Lane, now buried deep beneath the foundations of the
Hilton Hotel. Margot Mason, a friend of Sheila's before we had even left
Bombay, lived in a small room with just enough space for a desk and
telephone.

Cheshire's Trustees, in whose name his first homes in England had been purchased, were about six in number. I assumed that the whole thing must be legal, since the Chairman, Sir Alfred Denning, was Master of the Rolls and the honorary treasurer, Sir Archibald Jamieson, was Chairman of Vickers-Armstrong.

During the autumn of 1954, a house in Bromley had come on to the market. Sir Archibald Jamieson and a friend had put up the money to buy it. Bob Worthington, a city accountant who lived nearby in suburbia and was a friend of Margot Mason volunteered to be Chairman as well as Honorary Secretary. This was Cheshire's idea of DIY and it had certainly caught on at that time. Rotary Clubs, Round Tables, Youth Clubs, Boy Scouts and Girl Guides rallied to a cause they could understand – providing a home for physically handicapped men and women. These helpers scrubbed floors, painted walls, worked in the garden and humped furniture for they could see the end at which all this activity was directed. Long before work was finished there were patients – as they were then called – waiting to enter the home.

Sir Archibald had sensed that something novel and exciting was afoot in the deliberate way this group of people from the suburbs was taking risks, which were quite out of the ordinary. He was a merchant banker who knew about men as well as money. One of his sons had won a posthumous VC in the war. St Cecilia's, in Bromley, was opened by Cheshire himself soon after he got back to England from India. Before that he had been in hospital. Sir Archibald was asked by Cheshire to become Honorary Treasurer of the Trust – at this time known as the Cheshire Foundation.

As there was nothing in the way of cash to take over he had paid £10,000 into the Westminster Bank at Bishopsgate. At this moment Cheshire had to go once more into Midhurst Hospital. Before we left India he had asked me to contact Sir Archibald Jamieson. We took a taxi from his house in Westminster to the Law Courts in the Strand to meet Sir Alfred Denning. In the taxi, as we bowled down the Embankment, he told me that it was in Sir Alfred's rooms that the infrequent meetings of the Trustees took place.

He said it was a good thing that a newcomer from abroad – and one in his early forties – should be joining them.

"We need some younger blood," he said. "Apart from Leonard, we are all ancient and are likely to fall off our perches any minute."

When we reached the Law Courts and I was introduced to Sir Alfred Denning, Tom to his friends, I sensed at once that I was on inspection. I distinctly remember looking out of the window of his room in the Law Courts, seeing the name on the street placard outside – Carey Street. I supposed this was the origin of the phrase, if you went broke. In his panelled room in Westminster Sir Archibald thanked me for taking on his job as Honorary Treasurer and as a Trustee. Sir Alfred then asked me, "What church do you belong to?"

"The Church of England," I had replied.

Somehow I think he looked relieved.

"There's not much to hand over apart from some money which I and a friend have put in. It's the responsibility of looking after it and for getting some more in which daunts me." Sir Archibald spoke with feeling about Leonard Cheshire.

"An extraordinary young man."

It had been Morarji Desai, Prime Minister of Bombay Province who had said to Leonard six months earlier, "You were a man of war, now you are a man of peace. Why?"

Cheshire had given him a gentle smile but no answer.

It was at my first Trustees' meeting that Sir Alfred asked me to visit Wardour Castle in Wiltshire. "They seem to be in trouble, would you mind having a look?"

Wardour Castle, near Tisbury in Wiltshire was a large Palladian house. It had been the seat for many generations of the Arundel family. According to Chambers Dictionary, Palladian means "of the style of architecture introduced by Andrea Palladio, 1518-1580". It was built round a rotunda – its imposing public rooms opening off the circular space beneath the cupola. The family had not returned to the place after the war and for a time it had been used as a college for the Roman Catholic priesthood, then as an expensive girls' public school – but the lack of heating and the dangerous state of the roof had caused the governors of the school to abandon it. By this time the state, in the shape of the Historic Buildings Society, had taken it over. They were desperate to find a user and had persuaded Cheshire to take it on. He didn't need much persuasion.

After the Trustees' meeting Sheila and I had tea with Margot in her Mews bed-sit. She said, "One of the difficulties which the Trustees don't know about but which unfortunately the neighbours of the Castle do – and after all they are the people who will have to keep it going – is that Leonard wants to use it to look after some of the many discharged prisoners from the country's gaols who are increasingly begging him to look after them and, of course, he has agreed to do so. A retired soldier, whose name I have forgotten, but whom I remember was the first VC of the Hitler war, had agreed to run the place.

Margot concluded, "There are enormous holes in the roof and snow is pouring onto the ballroom floor where the inmates sleep on mattresses."

Sheila insisted on coming with us "to have a look". We drove there in Margot's little car. Neither of us had, at any time in our lives, ever spent a colder or more uncomfortable night anywhere. Margot, having been secretary to Earl Ferrers for five years in Staunton Harold (Cheshire's third home in England), knew a woodworm-rotting stately home when she saw one. "We'll have to go there but it won't be much fun," she said.

It was in fact truly awful and we felt desperately sorry for the VC and his charges. I think that night was the beginning of Sheila's frequent chest complaints.

Without being in any way an expert in house building or in the restoration of ruins, I knew instinctively that the lowest estimate imaginable for repairs to the stately ruin was going to be at least £100,000 and probably more. Then, by chance, I remembered that Percy Seymour, a contemporary at Cambridge, lived in the neighbourhood at a property called Maiden Bradley. The VC told me he was now the umpteenth Duke of Somerset and one of the fiercest opponents of the Cheshire enterprise. I also remembered that Alan Houseman – my closest English friend at Clare – and I had often flown our old Avro 504s from our summer camps with the Cambridge Air Squadron at Netheravon on Salisbury Plain to land in the park at Maiden Bradley. The 504s, complete with a ski between their legs, had been even more ancient than the Wapitis.

Margot, Sheila and I had drinks with Percy before lunch next day – now His Grace – and his wife, at which friendly reunion we heard even more reasons than we had already formulated ourselves, as to why there could be no – repeat no – justification for trying to turn Wardour Castle into a Cheshire Home. So I went back to the Law Courts in London and told the Master of the Rolls the sad story.

He said, "I thought as much. I'm sorry about your bad night but someone had to look. Some time I would very much like to meet your wife."

So I got off to a bad start. It was about this time that I had a wheeze about Sheila. She had been working hard choosing and buying furniture for 32, Chester Street and there had been little chance for socialising and making friends in London. I was a member of the Traveller's Club and one day in the bar I mentioned to Billy Buchan, grandson of the creator of one of my heroes, Richard Hannay, that I thought it would do no harm if Sheila had a bit of social publicity.

"You have something to do with PR, don't you, Billy?" I asked him in the downstairs bar.

"Indeed. It is true I have a room in Curzon Street and a brass plate outside it. What can I do for you?"

All he needed, apparently, was a photograph and a few words of description. So I gave him a Lenare photograph of Sheila taken in her white sari, with a simple sentence saying that her brother, Leslie Sawhny, was married to the sister of J R D Tata of Bombay. I didn't say a thing about who J R D Tata was. The photograph and description appeared the following week in the *Tatler*.

It was the first time that Sheila and I had ever had a proper row in our married life.

"If you ever do anything like this again I will probably have to book my passage back to India."

Happily the storm blew over almost as quickly as it had appeared on the horizon. One reason for it, I think, was because, just that afternoon, she had bought one of the best and longest lasting pieces of furniture we ever possessed. It was a large cabinet made of a light wood with wrought iron curlicues within its top panels and a green painted wooden platform, which could be lowered to form a perfect bar with painted glass shelves for bottles and glasses, and a cupboard beneath, in which the overflow of alcoholic reserves could be stowed. In fact it was the perfect bar. It is with me still nearly sixty years on.

"The antique shop from which I got it," she said, "told me it had belonged originally to Ian Hay, the writer."

From the depths of my brain I dragged up the memory of once reading his most famous book, *The First Hundred Thousand*, about the First World War.

34

The British Commonwealth

*"Not a day passes over the earth, but men and women of no note
do great deeds, speak great words and suffer noble sorrows."*
                                                        Charles Reade

It was about now I decided that I must get down seriously to finding a
proper job and start a new career, now that Leonard Cheshire had come
back from India and had set forth on his next operation. He had decided to
charter a Dakota once or preferably twice a year to take twenty or so of his
Roman Catholic patients to Lourdes. He had by now converted to the
Catholic faith soon after nursing his very first resident in his aunt's house,
Le Court, in Hampshire. Bill Dykes had died in his arms and had persuaded
him to make this great change in his own life only a few days before he died.

Apart from the disabled passengers, this venture would also need about
a dozen helpers to look after them. Margot asked Sheila if she would come
along as a helper. Sheila reckoned that Mona could cope with Venetia and
Robin for the three days trip.

"Of course," she said.

It was in this way that she came to see a miracle at close quarters. She
was given a middle-aged man who suffered from osteomyelitis and who
lived in a wheelchair which she now pushed. The man's home was at Staunton
Harold, Margot's old home when she had been working for the Ferrers
family.

"It was an astonishing experience," Sheila told me when she got back to
Chester Street. She had found the atmosphere in Lourdes to be a curious

mixture of commercialism and holiness. It was also hard work, as she had to manoeuvre a loaded wheelchair from aircraft to bus, then to hotel, then to the Stations of the Cross and finally up a hill to a cave, which she could not enter herself but where, in the case of her passenger, the miracle took place.

"When we met first at Kings Cross Station," she told me, "he couldn't walk. When he came out of the cave there was no sign of the wheelchair," she said. It had in fact been handed back to Margot. "My chap was given a stick. I had to help him along but he got back to our bus at the bottom of the Stations of the Cross, under his own steam. If that wasn't a miracle I don't know what is."

I reckon I had experienced one, too, in the City of London while Sheila was away. I was lunching at the City Club with an old friend, Bernard Greer, who had been chairman of a well-known ancient Calcutta Merchant House, Turner Morrison & Co. In the bar before lunch he had introduced me to an old Bombay "Koi Hai" (an old hand). I had known Leslie Gwilt for a long time in Bombay. He had joined us for lunch. Over the port he said, "Have you ever heard of the Commonwealth Development Finance Company?"

"Isn't that the government show that put up a black over ground nuts, somewhere in Africa?"

"No, it isn't," he said, pushing the port decanter in my direction. "That's the public sector's equivalent of CDFC. The one I'm talking about is in fact the CDFC – the Commonwealth Development Finance Co Ltd. The Bank of England got it off the ground together with a number of the largest companies in the country, all of which took up shares. Lord Godber, Chairman of Shell, is its chairman. They aim to start up green field projects in the Commonwealth and support existing ones that are weak. They already have a large portfolio in India and I happen to know they are looking for someone who knows India well."

He gave me the CDFC telephone number and the next day I found myself in Old Jewry on the opposite side of a desk talking to a man called Stanley Hoar.

"Would £3,000 a year be all right?"

I said gratefully, "Certainly it would. Especially if it means paying visits to India." It did.

There seemed to be rather few of us in CDFC when I started working in

Old Jewry, just off Cheapside. Half a dozen young men seemed rather few with which to develop the British Commonwealth. I was particularly happy at this moment because, apart from having landed a job, to Sheila's and, to my amazement, Duggie, who by now had resigned his commission in the Indian Army, had managed out of the blue to send us by air a real live Indian cook. His name was Munnar Khan and he was a dual-purpose operator in both European and Indian cuisines. I had forgotten in the hurly-burly of house hunting that Duggie had been put in charge of the Taj Mahal Hotel (among other companies) by his new brother-in-law, Jeh Tata. The hotel was now known far and wide as "Duggie's Horse", so smartly turned out were the staff. The Rendezvous Restaurant on the ground floor, close to the Gateway of India, was acquiring the same kind of worldwide reputation that years later in far distant Padstow (Cornwall UK) was to be won by Rick Stein.

Apart from his cooking, Munnar Khan was an excellent all-rounder who took a heavy burden of work in the house off Sheila's shoulders. He also liked children and dogs.

So I was not as worried as usual when Sam Samways, the CDFC Managing Director, said on my first morning in the old Jewry office, "We're going to throw you in at the deep end. You and I are off on a quick circuit to Nigeria, Ghana, and Sierra Leone, about three weeks of circuits and bumps – isn't that what you call it in the RAF?"

I discovered in the BOAC Boeing to Lagos that CDFC had advisory contracts with the governments of Nigeria and Sierra Leone. "Advice about what?" I had asked.

"Finance and industry," was the reply; they all want a steelworks or an airline. You must polish up your Nos and Nyets."

I hardly had time to take in the west coast of Africa, a continent I hardly knew, but we met many pleasant people, mostly English members of the Foreign and Colonial Service and a few business folk. I made contact with De Beers who owned valuable diamond deposits in a swamp in the middle of the jungles of Sierra Leone. Teddy Dawe took me to this outlandish place in his comfortable jet aircraft and we became friends for life. His wife, a beautiful Alsatian, became another of Sheila's corps of friends. Sir Maurice and Lady Dorman, the last English Excellencies of Sierra Leone before that colony's tragedy of independence were friendly and helpful. With their help and that of Mr Milton, the Prime Minister, I sowed the seeds of another Cheshire Home. Then Sam Samways was summoned home to Old Jewry. I was told to do a few more circuits and bumps before following him two days later. I had planned to fly home via Paris and it was only after Sam had gone that I discovered I had almost run out of travellers' cheques. So when I landed at Charles De Gaulle Airport in the early morning of the next day the only thing I could do was to ring up Vivianne Clive-Worms, former wife of Robbie Clive, to ask for her help. She lived quite a way beyond the Arc de Triomphe, a fairly long taxi drive from the St James and Albany Hotel where I planned to stay. I would ring her bell, she would throw out 5,000 francs from her third-floor window in a weighted envelope and I would reimburse her via her London bank account.

I took the first taxi I could see that was passing in front of the hotel. It seemed to me rather a small taxi and the driver rather large. I didn't dare ask him if he would mind waiting at my destination in the dix-septième arondissement, while I exchanged money and greetings with Vivianne. If he decided not to wait what would I do? Would I ever find a taxi out there in the sticks at six o'clock in the morning? He seemed a friendly type; he had to spend some time squeezing me onto the narrow back seat of his small cab (I had just had my second hip replacement operation and had found some difficulty in moving about).

As I got out I did in fact have the courage to ask him to wait – "only a few minutes". With a smile and in a broad South of France accent he said, "Bien sur, Monsieur."

The money-changing operation over, he insisted on squeezing me into the front seat by his side. As we cruised down the Champs Elysées he asked how I had become so stiff. I told him I thought it was the result of playing too much rugby football in my youth. His eyebrows rose at once. "Vous avez joué au rugby?" he asked, in a surprised tone of voice.

"Ou ça?"

I told him I had played in the South of France, the home of French Rugby. At once he was all smiles.

"Moi, j'ai joué pour la France. Le grand Jean Pierre Rive lui même. Il était capitaine d'équipe."

I remembered the brilliant French forward who ran with the ball like a bullet, golden hair streaming in the wind behind him. He had always been a favourite of Sheila's, when I had taken her to matches at the Stade Colombes. I hardly dared look at his meter.

"C'est combien que je vous dois?"

He seized my hand, as he replied with a broad smile on his face, "Pour vous, Monsieur, c'est gratuit."

I thanked him profusely, for such a gesture had never been made to me before, not in London, nor Paris, nor New York, nor yet in Bombay – a free ride in a taxi of well over seven miles. Wonders never ceased!

The concierge, who until that moment had been professionally grumpy, got me a ticket for the Lido that night in double-quick time plus a smile as he steered me respectfully across the hallway of the hotel towards the lift. How could he have known?

The concierge always knows everything, I told myself!

35

Duggie

"A Renaissance man in India"

Wilfrid Russell

The CDFC telephone operator rang through to my new office in Old Jewry.

"A Mr Saklatwalla from Tata Sons London office is calling for you, Mr Russell. Shall I put him through?"

"Yes, please." I knew Behram Saklatwalla, who ran Tata's London office, through Duggie. Why should he want me? His Parsee name was well known in London, his father had been MP for Battersea since the days of Campbell-Bannerman.

"Wilfrid, I'm afraid I've got bad news."

My heart sank; he went on, "Duggie has died, suddenly, no pain apparently." They always say that.

The drive home from the City to Chester Street was the worst I had ever experienced, worse even than the one from St George's Hospital to Sewree. Thank heavens I was alone and driving myself. How on earth was I going to tell Sheila? She was in the kitchen with Munnar Khan when I got home. I said, "Could you come up to the drawing room, darling, I've something to tell you."

She must have thought it was something I didn't want Munnar Khan to hear.

I sat beside her on the sofa – something I rarely did.

It was like a sandcastle on the beach collapsing under a strong incoming spring tide. Sheila, who seldom cried, wept her heart out – all she could say

– and she kept on repeating it, was, "But he always used to give me his share of our sweets."

There were other things, of course, with which messengers of bad tidings are familiar. I was hard put to it not to break down myself. It had been a heart attack in their flat near Kemps Corner, Behram told me afterwards. Duggie had been in Breach Candy Hospital for about a week, nothing serious so he had gone home and that was that.

He was only forty-three when he died. There had been a crowd of more than a thousand ordinary people who had walked behind him to the crematorium; then the electricity in the furnace had broken down. His ashes were placed, by Dabeh, inside the wall of the Tata Cancer Research Laboratory at Poona.

There was an obituary in the London *Times*. The way he had handled the same situation himself twenty years before when he had cast the Duke into the Ganga at Hardwar must have been, I thought, more dignified and there had been nobody to keep him company then save the Brahmin priest.

36

The Three Dinner Parties

"Oh some are full of red wine, and some are fond of white,
And some are all for dancing by the pale moonlight."

John Masefield

Sheila never forgot him, yet there was no outward sign of grief after that tragic afternoon. There was one new event, which outwardly occupied her attention at this time. Sonny's twenty-year old daughter, Moneesha, attractive, witty and undisciplined, turned up in London. Sonny had telephoned from Bombay to say she would be coming and would Sheila keep an eye on her. She had been to school in Bombay and been more than a handful for Phyllis, her mother, so that eventually Duggie, off his own bat, had sent her to a girls' boarding school in Bangalore for which he paid all the fees. At twenty she was more or less educated, certainly more attractive than she had been at sixteen, but she was still a handful.

She had already found a bedsit just off the Kings Road on her own. She had Sheila's natural dress sense but she had never worn a sari and never would in her life.

Sheila did her best "to keep an eye on her" but it was not long before that task would fall on to the shoulders of her first husband, John Cherry, a nephew of Air Vice Marshal Sir John Grandy.

Sheila deliberately had not invited her to the first of the three dinner parties, which are described in this chapter. The guest of honour was Paul Mellon. Our idea had been to assemble half a dozen of his closest English men friends most of whom had been up at Clare with him.

Paul sat on Sheila's right. On her left was John Tallent who played rugger for England, and later captained the national side and later still became President of the English Rugby Football Union. Other guests were Bryan Pope, Gordon Mackay and George Waller, later to become a well-known judge.

Munnar Khan produced a wonderful dinner (English style) and Mona helped with passing around the dishes. Venetia and Robin went to bed early. George Waller had been in RAF Coastal Command during the war. Bryan Pope had played scrum half for England and had kept me, quite rightly, from ever playing rugger for our college. Gordon Mackay had been senior prefect at Marlborough and was to be a lifelong friend of both Sheila and myself. Clare had never been a horsy college so Paul could not talk horse with any of us. But he spoke a lot about pictures with his hostess and a good time was had by all. Looking quite serious he did warn us, "Next time any of you come to America, if you're on an American ship, take good care the crew don't beat you to the boats." There had recently been an embarrassing episode on an American ship.

The second dinner party was quite different. It was for one or two senior city gents on the board of CDFC. It came to a disastrous end but that didn't seem to matter. Sheila took it in her stride. The most prominent guest was Sir Duncan Oppenhein, Chairman of British American Tobacco. He was an experienced artist in his spare time and exhibited annually at the Royal Academy. He and Sheila had much to talk about. Then came the crash.

Just as the sweet was being cleared away there was a crash like a V2 arriving without warning. The rope that held up the ancient food lift, which operated between the dining room and the kitchen, had sheered in two just like the rope holding the climbers of the first descent of the Matterhorn.

Munnar Khan was covered in broken crockery, which Duncan Oppenheim and the other guests cheerfully helped to clear.

Another couple, John and Daphne Glyn, came into my life again unexpectedly the other day. He had been an orthopaedic specialist, familiar with my five hip operations; she had been one of the best-known physiotherapists in London with a practice in the West End. Their two children, Ian and Gillian, were the same age as Robin and Venetia. They had come to Rock every August.

Fathers and Mothers became as close friends as their children. The renewal after a twenty-three year interval was via the Rock to London telephone grid. I had told Daphne about the dinner party accident that had been included in this book about Sheila. Daphne reminded me with a laugh that she and John had been present at that famous dinner.

"I remember how amazed I was when Sheila's calm reaction to the crash had been: "Don't worry, please, we'll have coffee with mugs upstairs in the drawing room. Munnar Khan will bring the mugs up on a tray." It was her tranquillity that amazed us most," Daphne had gone on.

The third dinner party was quite different to its predecessors. Sheila was not the hostess this time but she played the most dramatic part in it – at least I thought so.

Once a year the Managing Director of CDFC gave a dinner in the city for the senior clerks and the junior executives, plus their wives. It was the responsibility of the managing director to decide where the line should be drawn distinguishing those who were below the salt from those who were above it. Sam Samways had to draw this India-Pakistan frontier line, which pleased nobody, especially not the wives. He also had to choose a restaurant, which usually was situated in a sort of no-mans-land between St Paul's Cathedral and the Mansion House. The party usually began at about eight p.m. Stanley Hoar, the senior of the two chief executives, did not believe in dry martinis before dinner, despite having held an important post for some years in Washington with the World Bank, so that we all had to put up with Tio Pepé before sitting down. The wine was usually a distant relation of the vin du pays, with which I had become familiar in Languedoc in the South of France. On this occasion the restaurant was below ground, somewhere near the Mansion House. As soon as the dinner was over and Sam Samways had finished his usual speech (CDFC could not possibly indulge in anything as risky as an office party), a silent button was pressed and everyone knew the official part of the dinner was over. Sheila and I said our 'thank-yous' and 'goodnights' and slipped up the circular steps that led to the street. There was a single street lamp near the exit and I could just make out the shadow of the Mansion House looming in the background. The dinner had been black tie; Sheila was wearing her fur coat over her white sari.

I went up the street looking for a taxi. Sheila stood waiting on the pavement; suddenly I heard a scream. I turned round, only to see a young man lying on his back in the middle of the road being booted, kicked and hammered on the head by six or more of what looked like his 'companions'. They were about twenty years old and were clearly enjoying this one-sided fight. They wore untidy, rough clothes. Just as I made an ineffective attempt to find a policeman Sheila slipped off her fur coat, dropped it on the pavement and ran furiously at the group, shouting in a surprisingly authoritative voice, "Stop that at once." She then placed her legs astride the victim's head and glared. The gang disappeared silently at speed in to the darkness. At that moment, Dixon of Dock Green appeared; almost simultaneously a taxi drove by. Sheila picked up her fur coat and before the Bobby could extract his notebook from his breast pocket we were inside the taxi and away.

There were not going to be headlines in the next day's *News of the World* about a Banker's Brawl in the City.

In the taxi on the way home Sheila said to me, "Do they really do that sort of thing in England? I thought it was only in India people behaved like that."

37

All This and Everest too!

"The South Col in Hyde Park!"

Earlier in this story I mentioned that Sheila and I had given a party in March at Bates Hill for the Everest Expedition minus John Hunt, the leader, and Edmund Hilary and Tenzing Norkhei, the summiteers. Hunt flew from London, Hilary from Auckland, both of them direct to Delhi – I have no idea how Tenzing met up with them; it's possible he had been among the general group of sherpas whom Hunt or Wylie had recruited in Katmandu.

1953 was the year of my second home leave from Killicks after getting back to India. 1953, of course, was also Coronation year. Sheila and I were determined to watch the Queen's Coronation procession down Park Lane after the Service in Westminster Abbey. I had booked a room with a balcony on the first floor of Grosvenor House which looked down over Park Lane. We had invited some friends to share some bottles of the famous Old Widow's sparkling wine, together with a cold lunch. There was an added attraction, of course, in the shape of the Queen of Tonga whose open carriage was several vehicles behind Queen Elizabeth II's own magic coach in the procession.

Sadly, like so many other people besides Sheila and myself, we had to watch it all through a curtain of monsoon rain in flaming June. Nonetheless we had won two Queens for the price of one, since the magnificent Queen of Tonga made her own priceless contribution to the general entertainment by sitting in her open landau, roaring with laughter, ignoring the rain.

But almost the greatest excitement of all came from over eight thousand miles away.

Sheila and I had spent the previous night at my younger brother Gilbert's flat in Knightsbridge. Next morning we set off across Hyde Park on foot in the general direction of Park Lane. There were thousands of people milling around. Suddenly I saw it – a newspaperman's breast high news-sheet with the startling words:

"All this – and Everest too"

After lunch, after we had toasted the two Queens, Sheila and I took a cab back to my brother's flat. On the way, inevitably, we found ourselves talking about Mount Everest and the men who had climbed it.

My memory, rather naturally, went back further than Sheila's. Like so many of my generation I had always been fascinated by the great mountain and had read many books about it.

At Clare I had known particularly well in the early thirties, one of the Clare Fellows, Odell, who on the 1924 expedition, was the last man to see Mallory and Irvin alive. He was on the north side of the mountain, of course. "I was on the Rongbuk Glacier, quite high up. A cloud parted and I could see two tiny figures, high on the summit ridge. They were moving slowly and they seemed to me to be going upwards; then a cloud blotted them out. I never saw them again."

I told Sheila how John Hunt, in between modern language classes in C House at Marlborough, had often pressed me to embark on a climbing career by keeping him company on one of the French Alps, the Meije. "It's an easy one, Wilf."

But sadly my feet were always cold. "I'll stick to skiing."

That was why Gunia, our old Mali gardener, at Bates Hill owned a clapped out, whitish sweater with faded light blue letters on it – CUSC.

Sheila, by chance, had played tennis nearly every morning for a week with George Lowe, the New Zealand climber who less than two months later, John Hunt would select to carve a trail across the steep ice slope below Llotse, which would lead from the Western Cwm to the South Col. It was in fact this dangerous route which had made final success possible.

The Swiss had been beaten by this slope the previous year. George Lowe climbed over and above the "epéron Genevois" (the Geneva Spur) and had scrambled down on to the South Col from above. The selected team of summiteers, plus John Hunt and the Sherpas, had followed in his ice steps.

Sheila and I remembered Major Wylie, a Gurkha officer who had appeared to be the expedition's adjutant. Sheila said his bread and butter letter, thanking her for the Bates Hill party, was the best she had received so far in her life.

I just remembered among the others George Band the geologist, I think, and Pugh, a young Welshman who was a cousin of a friend of ours in London, Liz Clifton.

We had all felt sorry for the Bourdillon brothers who got so near, and yet so far, when their oxygen had run out.

When I saw – years later – the amazing photographs, which Hilary had been able to take during their short fifteen-minute stay on the summit, one of them stretching away to the North, soaring over the tiny dotted clouds to the far distant plains of Tibet, I thought of Llasa and the Potala, of Colonel Leslie Weir and his wife Thyra. Fifty years later I heard on the TV the story of how Hilary had shouted the astounding news to George Lowe, his chum from Auckland, when the latter had charged through the snow out of sight of the base camp to meet the two climbers. There were no radios in those days, so the expedition members, who had watched them for several hours coming down over the South Col and Lhotse face to base camp, had not known whether it had been success or failure. One New Zealander had then put his arms round the shoulders of the other and said, "We knocked the Bastard off."

38

Amy

"I see we are both in Fancy Dress."
Motilal Nehru

It was 1966 – we had been living in England for ten years. I was convalescing from my third hip operation in the most delightful of all recovery homes imaginable – Osbourne House – overlooking Southampton Water. There was a small, comfortable hotel in the grounds where friends and relations of the patients could stay. It was dusk and Sheila was walking back to the hotel along a path which I am sure Prince Albert must have used often enough a century ago; somehow her outline looked stronger and firmer than ever. We had just made the decision that she would have to fly to Bombay at once. Mona had telephoned through from London with the contents of a cable from Poona, that my mother-in-law was seriously ill. She was staying with a friend at Koregaon Park in Poona, the famous Indian Army Cantonment a hundred and fifty miles inland from Bombay, cool and comfortable at 3,000 feet. If you drove there from Bombay, half way up the ghat (the hill) you were level with the Duke's nose. You didn't have to ask which Duke the perpendicular cliff with its jutting proboscis was supposed to resemble.

I was due to go home from Osbourne House in two days time. In the meanwhile Mona and Munnar Khan would be at Chester Street to look after Venetia and Robin. So Sheila booked herself on a Tata Airlines Constellation. She only had a few days with her mother. Amy's fifty years in India had been broken only once by that single return journey to England with Sonny in 1920. It had been the only time she had seen her home in Berkshire since the turn of the century. She died with Sheila by her bedside.

Before I attempt to describe my own feelings, which were full of admiration as well as love, I feel I must tell a story which at least for me somehow describes how deep is the understanding between Indians and English who have lived for any length of time together in the subcontinent.

Even before the Nationalist Party, the Indian National Congress, had been formed in about 1885 a gigantic conference was held annually in each large city in turn, at which the stars could mingle with the rank and file. The agenda became increasingly nationalistic as the years went by.

Proceedings were held in English and there was a maximum of publicity. In 1943 when the military threat exerted by the Japanese had become serious, Lord Wavell had no hesitation in slapping Nehru, Mahatma Gandhi and the rest into gaol in Poona and Ahmadragan. My old poetry friend, Sarojini Naidu, was with them. She looked after the Mahatma in gaol who, on that occasion, came close to death.

This story concerns the annual meeting, which had taken place many years before, in 1919, at Lahore. My father-in-law, the Duke, had told Amy that he thought she really ought to put up a show, wear a sari and go to the Congress session, more as a mark of respect than anything else; he had no intention of going himself. Amy had never worn a sari in her life. But she obliged her husband and tried her best to put it on properly. Alas, it was not a success.

As Amy Sawhny entered the large Conference Hall who should she bump into at the entrance but Motilal Nehru himself, the father of Jawaharlal, the star, too. He had never been seen in anything but the smartest of Saville Row suits. On this particular day his old Hanovian son, Jawaharlal, had persuaded his father to put on an Indian homespun cotton dhoti, a similar garment to that worn by Mahatma Gandhi. As soon as Motilal recognised his English friend, his face had lit up in a warm, delightful smile.

"Ah, my dear Amy," he had said with genuine relief in his voice, "I see we are both in fancy dress."

Fortunately there were no TV cameras in those days. It would be doing Amy Sawhny a disservice to call her ordinary.

Ian Botham, when asked by a journalist who was interviewing him at

Heathrow on his return from a cricket tour in Pakistan, what sort of a place it was, had replied, "It's the sort of place you'd send your mother-in-law to."

Amy was as unlike the London pantomime mother-in-law, as it was possible to be, yet it is still not easy to describe her, except by what she did. She was essentially a doer rather than a thinker yet she never appeared to be doing anything in particular. Drawing rooms, sitting rooms and gardens seemed to appear around her as if by magic.

She didn't come to our wedding. I had been surrounded then for a fortnight by one of the worst battles of the last war and anyway she lived 1,500 miles away from Bombay and the Duke was ill.

I couldn't go to her funeral because one of my hips had collapsed. This happened several thousand miles away from her deathbed. We were, I think, as close to each other as any son and mother-in-law could be; in fact I loved her dearly and she took the place of my own mother for most of the twenty-one years I lived in India.

She was one hundred per cent English and yet she was profoundly different to the many English women who lived in India in those days. She was not smart in the accepted sense of the word, yet she had style. So far as I know she only wore a sari or a Shalwar Kamiz (Muslim blouse) once in all her years there – Motilal Nehru's "fancy dress" had been an apt description. With her it was always a case of sensible shoes and unmistakably English country gear.

Of course, in addition, she had a sense of humour and she was a strong character. I could never forget that she had eloped from a British Government House with an Indian lawyer in 1908. Sheila didn't seem to know exactly what part of England she came from, although it was possibly Berkshire. I only guessed that her maiden name was Edwardes because that was Sheila's second name.

The greatest thing she ever did, apart from creating and bringing up (with the help of Des Raj Sawhny) one of the finest families in India was to rescue such money as she had in the middle of the 1947 holocaust and take it and herself to safety 2,500 miles from Lahore in the Punjab to Wellington in the Nilgiri Hills of South India. Once there she built a new life in an old bungalow below the Ooty Club in a totally new atmosphere. Yet somehow it remained the same as it had always been, English comfort and good taste

— in the middle of India, a subcontinent that must have been so very different to her home in England, yet which she always felt to be the same. A good Latin sentence for her grave might well have been the same as Christopher Wren's in the crypt of St Paul's Cathedral — "Si monumentum requiris circumspice".

I loved Ooty because Mother had made yet another of her homes there in a bungalow she rented from the Club. It was hideous from the outside but the inside glowed with warmth. The silver shone, the chintzes were gay, in the proper sense, and her tables were covered in photographs of her children and her friends.

The visit I remember best was in the autumn of 1951. Venetia had been born in July and we had flown down to Coimbatore by Tata Air Lines. We had with us Nanny and the two Pekes. Venetia travelled in a carrycot. Mrs Sawhny had waited a long time for this grandchild. In the evening, over the log fire, when Venetia had been tucked up, Sheila and I gossiped with Mother about the old days. Her greatest asset in the long struggle had been her unquenchable Englishness. There is a paradox here somewhere, for Englishness in India has often meant insularity; the pride that so many English women have shown before the brown-skinned people of the country they had chosen to live in.

Mother's Englishness was of a different kind — the understanding of the aristocrat; there was no mistaking that she was English; her tweeds, dogs, her smartness and her style of clothes — they were all in character. Yet there was something deeper still than just appearances — it was a determination not to compromise with people, principles or problems. It shone through all she said and did. But even that quality would not have made Indians love her, for they shy away from uncompromising attitudes; it was her love of humanity.

She had been married to an Indian for thirty years; she had become intimate with his relations and with Indian people over three generations. She had never learned an Indian language and her Hindustani was the laughing stock of her children. She loved India and its people but in her younger days there had been few English people who would talk to her. Yet she was ready to criticise the many things offensive to her principles done by Indians.

39

Carry Your Bag, Sir?

*"Those were the days when well-to-do people travelled with
mountains of luggage, including unwieldy cabin trunks."*

                                                        W F Deedes

On my last business visit to New York for Killicks, a short while before we
left India for good, I had some curious experiences that were connected in
an equally curious way together – in fact they spilt over into my second
career and were connected too, with the carrying of small parcels by hand
on airliners. At least one of them looked every bit like a parcel bomb. It was
the first one, which, strangely enough, had brought me from a great distance
into touch with Buckingham Palace, the inside not the outside.

Phillip Brothers, our German-Jewish Agents in Pine Street, New York,
which runs parallel with Wall Street, used to lend us an office when we
visited them, a comfortable room complete with desk, telephone and privacy.
They also arranged for Sheila and myself to stay either in the Hampshire
House or the Essex House, luxurious apartment blocks overlooking Central
Park from the south. All these amenities, of course, were free. The first
phone call I always used to put through on arrival was to Paul. On this
occasion I picked up the phone and asked the Phillips' operator please to get
me Mr Mellon at Upperville, Virginia. Paul's voice came through. I said,

"Will next weekend be all right for me to come down to Upperville?"

There was an unusual pause at the other end of the line; unusual because
Paul was a swift operator on the phone. Somehow, I sensed there was
something wrong.

Then he said firmly; "Would the following weekend suit you, Wilf? You see I have the Queen of England coming to tea with me next Saturday."

I should have guessed. I had read in the *New York Times* that morning of the private visit of Her Majesty to Kentucky where a number of American race-horse breeders and trainers lived: this visit was clearly just two race horse owner-breeders having themselves a good old gas together. Thus it was the following weekend that Bunny Mellon invited me to her bungalow at Little Oak Spring where, over a pre-lunch dry Martini, she asked if I could do her a favour.

"It's a strange request but Syri Maugham told me the other day about some charming tiny papier mâché coloured birds which, apparently, are only made in India. Could you possibly get some for me? I want them for our drawing room in Antigua."

I said I would certainly try. I thought at once of Rudi von Leyden. This was right up his street. But who was Syri Maugham?

Then she offered me a second Martini. When that had gone she said, for no good reason; "Martini number one is normal good manners, on both sides, Martini number two is good fun. But don't ever forget that Martini number three is deadly."

It was the only piece of advice I ever took in America, especially if it concerned American Martinicles, as Jack Masters used to call them.

Back in Bombay Rudi von Leyden had never heard of the birds. But Sheila said firmly, "I'll find them for you." Next day she mentioned at chota peg time, "I've got your birds."

The following day Francis, our driver, lugged a large gunny sack up the staircase of Bates Hill. Like a magician Sheila dipped her right hand into the sack, pulled out two handfuls of straw in the middle of which were two whole flights of the most exquisite tiny papier mâché birds – baby kingfishers, blue tits, yellow tits, and even one miniature bird of paradise.

"Where on earth did you find them?" I asked. "And so quickly!"

"Hebbie," came the answer – the young Maharashtrian artist who had taught her to paint (K K Hebbar).

My next trip to America was on a Tata airliner, a Constellation. I lugged the gigantic sack from Santa Cruz Airport, Bombay, to Kennedy Airport,

New York. I didn't dare let it out of my hands or sight; the contents, packed in straw, were too precious and too fragile to hand to anyone. It was only by leaning rather heavily on the Tata name that I was given the rear seat in the first-class cabin and so could lower this unconventional piece of hand baggage gently between the back of my seat and the air hostess' cubby hole.

Bunny Mellon's gratitude was sincere and there was also a good deal of amazement in her voice. "How on earth did you do it?"

"It was Sheila," I replied and indeed it had been – it was in fact the best bread-and-butter letter that Sheila had ever sent to anyone. A long time later I learned who Syri Maugham was and what she did.

The next parcel adventure was prosaic in comparison and caused me less anxiety. The Newbolt family, my mother's long line of canons, minor canons, parsons (at least one of them of the hunting variety) went far back to one distinguished exception, a judge. Sir John Henry Newbolt, Chief Justice of Madras, who in 1810 had married Lady Digby of Sherborne and had taken her off in an East Indiaman from Southampton to Madras. His family portrait was kept proudly at this time by my Uncle Bobby, Canon of Chester Cathedral, the last male member of my family to whom I had been able to say "farewell" before setting off in January 1935 for Bombay to make my fortune.

On one of my business trips from London to India after my retirement from Bombay I asked him if I could have *The Judge* copied as I would like to give a copy of the portrait of the eighteenth-century Chief Justice to the present holder of that ancient Office so that hopefully he would hang it up in his Chambers in the Madras High Court. Uncle Bobby thought this was a great idea. Walter Langhammer, who had retired from Bombay to North London with his Jewish wife, did an excellent job, including having the copy framed. But it would certainly not fit into any jute bag I was likely to find. So what was I to do?

Tony Adams, of CDFC (Commonwealth Development Finance Company) the firm in the city where I was now working, and I were negotiating a low interest rate loan of £500,000 to the Mysore Paper Mills in South India – (rather appropriate under the circumstances). But we still had to carry the framed portrait (eighteenth-century wig and all) to Madras, via Bombay, Delhi and Calcutta.

Because there were two of us, twice the amount of social grease was necessary for it to be allowed on board at each stop. The internal airline aircraft was half the size of the Constellation but fortunately it was still part of the Tata empire. Pushing the picture behind the two back seats in the first-class cabin required almost the same degree of delicate handling as the birds. And when His Honour the Chief Justice received the parcel, with genuine surprise and gratitude, his Head Clerk nearly killed himself by falling off an antiquated ladder up which he had climbed in order to hang the picture, which he placed so near the high ceiling of the Chief Justice's chambers that you could hardly see it. There were no other pictures in his Chambers. I had taken the precaution of having the seventeenth-century judge's CV painted onto a large golden panel, which was just readable from the dusty floor of the twentieth-century CJ's private chambers.

The third and last parcel, which I had to convey by air over long distances, was potentially the most dangerous of all three, though deceptively light to carry. CDFC occasionally would send me back to India on short trips, usually to Bombay, where with the help of the World Bank, we had set up, in Bombay, a miniature development bank. It was called the Industrial Credit and Investment Company of India, ICICI. Its executive Chairman, G L Mehta, was a charming, orthodox Hindu, who had been independent India's first Ambassador in Washington. Just before I left London on one of these trips, Sheila had asked Afsar Qizilibash, daughter of my old friend Muzaffar Qizilibash, to tea in Chester Street. Afsar, who was nothing if not energetic and forward thinking, said immediately after hearing about this journey, "Would it be going out of your way to come back through Saudi Arabia? I have something I must give as a present to one of the Saudi Princes."

Afsar was already, at thirty-something, influential in Pakistan where her father had told me she was likely to become a minister in their government. I felt sure that Stanley Hoar, the Managing Director of CDFC would not object; it was possible that he might even approve.

I said, "Yes, of course. What is it?"

I almost said, 'I hope it's thin, flat and not too heavy.'

Afsar quickly replied that it was quite small and very easy to carry. She asked us round to her flat in Fulham for a drink that night. It turned out to be an expensive, and I thought, vulgar, cut-glass bowl, presumably to hold flowers, which, apart from having to be carried by hand, would have to be carefully packed in a square cardboard box. Did terrorists carry square bombs, I wondered?

After a second whisky in her flat that evening, it didn't seem to be as alarming a venture as I had anticipated. Next day Stanley Hoar approved of the diversion to Riyadh, capital of Saudi Arabia. Sheila, of course, would not be able to leave the children. There was no trouble on the outward journey to Bombay and back to Arabia via Bahrain except for the discomfort of having to carry a square cardboard box on my lap – rather like Mr Kyipup's Homburg hat. That is until Air India's Boeing landed at Bahrain, where the customs officers insisted that I undo the package myself; they left me, with grim pleasure in their eyes, to repack it after they had scrabbled about inside it for a good five minutes.

The same thing happened at the enormous glossy, newly built Saudi Arabian customs palace on the main land across the half-mile of Persian Gulf waters which separate Bahrain from the Arabian desert. The dirty looks I had to endure were heavy with suspicion. Curiously enough I was ushered through the customs at Riyadh with speed and no demands for me to unpack my parcel were made.

Did Afsar have a James Bond means of communicating with her Saudi Prince? She had insisted to me that the gift was both expensive and that her Prince was very important.

I stayed in Riyadh with a Palestinian Professor of English at the University, to whom I had an introduction from London and who lived in an air-conditioned cottage on the outskirts of the town. He was a delightful host and insisted that I should be careful once inside the Royal Palace.

"Careful of what?" I asked.

He said that I should not risk dropping my gift or even looking like doing so. He also told me how to find my Prince from among the large number available. "He's fairly near the top," he said, "so you must really take care."

He bravely dropped me outside the palace gates and explained in Arabic to the guard who I was and the purpose of my mission. The Guard platoon and its heavily armed commander looked formidable. The Professor then drove off saying,

"They will probably send you back to my house in a Rolls Royce." Big deal, I thought.

Then came the last and most terrifying part of the journey, a sort of Hilary Step just below the summit of Everest. An armed corporal led me into the palace and left me at the bottom of an immense marble staircase, where there was a landing in the middle, leading to the upstairs floor. On each step of this marble staircase was an armed Saudi soldier standing to attention, his AK47 rifle held loosely across his chest, at the ready. By this time I felt like a piece of jelly and, of course, tripped up stepping out onto the landing. My problem then was how to hold onto the cardboard box containing the glass bowl safely. I managed to do this and regained my balance, sweating; none of the soldiers moved an inch. I wondered afterwards what a clip of AK47s would feel like.

At the top of the stairs there were more soldiers. A servant came out from behind a beaded doorway and indicated that I should come through into an antechamber. He then explained, in broken English that I wouldn't be allowed to meet His Royal Highness, presumably he was so Royal and so High. Instead a curious and rather untidy-looking little man appeared from behind a curtain and asked me what I wanted! I said I had come on behalf of a Pakistani lady who was known to His Highness and that I brought a gift for him from her and would he be so kind as to present it to him. Then with immense relief I handed over the box to the dim-looking chap in this dimly lit back room, who said casually, "By the way, I am the Prince's doctor!"

✳

"Those were the days when well to do people travelled with mountains of luggage including cabin trunks." So wrote Lord Deedes at the beginning of his delightful book, *To War with Waugh*! I don't think Lord Deedes was particularly well to do in those days, the early thirties, although the *Morning Post* certainly sent him off to Ethiopia on the SS *General Metzinger* from Marseilles with a mountain of luggage – "It had taken two taxis to convey me and my gear from my uncle's house in Bethnal Green to the station."

Sometime in 1963, I think it was, Stanley Hoar had sent for me and said solemnly, after asking me, surprisingly, to take a seat opposite him at his desk:-

57 Two lovely ladies: Margery Baker and Sheila Russell (1960).

58 Bernard and Diana Greer at their home at Aberystwyth (1985).

59 Nawab Muẓaffar Ali Qiẓilibash with his daughter Afsar (on left)
at Eton on 4th June 1964.

60 Sheila after a flying lesson.

61 Wilfrid with Sheila on the links at St Enodoc.

62 In memory of Venetia: a sculpture of the Madonna and Child by Venetia. Photographed by Henry Grattan.

63 Venetia in an acting role.

64 Robin and Sheila with Fleur and Berty.

65 Sheila and Robin at Clare College.

66   Robin, Sebastian, Bertie and Fabienne (1996).

67 *Sheila's favourite Pekinese – Fleur.*

68 *Sheila with her favourite dog Fleur.*

69 A Convent in Goa: *a watercolour by H A Gade (1953).*

70 A Fish Supper: *by Renig, the daughter of K K Hebbar, painted at the age of ten.*

71 Mountains in India: *a watercolour by K K Hebbar (1952)*.

72 Mahabaleshwar in the Monsoon: *a watercolour by K K Hebbar (1952)*.

73 Juhu Beach near Bombay: *a watercolour by A K Ara.*

74 Dal Lake, Kashmir: *a watercolour by K K Hebbar (1952).*

75 Roses in a White Vase: *an Oil Painting by A K Ara (1955).*

76 *Still Life:* Pink Carnations in a China Mug: *a watercolour by Sheila Russell.*

77 Flowers in a White Vase: *a watercolour by Sheila Russell (1965).*

79 *Sheila Russell.*

78 *Sheila Russell.*

80 *Mimosa blossom at Lower Cole, Rock, overlooking the Camel Estuary: a photograph by Henry Grattan.*

81 *Summer flowers above the Camel Estuary: a photograph by Henry Grattan.*

82 The author in the Chindit hat worn by Jack Masters: photographed by Henry Grattan.

"The Chairman, Lord Godber, (Chairman of Shell at this time) has decided to spend six weeks in India having a look at our investments there. Lady Godber would be going with him. He asked me yesterday, whether you and your wife could accompany them, since between you both, your knowledge of India must be quite extensive."

I said immediately I didn't think Sheila would want to leave our two children in England even though we had a living-in Nanny but I would, of course, obey orders and enjoy doing so. It was in this way, shortly after 8.30 a.m. a few weeks later, a large hired car arrived in Chester Street with a bulging boot.

Lord and Lady Godber, surprisingly for eminencies, were squashed onto the back seat. In front, of course, was the chauffeur. They had driven to our house from their London flat in Princes Gate to pick up their ADC. I stowed my modest suitcase and BOAC airbag on the floor beside the chauffeur and sat in front with him, as all good ADCs do. Sheila waved us goodbye from the front door.

My troubles began at Heathrow where I leapt out of the enormous limousine and tried to open the back door so that my distinguished passengers could get out. It wouldn't open. I pulled hard several times with no result. Panic was beginning to set in when I spotted a tough-looking black porter who had been watching my efforts with a professional and disdainful smile on his face. I looked despairingly at him. He then moved with surprising speed in my direction and whipped the door open in a trice. It was my worst moment of the whole six weeks. I didn't even count the mountain of luggage as it tumbled out of the boot. The black porter organised a team in no time, then an efficient chap, in a pinstripe suit, from Shell, sprang from nowhere and took our tickets and passports, which he returned to us in the VIP lounge half an hour later.

In the comfortable waiting room Lady Godber suddenly asked me what I thought I should call her. In all honesty I had never thought about this. I looked and felt rather helpless. Then she said firmly, "I think it should be Lady Vi." Brilliant, I thought, and so it was, for much more than the next six weeks. When at about 11.30, Lord Godber said to me, "I wish it was dry Martini time," despite Bunny Mellon's advice, I knew the six-week trip was going to be a success. Lord Godber, I learned later in the City, had built up the Shell business in America over several pre-war years thus becoming Sir Frederick Godber. His peerage came in 1945, when he could have taken over – but to his immense credit did not – the sixteen per cent of Shell Transport and Trading, which belonged to the Dutch, and which had been in German hands since May 1940. This, I think, was a courageous and honourable thing to do.

My heart, however, sank when we arrived at Karachi. It was then that I was first conscious of the true size of the mountain of baggage – fourteen pieces, not counting my own little heap of three.

This book is meant to be the story of Sheila's life, not of mine, so there will be no detailed description of the next six weeks other than to mention that there were some places, particularly Mount Abu, north of the great mill town of Ahmedabad, where the visit does have to be described. It was an out-of-the-way hill station, close to the magical deserts of Rajasthan, where I had to steer Lady Godber firmly away from the violently erotic sculptures of the Jain Temples where the local millionaire, Sir Purshotamdas Thakurdas, Killicks' close business associate, a Jain, was determined to take her and Lord Godber, In planning our route he had said he particularly wanted to go "off the beaten track" providing it was at all possible, rather than fly in comfort direct from Ahmedabad to Delhi.

I had worked out with Sandy Smith of Burmah Shell in Karachi a route from Bombay to Ahmedabad inspecting on the way one or two of CDFC's investments. Sandy had pointed out to me that we would have to spend a night in the comfortable Shell bungalow in Ahmedabad and then proceed by car via the Mount Abu temples into the "off-the-beaten-track" jungle to a Maharajah's country palace near the borders of Rajasthan. (Sandy Smith had been the first British paratrooper to land on Pegasus Bridge in Normandy at 4 a.m. on the morning of D-day in 1944.)

My admiration for both Lord and Lady Godber, already high, rose higher still when our hired car arrived at the broken-down and clearly badly run so-called hotel which its princely owner had been trying to make money out of by telling all his friends that it was a comfortable hostelry in the middle of a picturesque but uncomfortable jungle. To start with there were not enough employees to cope with the fourteen pieces of luggage; the bedrooms contained only string beds, in Hindi, charpoys.

There were creaking electric fans hanging from invisible ceilings covered with spiders' webs – and a curried dinner, which was even too hot for my old timer's taste.

Yet they made no complaints and indeed seemed to enjoy it all. We were rewarded next day when we were taken round one of the most beautiful and remote of Hindu temples in the whole subcontinent. We spent the next night in a small dak bungalow – dak being the Hindi word for the Moghul postman's night shelter. All this had been organised by Burmah-Shell's jungle representative.

As our car drove out onto the country road that would take us to Udaipur I spotted two simply dressed Hindus, each wearing a dhoti and a black pill-box hat, arguing fiercely with each other in the middle of the road. They paid no attention to our car. "Who would they be?" Lord Godber asked with some curiosity. It so happened that I recognised one of them.

"They don't look much like it but actually they are a couple of Bombay's multi-millionaires. They are probably here to pay their respects to Kali, the local Hindu Goddess. They are probably arguing about the current bull market on the Bombay Stock Exchange."

Sadly we could only stay for half a day at the comfortable, professionally run hotel on the small island in the middle of the magic lake at Udaipur (owned and run by Tatas) where Dabeh had designed the interior décor in traditional Rajasthani style carried out with all her French artistic skill. Next day I rode with Lady Vi, on the gold caparisoned backside of the most Royal elephant of the Jaipur stables, which took us slowly and solemnly up a steep track to the Palace of Amber where all the interior walls shimmered with tiny mirrors. It was indeed a wonderful experience they had both said later to Jai, His Highness the Maharajah, who as a younger man had spent two years at "the Shop" in Woolwich. So we came to Delhi where there was a letter waiting for me from Sheila which reported that Robin had been chased downstairs by Venetia into the basement of the Chester Street house, where he had slipped on the kitchen floor, slid and crashed into the glass of the downstairs bathroom door. He was now safely in the Great Ormond Street Hospital for children where apparently he was making good progress. "Don't worry, darling, he'll be OK; but I'm glad I didn't come with you."

In Delhi, Burmah-Shell took over the caravan, including the fourteen pieces of luggage. Next day Lord Godber insisted that I accompany him on his formal visit to the famous American economist, Professor Galbraith, whom Jack Kennedy, the American President, had just sent as his ambassador to Pandit Nehru's government. We were due at the US Embassy at twelve noon. At 12.30 when Lord Godber was sagging under the torrent of the Ambassador's statistics he leant over to me and whispered, "Isn't it about Martini time?" So I invented one further appointment. The garrulous and domineering diplomat then let us go.

The rest of the trip went well except for the inevitable tummy upset at Madras, which hit us all. Back in Bombay Sir Purshotamdas Thakurdas presented Lord Godber with an enormous silver filigree imitation of a gateway arch, copy of an eighteenth-century Moghul original at Ahmedabad, which he had organised as a gift to the noble Lord. Six months later I stumbled on it in the cellar of the Godber country house in Mayfield when I was searching for a bottle of French Vermouth.

We said our goodbyes at Santa Cruz airport in Bombay where the Godbers boarded a 707 for Heathrow. I was going on to Nairobi – the Commonwealth still had to be developed. "You must bring your Sheila with you to Mayfield when you get back," Lady Vi had said. I was sorry to see them go but watched the last of the fourteen-bag mountain disappear into the Boeing's hold with a sigh of relief.

40

A Cherry Tree in Chester Street

"Loveliest of trees, the cherry now
Is hung with bloom along the bough..."

A E Housman

We were lucky in Chester Street, No. 32 being on the corner of the eastern end; we had a garage at the bottom of the small garden which Sheila soon got going after it had suffered several years of neglect. I watched the cherry tree she had planted next to the garage door every morning when I got into the car to drive Venetia and Robin to their schools. With the passage of the years it had grown surprisingly fast and every spring its pink blossoms seemed to challenge the early Victorian bricks that surrounded it. It was, I swear, the only cherry tree between Grosvenor Gardens and Sloane Square, where I dropped Venetia, who had met her lifelong friend there, Marina Dracoulis (Greek shipping family).

I then drove round the corner to Hill House, highly popular at the time because Prince Charles had just left it, where I dropped Robin off. Occasionally I had to park the car, easy in those days, if we were early and joined the queue of fathers doing the same thing. Sometimes I found myself in front of or just behind Reggie Maudling, Shadow Chancellor of the Exchequer who also lived in Chester Street – he shared one half of a divided house with Lionel King-Lewis, our doctor, whose son, Peter, was Robin's very first school chum. I then drove east to Old Jewry where there was a basement garage. I was very spoilt.

Lionel King-Lewis had his moment of glory in 1964 when the Prime

Minister, Harold Macmillan, in the middle of a cabinet meeting, suddenly felt the early pains of the illness that put an end to his political career. With true Macmillan courage he refused to leave the cabinet room until a doctor turned up who in this case was the locum for the Number Ten regular GP who was on holiday. So Lionel drove at breakneck speed to Downing Street where he examined the Prime Minister and gave the media a photo opportunity in the Cabinet room by holding up to the cameras of the world a specimen of Macmillan urine in what looked suspiciously like a wine glass. The contents on the front page of the *Evening Standard* that afternoon looked more like a glass of Chateau Lafitte than anything else!

A year or two before, soon after we had settled in, Sheila had said, "Isn't it about time we found somewhere to go for the summer holidays?"

After much discussion we boiled down all the possibilities to a short list of two. The first was in Dumfriesshire where Toni Hesketh, now Toni Thomas ran, together with her ex-Calcutta tea-broking husband, Philip Thomas, a Stately Home Hotel. She was Venetia's godmother. The hotel was a few miles from the Solway Firth, close to several golf courses.

The other was a holiday resort called Rock on the Camel estuary in North Cornwall. The River Camel flows into the Atlantic in the middle of the North Coast of Cornwall. It also boasted one well-known golf course and possessed a good surfing beach at Polzeath where my mother had taken my brothers and myself for summer holidays before the war. It was also John Betjeman country. I think this tipped the scales. We chose Cornwall. Sheila, of course, did not know either. I plumped for Rock, which is several miles up the Camel estuary from the Atlantic, in favour of either New or Old Polzeath. My memory whispered to me that there had always been something rather unexciting about both of the Polzeaths. We were nearing perhaps the end of a long era of snobbism and class-consciousness, or maybe it was something else? I had never been to Rock but somehow it had always sounded smarter and less conventional.

We drove down there on an empty road; Salisbury Plain was like a green Sahara Desert. The drive from London took us eight hours. We descended at the Rock Inn, opposite the small port of Padstow, then virtually unknown to the outside world.

After Sheila had unpacked and put the children to bed we had dinner in the hotel dining room – it was the coxswain of the lifeboat (we were told afterwards) who had carved the leg of lamb in the middle of the dining room wearing a chef's white hat.

Then we strolled along a narrow road, the estuary on our left. We took a turning up to the right, where a signpost pointed to the St Enodoc Golf Club. It was there, just as the sun went down, that we overtook an elderly lady. We fell into conversation with her. Clearly she was an old inhabitant.

"My name is Bannerman," she said, as if she had known us all her life. "People call me Ban. Why don't you come and see my little house? It's up this road and overlooks the water."

Sheila said, "Why not? How kind of you to ask us."

She showed us a tiny bungalow, which looked out across the Camel Estuary, where many small boats were anchored. "It's called Sandy Cole. I let it for the holidays and live in my caravan over there." She pointed towards a clump of macrocarpa trees. We spent the next five Augusts in Sandy Cole.

As we said goodnight a beautiful girl came running out of the small house to meet her grandmother. "Oh this is my granddaughter, Susan Walsham." Sheila said hello to a girl who, as a woman, was to become the very best of her many girl friends in England.

This is where I have to emphasise the violent change that was taking place for Sheila, who had to embrace a new way of life among, for her, a virtually new and unknown people. The English people she met now were quite different (especially where the women were concerned) to those among whom she had been raised in Lahore and the Punjab. I choose the method I do (of personal description) in order to show not only how different the English in England are to the English in India whom she had known all her life, but also how much better they were, in England: – in intelligence, hobbies, interests, backgrounds, war records and kindness (lack of socialism).

I thought hard about this and decided on a detailed description of the English among whom she would now and did live for the rest of her life. In effect, the county people among whom she would now build a new home and a new life were, admittedly, above average. This and the beauty of Rock, Padstow and the North Cornwall coastal area was the magnet which attracted us all so strongly that we decided to retire there.

This is somewhat akin to the problem that faced John Masters in 1948 when he had been writing his famous novel *Bhowani Junction*. I would not change the 'personalisation' principle – I am proud of England and its leaders in the upper middle class, as was Sheila from her own specialist point of view. Generalising descriptions are not my genre and never will be. They are part of the 'I was there' principle. The people in Part 2 tell of the old British Empire type. The Bombay 'Indian' English increasingly come across as new Labour Blairites.

India wins in the long run because they do not and never did believe in the Blair philosophy. Sheila and her family somehow managed to fuse together the old British India with their own version of the New India.

41

Rock – A Magic Place

"We used to picnic where the thrift
Grew deep and tufted to the edge…"

John Betjeman

There was no question of us finding ourselves between a Rock and a hard place. Sheila only went back to India once after she, the children and I had left it for good in 1956. There is a big difference between leaving a land like India and "staying on" which Celia Johnson depicted so strikingly in the television play. There were two reasons for this so far as Sheila was concerned. The first was that Sonny had married again in America after Phyl, whom Toots Williams had likened to Naomi Campbell and Claudia Schiffer combined, had sadly died of cancer. He had left Golodetz, married again in America and lived out his happy and successful life on Long Island where cirrhosis of the liver finally dealt him its mortal blow. Sheila loved him and missed him; his daughter, Moneesha, whom she had so many years ago tried to protect when she first arrived in England, had bravely defeated cancer herself, had become a gifted cook and then married her second Englishman. She lived in Putney and somehow, in true Sawhny fashion, managed to get her daughter married in California. She still travels the world.

Dabeh lived out an unhappy life in the Taj Mahal Hotel in Delhi until her slim emaciated body was laid out on the Towers of Silence hidden on top of Malabar Hill where the vultures hovered. So Sheila had no one left in India to visit. Yet she never gave up her loyalty to and love for the land of her birth. There were occasions in Rock when she wore a sari. Then nearly everyone in Cornwall looked at her and was stunned by what they saw.

The second reason was that, as perhaps was to be expected, she had come to love England. She was, like all her family, a 'doer', although her doings were scarcely ever noticeable. For instance, she had never mastered changing gear in a car, so it was, I knew, an act of courage when she made herself learn how to drive and earned her driving licence. From now on she always shared the driving from Cornwall to London, 300 miles each way. Even with an automatic gear change she often ran into various walls in and around our garage; but still she carried on. The advance she made in painting was remarkable, especially in oils. In London her teacher had been employed by the LCC, which had pleased her (and me) since her lessons were free, gratis and for nothing. It was the only thing that Labour, either New or Old, had ever done to please me. Embroidery she had learned to work at with skill and contentment from Bunny Mellon.

When she decided to take up bridge seriously she put herself in the hands of Trevor Jones. Her life in England at that time was full to the brim.

The solid foundations of a boarding school education for Venetia and Robin (Venetia went to Wycombe Abbey, Robin to Eton) gave her real satisfaction. She was only sad that she was so weak at the piano because she knew that if she could have played it at all well she would have made me particularly happy. But she adored, if I can use that much overworked word, the ballet. I wished so very much that she had lived to see the tercentenary Russian celebration of the St Petersburg ballet in June 2003. She would have thanked Mr Putin in person, if that had been possible, especially the staggering performance of *Swan Lake* (all this, of course, on TV).

Sheila very soon fell in love with Rock; we rented Ban's bungalow, Sandy Cole, for the next six summer holidays. Then I persuaded Ban to sell us the bottom of her garden. Like the developers whom we were always cursing, we built our own house on the slope leading down to the Camel estuary. With the help of a London architect- curiously he was called Russell – Sheila designed the perfect house. In true Tata style – unlike the Taj Mahal in Bombay – it was built, not the wrong way round, but upside down.

The bedrooms were sited below the sitting room. When we had cut down Ban's macrocarpa trees the view over the estuary was far better than anything you could find on the Cote D'Azur. The deeds were in Sheila's name.

42

Lower Cole

> *"Lark song and sea sounds in the air*
> *And splendour, splendour, everywhere..."*
>
> *John Betjeman*

It was Donald Bousfield, a house tutor at Eton, who christened Sheila's house at Rock, Lower Cole. Like many other schoolmasters, he and his wife, Pamela, had a seaside home in Rock. It happened to be situated bang next door to ours. The Bousfields had three daughters – Diana, Caroline and Vanessa.

Venetia (now known as Goop – nobody knows why) became a close friend of Vanessa. Robin had been put down for my old school, Marlborough. I had always felt deep down that Eton was in fact the best boys' secondary school in the world. I also knew that every Eton house tutor's list was full up with candidates for the whole of his seventeen-year stint as a housemaster. Despite this knowledge one day I asked Digger Bousfield if by any chance he had a vacancy. "You're very lucky," he said. "One father has only just fallen out and I haven't had time to fill the hole."

So Robin had five happy, productive years, first at the Hopgarden, Donald Bousfield's House, then at Carter House with Raef Payne. After a year, Robin was persuaded by his classical tutor to have a go at a college scholarship, which if he won and provided he wanted to stay on in his House he would become an Oppidan Scholar, that is if he would stay in Bousfield's house in the town and not have to live the monastic life of a King's Scholar "in College". Oppidan scholars' parents paid the normal fees.

Henry VI had apparently left sufficient cash for the free education of seventy exceptionally clever young Tudor gentlemen. Robin and Donald Bousfield politely left it to me to make the decision. I felt I owed it to Donald Bousfield as much as to anybody else to plump for the Oppidan way up the ladder. It was about this time that I was introduced to Sir Alec Douglas Home at a Commonwealth party; I asked him for his expert view.

"Which is better, sir, to be a King's Scholar or to be an Oppidan Scholar?"

There was no hesitation in the answer. "I myself would say Oppidan Scholar every time, provided the boy's father could afford it. Are you the father?" and his eyes twinkled. He suggested we have a drink.

I replied, "Yes, sir, I would like that."

And then the Shadow Foreign Secretary said, "It's really up to your bank manager, isn't it?" I thanked that delightful man for his advice.

Robin's effort to be accepted by my old college at Cambridge, Clare, was surprisingly difficult considering that he had won an exhibition and that his father and grandfather had both been up at Clare, in 1890 and 1930, respectively. But the era of political correctness had arrived. After some ironic backchat from the then Admissions Tutor, Robin was ungraciously allowed into the college, which many years earlier had at the hand of his father's closest friend in Clare, admittedly an American, benefited in one way or another by the equivalent of fifty million dollars.

Robin got a scholarship in his first year, in Anthropology. His father cast an impolite thought in the direction of that Senior Tutor (whose name did in fact indicate German ancestry): "Up yours," I thought.

Venetia, three years ahead of Robin, had won a scholarship both at Girton, Cambridge, and Somerville, Oxford. Clearly she couldn't go to both so she chose the same college as Margaret Thatcher had done before her.

How was it then that Rock presented itself as such a special place both to Sheila and myself, and to our two children?

43

Peter Pan

*"...a little boy named Peter Pan, who had flown out of the
window when he was a baby and never would grow up."*

J M Barrie

The first person we met in Rock, after Ban and Susan Walsham, was Ken
Duxbury. He lived like Robinson Crusoe on the golden sandy beach that
stretched from the Rock Sailing Club, just below the Rock Hotel, towards
Daymer Bay and the Atlantic Ocean.

On our first morning we dashed along the beach, Sheila, Mona and the
children wondering at what point we would plunge into the water. Before
we had taken off our sand-shoes we saw him—what appeared to be a
bronzed, naked young man scrubbing the hull of an upturned dinghy. When
we looked more closely we could just make out a sort of G-string; otherwise
he might well have been the famous castaway on Tobago Island. There was
no question of introductions. Within a few minutes we learned that he gave
sailing lessons in his dinghies – there were two of them, *Whisper* and *Louise*
– and that he had only been here for a few months and slept on the dunes
above the beach.

Finally, he told us he had been a sub-lieutenant in the Royal Navy
during the last two years of the war and had served on the Arakan Coast
of Burma. He and two friends had recently sailed from Cardiff to Cornwall
where he had left his fellow crewmen to continue their voyage to Lands
End while he had stepped ashore on this very beach with a rucksack and
nothing else.

"There was a magic about this estuary — I didn't even know its name — which I couldn't resist," he said with a smile like that of Lord Louis Mountbatten. We talked while the children had their first swim. His name, he said, was Ken Duxbury. And when he also said quite casually, that he had discovered that John Betjeman was a frequent visitor to Rock we knew that we would become friends. Sheila and I swam too. We arranged that he would teach Venetia and Robin how to sail, in *Whisper* and *Louise*.

It was during our first summer holiday at Sandy Cole in 1958 that we met Betjeman in the flesh. It was in Sandy Cole. Ban had come over from her caravan in the trees for a cup of tea with Sheila. The children were next door at Spindrift with Mona, getting to know the Bousfield children. Suddenly he came in. I remember having seen him in the distance at Marlborough during his last term when I had been a new boy.

During the few years between then and now he had begun to make a name for himself as a poet. He knew a lot about the Church of England on which he was already an expert. He knew all about my grandfather who had been a Canon of St Paul's Cathedral for forty years. I always regretted this was the only occasion that we met. John Betjeman had read the lesson when Sue Walsham married Chris Harbour in the Naval Chapel at Portsmouth. Sue had been given away by Rear Admiral Sir John Walsham. Sheila had attended the wedding.

That first summer the Bousfield children made good use of the natural swimming pool on the way to Pentire Head where, at low tide, the tiny cowry shells were washed up onto the sand; those shells, so small they were almost English pearls, of which Betjeman wrote in "Summoned by Bells";

> *"In all the roar and swirl*
> *The still and small things gained significance*
> *Somehow the freckled cowrie would survive*
> *And prawns hung waiting in their watery woods…"*

Someone had carved a diving board into the rocks. At high tide we could dive into the ocean waters. The remains of that diving board were still there in 2003. Many generations of lucky children had swam in this magic pool, where in my teenage holidays I had often looked out to sea to the unknown, to the Camel Estuary where the Westropp twins, Celia and Lena, daughters of my father's best friend in Cairo and my guardian since he died had swum the two miles from Stepper Point to Daymer Bay and back. On our way back from Pentire Head to Rock we were in Betjeman land.

> *"To hear blow flies settled upon squashy heaps*
> *intent and gorging at the garden gate.*
> *Stink of solignum on the wooden fence;*
> *mint round the spring and fennel in the lane.*
> *And honeysuckle wafted from the hedge..."*

It was in the middle of our second holiday in Ban's cottage when we suddenly realised that Rock, outwardly unimpressive and certainly no Victorian seaside resort was, as our Peter Pan had said, truly a magic place which, so far as London emmets were concerned, was in a social sense run by a prefectorial social group of which undoubtedly, Geoffrey and Helen Greaves were at the top of the ladder.

Geoffrey was a great gardener, he also had a large-scale map of Rock covering the wall of his dressing room. Between the ninth and the eighteenth holes of the big course, he once told me how he had ended his war shaking hands with Russian soldiers somewhere near Potsdam. Jack Hawkes, who owned large tracts of land near Dorking, was his best friend. He, poor chap, had been in the 51st Highland Division so had to travel from St Valery to a POW camp in Poland where he stayed until the end of the war. The next memorable picture I keep in my mind from those early days at Rock was of the two friends playing chess together in the streaming sunshine on the balcony of their cottage, which overlooked the estuary on the other side of the narrow road.

Another outstanding warrior and his equally outstanding wife was Mike Austen-Smith. A long-standing member of the territorials he had joined the HAC, the Honourable Artillery Company, the oldest regiment in the British Army, shortly before the outbreak of war and got his de-mob suit in 1956 as Colonel, commanding the regiment.

He and his wife, after the war, formed a successful architectural partnership. He was an all-round operator, if ever there was one, gardener and eventual writer. His war memoirs based on letters written to his mother from North Africa and Italy made one of the best war books of World War Two that I ever read. I gave a copy to Robin. Inette, his wife, did everything well that she touched. She ran a successful anti-bureaucratic society to protect Bodmin Moor from Blair-like deadening bureaucracy. She, with Monica Pethybridge was a devoted Glyndebourne loyalist.

Their summer house in Rock, with its snake pit, was a well-known party centre. Their second summer retreat was an old mill, near Advent, a Cornish village near Camelford, which they transformed into an ancient and modern water mill where they cheated SWEB (our local electricity board) by generating their own power from their own stream. Mike had many letters after his name, starting with MC and ending with OBE.

There were two other couples who cannot be left out of my list especially as I had extra-curricular connections with both. They were emmets too, of course, weren't we all?...

Richard and Joan Bevan were both thinkers and doers. Joan was at the centre of most charitable gatherings, particularly the annual cancer research evening. She used to come to me to borrow the St Minver Silver Band's trestle tables for the platters of food which she and her friend loaded onto the groaning tables. I played the trombone in the band and had a key to the band room. Oddly enough, Joan also owned a gold mine in South Africa. She had all the virtues, charm, kindness and energy. Richard had been Chairman of the Gresham Club in the City of which I had been a member for many years. His main contribution in Rock had been organising the raising of a startling sum as our contribution towards the building of the Duchy Hospital in Truro. I think it was to be the only private hospital in the county and it cost plenty. I could sympathise with him from my own experience in Bombay. As we all entered the three-score years-and-ten age group Sheila and I saw less of them, especially as they sold their delightful property on the estuary, Gentle Jane, to a scion of the Rothschild family. I was touched when they came to Sheila's funeral in 2002.

Then there was dear old Toddy Urling-Clerk, a retired jobber on the Stock Exchange who was another Dorking landowner. His wife, Joy, worked in tandem with Joan Bevan. Her speciality was trudging around the extended village with copies of *Link*, our village magazine. She and her numerous friends, which included Sheila, all had beautiful gardens.

Toddy who had fought a tough war in the Middle East – he actually suppressed a mutiny of free French prisoners all by himself – had been a good friend of a good friend of mine. Peter Clapham had been at Marlborough with me, also at Clare. He had joined the RAF as an observer. In due course he became the most effective night fighter navigator – radar controller in the RAF and was Basil Embry's permanent night eyes. Their most famous exploit had been the taking out at fifty feet of the Gestapo HQ in Copenhagen without disturbing a brick from the houses on either side. Poor Joy died soon after Sheila. Toddy was cared for by an impressive Zulu nurse, to whom he was devoted.

Then there was Monica Pethybridge, who like my old friend the Maharajah of Porbunder in India, had in her time led a string quartet, which had favoured the works of Wolfgang Amadeus Mozart. Like me she knew her way round Munich, the musical capital of the world. She with Inette Austin-Smith and Meg Squire were loyal summer visitors to Glyndebourne. No wonder Rock was a place of magic.

There were others, perhaps the most striking of whom were Geoffrey and Meg Squire. Geoffrey used to play the organ at St Minver Church and when Venetia married Thomas he played the Wedding March on the same organ, plus all the hymns, the 23rd Psalm, etc. At the reception I remember talking to him about the Hindu Khush. His career had been a conventional one in the Indian Army. At the beginning of the war I used to watch the medieval Vickers-Armstrong troop-carriers take off for Gilgit from the RAF airfield at Risalpur near the Khyber Pass. It was the most distant outpost of the whole British Empire, nestling as it did, in the middle of the Karakoram mountain range; flying in to the remote valley between India and China was the only safe way of entry to the valley between the high mountains, which enclosed Gilgit. Geoffrey's regiment was stationed there. Meg, was in my view, the best dressed and most beautiful of the English women in Rock. She had the smartest and most extensive wardrobe of the lot, just as Sheila with her saris was her opposite number in the admittedly small group of expatriate women in our village. There were, of course, others who will appear later in this story.

44

The Flying Dutchman

"We were a gallant company,
Riding o'er land, and sailing o'er sea,
Oh! but we went merrily..."

Lord Byron

By now Venetia was at Somerville (Oxford) and Robin at Clare (Cambridge). It was still in the distance in our imagination but nonetheless that prospect could be firmly made out on the horizon, when parents, if not children, begin to think about birds leaving nests. Neither of ours had thought little about this.

Venetia had a ten-foot dinghy, which had been built by the grown-up Peter Pan's sailing school and boat building business, Westerly Boats, of which he had become senior partner, a successful example of private enterprise. He had also, believe it or not, built his own house in the middle of our village. Looking ahead I asked him to advise me on the best sailing dinghy for our family. I thought, perhaps, that Sheila might like to be taken out of the estuary into the Atlantic Ocean by Venetia on calm days in June. This did not materialise but when winter came we all went to the Boat Show at Olympia and I bought a sixteen-foot Wayfarer, which we christened *Pickereel* (from Kipling's *Just So Stories*). Its number was 221: – it was the first Wayfarer to be introduced to the Camel Estuary. Before the summer holidays came round again Westerly's had added this type of dinghy to their growing fleet.

Ken Duxbury taught the editor of the *Sunday Express* how to sail. From then on the *Sunday Express* carried each week a four-column article on sailing by "Our Yachting Correspondent". Ken now has a dozen books about sailing and other subjects to his credit and during the last ten years has earned himself a satisfactory annual income from his watercolours of Betjeman land.

Robin's dinghy (Venetia's look-a-like) was called *Fried Potato*. Sheila spent much of her time looking after our matelots' gear. With the help of a pair of powerful binoculars, we spent many anxious hours scanning the Camel Estuary, from Padstow to the Doom Bar, searching for two quite separate and solo dinghy sailors.

There was one adventure, which happened to me and was sufficiently upsetting that Sheila ultimately had to nurse me back to a state of walking wounded. There was on our beach one eccentric yachtsman whom Ken assured me later, besides being middle aged, was apparently an over-confident and none too skilled helmsman. His name was Skipper Herring. He owned a large Olympic class, twenty-five foot dinghy, called *The Flying Dutchman*, which he sailed alone to such distant places as Newquay and Mother Ivy's Bay. He frequently invited me to accompany him and, as with my previous experiences with mountaineering and John Hunt, I invariably excused myself. When the accident happened I had just recovered from a third hip replacement operation; my back felt like jelly. The London osteopath had asked me to wear a stiffening waistcoat jacket under my shirt. One morning when a force five wind was blowing against an empty beach there was Skipper Herring and his formidable yacht. Once more the invitation came – it was to be the last – and inevitably I had to give in. I put on my Mae West, clambered on board and we were off up the estuary, in a flash, heading inland in the direction of Wadebridge.

"It's blowing too hard to go outside," he shouted at me over the howling wind.

We roared up the River Camel at what seemed to me to be about forty knots. Soon we ran out of seawater and opposite Cant Hill Skipper Herring went about. He had no option. Inevitably we capsized. I sank to the bottom and when, after what seemed an age I shot up to the top, my internal waistcoat had swollen so tight that I could scarcely breath. I could see the capsized yacht but there was no sign of its skipper.

Then, mercifully, the cavalry arrived. I had no idea that Robin had been taking a sailing lesson with Trevor Evans, one of the Westerly partners. Trevor with the wise instinct of the professional had trailed Skipper Herring and his clumsy passenger, keeping us in sight from half a mile astern. Just as I surfaced Trevor dived overboard from the Westerly Wayfarer, which his young pupil then took over. Within five minutes I was lying breathless on a pebble beach while Trevor tore off my Harley Street waistcoat and Robin sailed his instructor's Wayfarer with due aplomb to the shore. In half an hour I was home and dry in my own bed and Sheila had taken charge. In a couple of days I was on my feet again. The Olympic yacht was eventually retrieved a mile upstream. Skipper Herring did not invite me to sail with him again. I reckoned that both of us had been lucky to get away with it.

It was during that summer that Sheila did come out with us on one of those glorious days when Cornwall beats the Côte d'Azur to a frazzle. Ken Duxbury took one of the Westerly Wayfarers and Venetia captained *Pickereel*. Nigel Donell, Robin's closest friend, joined our crew and Fleur, Sheila's black Pekinese, came for the ride. Sheila had filled up a large picnic basket, which contained one bottle of gin and two of tonic water with ice in a separate container. We dropped anchor in a cove, near Stepper Point, where Ken climbed up the vertical cliffside and Fleur chased her own tail on the golden beach. We had by now left the bucket and spade era and had arrived at the surfing and sailing age. How can we ever have thought seriously about Dumfries and Kirkcudbrightshire? Sheila did not seem to be homesick for Hindustan.

45

The Visitors' Book

> *"From August 1963—*
> *Bernard, Diana and Helen Greer*
> *To October 2002*
> *When you, darling Sheila, were lost to view*
> *The Guest book is full of Dawes and Beresfords*
> *Donnells, Sawhnys to Russells, an occasional Ruck-Keane,*
> *Of happiness and friends and a house that is always full."*
> *Wilfrid Russell*

Lower Cole with its superb view and Sheila's burgeoning garden compelled us to invite many friends to stay throughout the summer months. The weather most years was usually good and by now – the early seventies – Sheila had a growing circle of friends.

Our longest and the most cosmopolitan among them, I suppose, were Robbie and Joan Clive who lived in a delightful house in one of the most glamorous of English villages, Ewelme, near Henley. John of Gaunt was buried in the fourteenth-century church, Anne Boleyn had owned what must have been almost the first of commuter cottages. Peter Fleming, with whom I used to play soccer in Delhi, lived at Nettlebed, a few miles away on the Oxford to Henley road. Robbie, a Wykhamist, who loved pictures almost as much as did Paul Mellon, used to work at one time for the Worms Bank in Paris and by now jointly owned a head-hunting outfit in London with a Tory MP. Joanie was an excellent all-rounder with above average good taste in dress, interior decorating and gardening. My early memories of her went back to my first post-war skiing holiday at Val d'Isère, in the French Alps. She was the only woman I ever saw skiing in a skirt. As she never fell down, her unconventional appearance didn't really matter. She was a better skier than many women twenty years younger that she was.

She was also a friend of Françoise Gaston-Breton. Sheila and I went on several exhilarating continental holidays with them. I could always leave the 'admin' side to Robbie. Our most exhilarating holiday was at Sorrento, in Italy, where you left the hotel in a lift that smoothed itself down the inside of a cliff to a comfortably equipped launch which took you to Capri and its famous grotto. The site above it of a Roman villa that had belonged to the Emperor Constantine, many centuries before, was the first example for me of an early Roman Mediterranean holiday home. Next door there was another equally well-known Swede who had written about him.

Gracie Fields owned a villa lower down and nearly on the sea with a beautiful swimming pool. We had lunch at an Italian terrace restaurant, fifteen hundred breath-taking feet above the Med. It was the best meal from a dizzy height point of view I can remember in my life because of its perpendicular position above the shimmering blues of the Mediterranean.

We walked in a perfect Italian garden above Amalfi in the late afternoon dusk. Joanie, courageous, sometimes foolhardy, had wandered off with Sheila; neither of them were visible. Robbie, always punctual, had gone to our five p.m. RV where the hotel taxi was to meet us (I had noticed on the way in that the gardens closed at five p.m.); my watch read four-forty-five p.m. I ran in a most un-English way all round the neat gravel footpaths shouting Joanie's name (not Sheila's) and found them calmly examining the outside entrance to a complicated maze. We just made the garden's exit with a minute to spare. Joanie's champion escape effort a year or two before had been to lose herself in the catacombs beneath Saint Marks in Venice.

Early on in our friendship I had discovered that Robbie was a direct descendant of Clive of India. I, more than Sheila, had bored them both often enough with my talk about India so when I discovered this rather dramatic connection I was taken aback and embarrassed. Every now and again Robbie would disappear for a fortnight to Wales where a cousin lived in Powys Castle. Robbie's forefather had hit India with the East India Company some two hundred years before Mr Charles Killick and Mr Robert Preston Nixon had stepped ashore at Bombay in 1857.

Another couple who used to come often both to Chester Street and to Rock put me into a long-term connection with 617 squadron, RAF – the Dambusters. Tony and Marjorie Iveson had first been introduced to us by Leonard Cheshire, who had taken over command of 617 after Guy Gibson had bust the German dams in May 1943 and had himself been shot down a few weeks later. Marjorie had been raised in Jersey so she was more French than English. When we met in 1962 she was a well-known TV producer – I think with Thames TV. She and Sheila hit it off well. Tony, like Charles Gardner before him, was firmly addicted to flying. He had joined the RAFVR in 1938. His first operation against the Luftwaffe had been in a Spitfire, somewhere off Lowestoft where he finally had to ditch in the North Sea and wait for half an hour sitting in his cockpit before he was rescued by a passing trampship. He then, wisely, transferred to Bomber Command (as I write he is Chairman of the Bomber Command Association) where he flew one tour (thirty operations) before his final posting to the Dambusters, at the end of 1943 after the Möhne and Eder Dams had been well and truly turned into a deluge of water by Guy Gibson.

Tony won his DFC attacking Bergen in Norway in 1944 by flying a bullet-ridden Lancaster safely back to the Shetlands, after giving his crew the choice of baling out into captivity or of returning across the North Sea in a colander. His most dramatic operation took place on 4th November 1944 when he and eighteen other Lancaster Captains led by Willy Tate attacked the Tirpitz which was sheltering at the head of Tromso Fjord, the most northerly of Norway's deep and precipitous rocky inlets. It took them six hours flying from Scotland to reach the target in perfect weather – good for bomb dropping but bad because of the danger of meeting enemy fighters. Fortunately none appeared. Tony met the CO of the ME 109 Squadron that had been entrusted by Goering to protect the Tirpitz from Bardufoss, twenty kilometres away, in 2002 at a meeting in Hollywood. The German Oberst, by then an American immigrant with plenty of dosh, told his story to Tony:-
"Our radar went US – unserviceable – so we missed you by five minutes. Hitler put me under solitary arrest. I'm glad it was not worse."

617 had an especially accurate bomb-sight. They were the only squadron in the RAF to be issued with this astonishingly accurate bomb-aiming device, which required five minutes straight flight before flying and dropping the bombs. They found their target surrounded by useless torpedo nets. They were aiming Barnes Wallis' five-ton bombs from a height of fifteen thousand feet. Willy Tate, appropriately scored a direct hit with his first bomb, the next Lancaster scored a near miss — twenty-five yards. Then came Tony Iveson himself with F.Fox. He scored a direct hit from 15,000 feet. There were a few more near misses and *Tirpitz*, with a sigh of despair, turned upside down and capsized. Most of Barnes Wallis' "children" had to carry their bombs home to Scotland. Two British battleships had been anchored in Scapa Floe for two years. They could now be released. Bomber Harris had told Winston Churchill he could do the job in four minutes flat and out of office hours. He did.

There were many others, of course, who came for weekends, notable among whom was Teddy Dawe, a director of De Beers who had an excellent taste in pictures and old furniture; he was also a first-class chef who cooked for his own excellent dinner parties; he travelled frequently between London and Johannesburg. I had met him originally in Sierra Leone where he was inspecting diamond deposits in the swamps of West Africa. Sheila was the guest of Teddy and his wife several years running at Ascot where her white sari came in useful and where, happily, she had no need to wear a hat. Teddy was close enough to Sir Phillip Oppenheimer to be able to borrow his box for at least one day of the famous week.

I have described the social structure of Rock as I saw it when Sheila and I first came to live in this magic village, which was run prefectorially as far as the retired section of our community was concerned. Geoffrey Greeves was its Senior Prefect. But as most people know this system always demands a senior master or mistress to be in charge. Quite frequently in a rural village situation these disciplinarians are married to each other. At Robin's school the masters were known as Beaks; they wore white bow ties all day. In the holidays Robin's House Beak was our next-door neighbour. In fact it was Donald Bousfield who had generously agreed to break with his Eton's rules by accepting Robin into the Hopgarden. By chance, he also chose the name of our own house when the time came to christen it.

"What's the name of the bungalow you used to rent from Mrs Bannerman?" he had asked.

"Sandy Cole," was my reply.

"Then I would suggest Lower Cole."

For me he was certainly the most senior of them all. Both he and Pamela, his wife, were always there yet you hardly ever saw them unless it was Donald lighting a bonfire at the bottom of his garden or Pamela working hard at installing a new gadget in their immaculate computerised kitchen. He scarcely ever wore a tie, certainly not a white one. Between them they wrote a delightful history of St Breward, a village on the edge of Bodmin Moor to which they moved when Rock began to lose its silver lining.

Rowlandson had made a number of drawings of the countryside around Bodmin in the late eighteenth century. He had a friend who lived at a place called Hengar Wood. Paul Mellon had sent me two copies of the catalogue of his own collection of England's finest draughtsman's work. "I expect you probably have a friend near you who is interested so I am sending you an extra copy." This is what Paul Mellon had written to me from the head office of his Bollingen Foundation, in New York. St Breward was, of course, only a few miles from Hengar Wood.

Most of Rock's house prefects played regular bridge together. They were well above the normal standard and they all had golf handicaps of between ten and twelve, most of them had been either City Gents with homes near Dorking or Sunningdale. Sheila used to say that in her experience Donald never made a mistake at bridge. I knew that years ago he had won a soccer Blue at Cambridge and had once actually played cricket for a minor county against Sir Donald Bradman in a touring Australian team. He certainly never wore his Hawks Club sweater in his garden; all this in addition to being Senior Maths master at Eton.

Another charming couple were Larry and Joan Dodd. Larry, after retiring from the Ghezireh Cotton Company in the Sudan, had settled in Cornwall as a Clerk in Holy Orders. His parish was at Stratton, in beautiful country on the outskirts of Bude, where he preached to a congregation, which included a Royal Navy widow called Joan. Larry was the equivalent, in the twentieth century, of the hunting parson of the nineteenth century. They got married, moved to Rock and lived happily ever afterwards, playing bridge and golf. Sheila enjoyed her bridge with Larry enormously. He was an excellent player with a gleam in his eye. Joan was the best lady golfer in the county.

Our political prefect was Elizabeth Coburn-Smith. Her husband, Jock, had flown with the South African Air Force in the Desert during World War Two. Now he was chairman of the local flying club. He used to take me on many pleasant flights in his own aircraft. Once we flew to the Scillies. On the way home we got ourselves thoroughly lost and had to land at St Mawgan, the nearest RAF station to Rock. Sheila, her driving skills by now well honed, had to drive twenty-five miles halfway round the estuary to bring us sheepishly home to Rock.

Another interesting and smart widow was Monica Pethybridge who had been a WAAF in World War Two. She was musical, amusing and energetic. She had played the violin all her life and when she lived in Bodmin, before coming to live in Rock, she had organised and led a well-known amateur string quartet. Her daughter Sarah had begun to take an interest in Buddhism and India.

One of the most interesting of our friends was Penelope Willis whose maiden name had been Tremayne. She belonged to an old Cornish family who owned a beautiful Queen Anne Manor House called Croan, situated halfway between our nearest town Wadebridge, and Bodmin – many years ago the county capital. Penelope was highly intelligent, beautiful and brave. She was the daughter of a well-known senior officer in the RAF, Air Marshal Sir John Tremayne. She married late. Before marrying she had spent some time in the Levant acting as special correspondent for the Sunday Times. She had been mixed up in the fighting in Cyprus at the time of the troubles between the Greeks and the Turks. It was during this time that she met and married her husband Tony Willis who had flown with 617 Squadron. She was also a writer of distinction and a composer of witty and beautiful poetry. Sheila and I got to know her well because she was constantly leaving her home in the Cornish countryside for distant places and we seldom knew where she had gone or when she was likely to come back.

On one occasion she asked Sheila for some letters of introduction in Lahore as she was going to the North West Frontier. It so happened that Sheila was able to give her an introduction to Sonny's old Afghan friend,

Prince Hissam el Effendi. Toots Williams, who has appeared on several occasions in this story, also knew Hissam and had given her a letter of introduction to him.

Many weeks later Penelope reappeared in Cornwall and we discovered that she had been into Afghanistan and the difficult mountainous country between the Khyber Pass and Kandahar.

Her next expedition had been to the other end of India, to Ceylon, where she had been kidnapped by the Tamil Tigers. She was kept a prisoner of these savage terrorists for several months, in the north of Ceylon. Eventually when she was extricated she wrote an exciting book about her adventure.

Several years later she had sent me through the post a parcel of forty pages of manuscript which she told me was the official log of her father as a young sub-lieutenant in the Royal Naval Air Service. In October 1914 he, with three other young pilots, had flown the first ever bombing raid to be carried out anywhere in the world, their ancient aircraft had been flown from Le Havre in France where they had been assembled from boxes to continue their journey by the French railway system to Belfort. Their target had been Ludwigshafen on Lake Constance in south Germany where they had been ordered to bomb any zeppelin they found there with four twenty-pound bombs, all of which were attached to their aircraft by a piece of elastic.

Her father had in fact found a Zeppelin on the ground and had dropped his small bombs, which had bounced off the top of the Zeppelin. He was shot at by a machine gun crew sited on top of the Zeppelin, who could not depress their gun sufficiently to hit him. He then drew his personal revolver from his belt and fired at the crew that had missed him. He had got home without a compass to the field in France, which was only about one hundred kilometres from where he had set off. Only one of his friends got home to their base in France.

In her covering letter to me Penelope said simply, "Could you tell me what I ought to do with these papers?"

I asked her if I could send them to Tony Iveson who has already appeared in this story as having struck the *Tirpitz* with a direct hit with a five-ton bomb from fifteen thousand feet. In this way the lengthy, well written, historic description of the first ever bombing raid in history, in October 1914 had reached the archives of RAF Bomber Command in 2003.

We had one naval officer, Peter Maslin, and his wife, Jane. Peter had taken early retirement to become a schoolmaster at Millfield before retiring to Rock. For several years he had been Navigator in *Britannia*, thus commanding the respect and admiration of us all. He was an ace bridge player and Sheila's favourite partner. I could always tell when he had partnered her by the glint in her eyes when she came home. After she died he told me that she always overcalled – he considered this was a sign of her courage and determination.

The most distinguished visitors of all, I suppose, who had honoured Lower Cole once in our early days at Rock in 1973 were Lord and Lady St Levan, whose family had owned St Michael's Mount at Marazion, with its medieval castle and chapel on the summit of its island citadel, from the time of Charles II at the end of the Civil War. Lady St Levan had collected a quarter of a million pounds from the people of Cornwall to build St Theresa's Cheshire Home. Lord St Levan gave some land opposite the castle on which a magnificent new home catering for forty disabled men and women was then built. At this time, Cheshire had to go off into Millfield Hospital in Sussex for well over a year. Lady St Levan was a sister of Harold Nicolson, my first lecturer on Germany at Viceroy Court in October 1944.

When they came to lunch with us I drove over to Wadebridge, met their car at the entrance to the Royal Cornwall Showground and navigated them to our home with its distant views of the Atlantic to the West. Sheila had given them a lobster thermidor, which she had cooked herself. Her well-known Bombay-style mouth-burning curries would not have been well received in John Betjeman land.

46

Betjeman on the Links...

"Dark of primeval pine encircles me
With distant thunder of an angry sea..."

John Betjeman

Sue Walsham was her Rock name. She was the girl who had rushed out of Sandy Cole that first night when Sheila and I had met Mrs Bannerman, in 1957. Her father was Admiral Sir John Walsham. Among Sheila's many friends, Sue was the one who replaced Kikuk Thadani as her closest. Kikuk and her ex-World Bank husband lived in New Hampshire near the American Canadian border for most of the year. She loved England and kept a flat in Kensington. There were also long phone calls from London to Lower Cole since her Indian husband wouldn't drive a car and didn't like our nationalised railways.

Sue was so truly magical I cannot describe her, just as Jack Masters had not been able to paint Victoria Jones of *Bhowani Junction* to his own satisfaction, and as a result Sheila had come to his help and this had contributed in some respect to the creation of that remarkable novel. Sue's husband, Chris Harbour, was the principal figure in a Vermeer-like picture which was to be seen by millions of BBC viewers when John Betjeman was carried up the tenth fairway of our golf course on his last journey to the tiny church of St Enodoc in a monsoon-like storm. Chris, more than six feet tall, was the leading pallbearer of one of our greatest Poet Laureates. Sue told me many years later that the pallbearers had stood motionless throughout the service in the tiny church; they wore no mackintoshes and the rain dripped off their simple clothes onto the floor. The storm raged outside an otherwise empty church. No Poet's Corner in Westminster Abbey for John Betjeman.

The church had been built in the ninth century AD and throughout most of the nineteenth century had been buried in the sands of Daymer Bay. The vicar of those days had to climb down through a small skylight in the steeple to take a solitary Communion Service, then climb up again to let himself out of the skylight into the graveyard. The church was extricated from its covering of sand towards the end of the nineteenth century.

It was about this time that Robin went up to Cambridge to my old college, Clare. The admissions tutor had not been helpful. Could it have been for some queer social or political reason? There was talk of a new fad called political correctness. At last he managed to slip through the net of prejudice and spent three happy years in the college of his father and grandfather.

He had then been articled to Price Waterhouse where, in due course, he passed his exams and became a chartered accountant. Then he disappeared from our view to their Casablanca office in Morocco, where he met a French girl called Fabienne Nucci whose family lived in Nice.

In due course they were married by the British Consul-General in Gibraltar. Thus Sheila was deprived of her first family wedding. In this way Robin became half-French just as Duggie, his uncle, too, had become half-French before him. Fabienne turned out to be more intelligent than his sister or himself.

Venetia – Goopy – swept through Somerville. She seemed to take Oxford more seriously than Robin had regarded Cambridge. She met an undergraduate, Thomas Whiffen, who had been at St Paul's where my father had also been to school in the eighties of the previous century. Thomas' father was the Vice-Chancellor of Newcastle University. Goopy then spent a year or two teaching English at her old school, Wycombe Abbey. Thomas Whiffen came down to Rock quite often and showed us that he was way ahead of both Sheila and myself whether it was in English Literature, Scrabble, mathematics or, as the years went by, in the arcane world of computers and the Internet.

He was also a serious member of the Church of England and a Lay Reader. Sheila and I were impressed by the way he ran the finances of his church in Winchester where he had lived since he had come down from Oxford. He also ran the finances of most of the secondary schools in Hampshire. By a curious chance the Newbolt family was an old Whitley clan.

They were married in our parish church at St Minver. I put up two monumental blacks on this occasion; the first when a letter arrived for Venetia the day before the wedding addressed to Venetia Whiffen. I said to Sheila, "I didn't know Thomas had a sister called Venetia!" And at the reception at the St Moritz Hotel, I so arranged the seating at the top table so that it scarcely accommodated all the relations of both bride and groom. In fact there was no room even for our old friend Canon Gent who had just married them.

They went to Paris and Rome for their honeymoon. When they had gone Sheila found Lower Cole as empty as I did. We knew that Robin and Fabienne would survive in the African Bush where Price Waterhouse had sent them. Happily we knew that Venetia also would have a very clued-up husband to look after her in the medieval wilderness of Winchester!

47

Bridge over the River Camel

"It's more than a game. It's an institution!"

Thomas Hughes

With her children off her hands, Sheila had to find a serious hobby, preferably one that was different, both from painting and embroidery. It did not take her long to make a choice. Rock, rich in so much, could also lay claim to the outstanding skills of one of the best bridge players in the land. Not only did Trevor Jones play top-class bridge, but he could also do the much more difficult thing – teaching other people how to play. Trevor did not live in Rock – he and his wife Pat, also a devoted supporter and teacher of the game, lived about twenty miles away at St Merryn, on the far side of our estuary. But they were willing to drive the twenty-five miles around to Rock in order to teach a gathering of some twenty ladies, and a scattering of gentlemen, the secrets of this ancient pastime.

It must have been in the eighties when Sheila signed on for their weekly class. She already knew the rudiments of the game and so was good material for the maestro. After a year or two she became enthusiastic. Trevor, by certain signals, had indicated that he was finding her a promising pupil.

Catherine Garnet, an Oxford graduate, told me at a county cocktail party that she had become in fact his star pupil.

At first I accompanied her to these bridge lessons but lagged several miles behind and soon gave up. Before I dropped going to his classes I discovered in a roundabout way that Trevor Jones in his youth had been a keen and talented cricketer. He had once scored a century for Somerset at

Leeds (sadly not Lords). I had to confess to him that on the only occasion I had played at Lords – for Marlborough – against Rugby – I had made six not out (we were rained off on the morning of the second day).

When I came to describe Sheila's ambitious efforts at learning how to achieve an average performance at bridge I asked him how in fact she did play. He said, "I first met Sheila in the 1980s at the bridge table – and how she did love her bridge. In the Rock area there were a number of keen bridge players and Sheila was one of them. She was not only keen and enthusiastic but also exuded personality and table presence. Like most of us she was always trying to improve.

"Sheila had one big advantage," Trevor went on. "She was charming at the table, both to her partners and to the opposition. Bridge players will know what that means!! It was indeed a lucky player who 'cut' Sheila as a partner, for then you didn't need all the high cards. You had the greatest asset – a good partner. Sheila will be greatly missed by her many friends."

As I have mentioned elsewhere, I think her favourite male partner was Captain Peter Maslin, while her favourite female partner was Vivianne Williams, who died shortly before her. Vivianne was the wife of Toots, who had danced with her at Falettis Hotel in Lahore two years before I first met her in the Meadow of Roses, three thousand feet above that other magic place – the Vale of Kashmir.

48

Summoned by String Quartets

> *"Let's all in Love and Friendship hither come*
> *Whilst the shrill Treble calls to thundering Tom*
> *And since bells are for modest Recreation*
> *Let's rise and ring and fall to Admiration."*
> Georgian ringers' rhyme in Church tower at St Endellion

At one point in this story I began to sag and believe that the forces of so-called modern England were about to overwhelm the magic of Rock. Although Sheila never spoke about such ethereal things as magic and matters of the spirit, I reckoned that I knew her well enough to be confident that she was not giving way under those malignant forces, if indeed they did exist. Anyhow just when I was at my lowest, a poetic mist settled on my gloom and somehow I knew that it had been conjured up by Sheila. Suddenly I knew that all would be well and that I would not have to look out for a Mullah in Rock. What could this be?

Then, equally suddenly and surprisingly I realized what it was. It was the St Endellion Music Festival.

From the summer of 1959 when Sheila first heard about this rural miniature of Glyndebourne, she had made sure that she always had a picnic basket and a rug ready for use in August, so that during the twenty-minute interval halfway through the concerts we could make sure of being there and of using them. In fact, for several years running we went together and sat in one of the local farmer's fields with our rug and a bottle of cold champagne.

The concerts took place at the beginning of August every year in the fourteenth-century early English Church of St Endellion which, in John Betjeman's words, watched over Port Isaac Bay, "like a hare, whose ears are the pinnacles of the tower and the rest of the animal was the Church, which crouches among wind-swept firs".

The magic of Rock had been rescued from oblivion by an inspired introduction to the Cornish cliffs of the unstoppable sounds of soul-inspiring English violins, violas, clarinets, flutes and French horns.

There are too many names connected with this extraordinary society that to record them all in this story would not be practicable but some, such as Roger Gaunt, Biddy Holden, Richard Hickox cannot be shut out as if we were closing the church door upon them.

The church was supported by a sizeable vicarage without whose assistance the adventure could never have been launched; they include Arch Deacon Pring, Parson Hocken, Prebendary Murphy and Canon Prior. I personally remember Vicar Prest whose term in the parish was hugely supported by a close friend of Sheila's, the wealthy patron of Michaelstow's ancient church near Camelford – Mary-Ide Warlow-Harry. The dilapidated vicarage would have collapsed almost before the society had been formed without people like Mary-Ide whose generosity flowed mainly from Wall Street. I am confident that Richard Hickox, who conducts the orchestra, will end up with a KBE – he already has a CBE. He has raised the standard of music on the Cornish cliffs to such a height that professional performers from all over England clamour to perform at St Endellion – for free.

Sheila's friend Mary-Ide created, with her skill at weaving tapestries and crocheting, the many flags that adorn the nave and the choir. It was Nicholas Roscarrock who loved the church's patron saint so much that he wrote a hymn in her praise.

> "To emulate in part thy virtues rare
> Thy faith, hope, charities, thy humble mynde
> Thy chasteness, meekness and thy dyetspre
> And that which in this world is hard to find
> The love which thou to enemies did show
> Reviving him who sought thy overgrow..."

All I can add to this fourteenth-century hymn is that Sheila's virtues exceeded even those of the patron saint of John Betjeman's favourite church on top of the cliffs, whose arms embraced Port Isaac's bay.

49

Mens Sana in Corpore Sano

"Oh, grim look of night! Oh night with hue so black!
O night, which ever art when day is out."

Wm Shakespeare

I have put off, for as long as I could, writing about Sheila's health. As a family, the Sawhnys had always enjoyed good health in the sense that, despite a higher than average IQ, they were all devoted to the outdoor life and essentially to English games. Golf was certainly their most popular family game. "The Duke", her father, would have played every day of his life, had it been possible. Yet he died young. In 1941 I arrived at their family house in Lahore only just in time to ask him for his daughter's hand. He had been wrapped up in a Kashmir shawl and was crouching before a blazing coal fire. He died, shortly afterwards, in his early fifties, of a heart attack.

Duggie was an all-round sportsman. His passion was riding, while Sonny followed the more conventional path of shooting and fishing. He always managed to get hold of superb shotguns, with which he pursued large numbers of pheasants, grouse, duck and partridges. He must have reduced considerably the fish population of most of the rivers in Kashmir in his enthusiasm for casting into pools where the trout were most plentiful and, despite his keenness on the consumption of Scotch whisky, he was the only Sawhny, apart from Sheila, who passed the three score years and ten mark.

Sheila was to be the oldest of the Sawhnys, for she reached the early eighties. Apart from golf, her favourite game undoubtedly was tennis. There was a distant Sawhny cousin who played tennis for many years at

Wimbledon. She and I used to play often on the glorious grass courts of the St Lawrence Gardens in Lahore when we were walking out in 1941.

Regarding whisky, I think Sonny must have heard somewhere a story told by Winston Churchill's private secretary, Anthony Montague Brown. It went: "When I was a young subaltern in the South African war, the water was not fit to drink. To make it palatable we had to add whisky. By diligent effort I learnt to like it," he had said, according to Anthony Brown. "I neither wanted it or needed it but I thought it pretty hazardous to interfere with the ineradicable habit of a lifetime."

I am sure it was that appalling winter night in 1957 which Sheila, Margot Mason and I spent at Wardour Castle that clogged up her lungs in some way; often she would have to go to bed for several days at a time. She also had several heart attacks, as a result of which she had to be flown off to the hospital in Truro by our county helicopter ambulance. Once the helicopter had to take off from the beach below Lower Cole and once on the road that ran beside the estuary. Her description of the heart cases reception area at Treliske Hospital made me think of early Hogarth prints – the overcrowding, the shouting and screaming of a multitude of other heart cases made alarming listening. As usual she took it in her stride. St George's Hospital in Bombay must have been like the London Clinic by comparison.

But she always recovered and it was not until the skin complaint of eczema took hold of her that her normal life style was seriously interfered with.

Up to now I have avoided trying to describe the real people of Rock, many of whom were her friends. The cosmopolitan outsiders about whom I have been writing, were after all "emmets" – temporary, sometimes semi-permanent, uninvited guests. After the millennium the two young Princes used to visit Rock every summer. They were brilliant at melting into the magic background but they, too, were emmets, even if rather special ones.

Venetia and Thomas came three or four times a year. Goopy loved animals even if not in the normal Sawhny way; and this was another minor divergence from her mother's tastes. First it was a parrot but, fortunately for us, it couldn't travel and had to stay in Winchester. Then there was Fin, an immense underbred mixture of a Doberman and a police dog. Poor Thomas had to exercise him, which he did religiously when he was at Rock, leaving Lower Cole every morning at about seven o'clock to walk him four or five miles along the beach. Fin was certainly not Sheila's cup of tea nor mine.

The only time I can remember her approving of Goopy's dress was the occasion of the wedding of her god-daughter, my niece, Susan, to Mark Ruck-Kean in 1976. I can't think why she didn't always dress as she did on that day. She wore a black skirt, a white silk blouse and a smart well cut black coat, the whole crowned by a thin black hat, which I couldn't begin to describe. Patricia Ruck-Kean was a friend of the brewing family of Courage. They owned a splendid Georgian House, complete with private chapel, somewhere near Banbury. We had been staying with Betty Halloran, an old friend of Sheila's and of mine, who lived near Reading. I had got ourselves truly lost driving from Sulhamstead to Banbury. Then, just as we reached the chapel we were suddenly overtaken, in the middle of a field on the Courage estate, by a white Rolls-Royce decked out in silver wedding ribbons, conveying the bride and groom to the church.

I remember at the overcrowded reception talking to Edward Courage who sat in a wheelchair, from which he had conducted the affairs of the Courage family business from a surprisingly early age. We talked about Leonard Cheshire, whom he knew, and admired. Goopy seemed to enjoy the occasion. I drank too much champagne and drove back to Reading faster than on the inward journey.

It is possible that Sheila's daughter had too spiritual a temperament for human clothes. She wrote good poetry, which displayed a heart that was both gentle and polite. She also painted surprisingly well but not often enough. She was best, I think, at still life.

With your permission, I will quote one of her poems. It is called "Fawley Mount". I know nothing about Fawley Mount, either what it is or what it means.

"The tossing trees
Silver blue and green
Sway in the wind like ocean weeds
Beneath a transparent air blue sea;
And we like strange shell creatures
Move as molluscs down the grassy paths.

And are there angels up above
That air blue dome
Who look as we look?
As we look deep into the oceans depths
And mark our Lilliputian labours
Our intolerable griefs?
And who weep with infinite pity down
Tears of love into our parched and scalding hearts?

A pheasant rises with a clap of wings
From bracken, little fir trees
And the green of birches
Seeded in the scrub.

The beetles move with purposeful intent
And deep within the wood
The leaf mould lies
In quiet damp, cool and sweet.

Venetia Whiffen 1995

The most influential person in our village, I suppose, was John Bray. Sheila had known his parents ever since we first arrived on that summer holiday in August 1957. They owned Bray's Central Stores, one of the two grocers' shops in the village. Leslie Bray, his father, was a smallish man, friendly and conscientious. Sheila liked and respected him as she also did his hard-working wife who plodded in his footsteps round the shop, collecting our groceries from their well-stocked shelves.

I had a strange Dickensian relationship with her husband after he told me at one of the church fêtes that their family was not Cornish. He had started life, he told me, in London as an assistant in a haberdasher's shop on Ludgate Hill, which was only a few hundred yards from St Paul's Cathedral.

"How odd," I had said, just as Sheila emerged from the second-hand books tent where Pamela and Donald Bousfield were selling dozens of old paperbacks for a shilling each. "My grandfather was a Canon of St Paul's. I know Ludgate Hill like the back of my hand." Old Leslie Bray had replied, "I used to know one of the Canons well, Canon Newbolt. I used to go once a week to his house in Amen Court, with other young men from the City. We listened avidly to his dramatic explanations of the Scriptures."

I stopped him and asked, "Was it by any chance the Amen Court Guild?"

Leslie Bray looked at me in astonishment, as did Sheila.

I went on, "As a boy of ten I remember those Thursday evenings when twenty or thirty young men twice my age invaded No 3 Amen Court and disappeared respectfully into my grandfather's study, its walls groaning with books and his writing desk full of quill pens."

In due course Leslie Bray handed over his shop to his son John, who had an adventurous and throbbing entrepreneurial get-up-and-go spirit which he employed to turn the modest family grocer's shop into a soaring business of estate agent and developer. When he inherited the business John Bray and his wife took over the Pavilion Stores, about five hundred yards down the road, which had previously housed three squash courts, where once the Prince of Wales, Mark 2, had played and where the new owner became known as Baron Bray of Rock.

There were times in his meteoric career when I began to wonder whether he might not be starting to threaten the magic aura of the place. So far, nearly fifty years later, that magic still prevails. The Central Stores became "Di's Dairy". Sheila made friends with the newcomers, Di and Tony Dunkerly, who provided her with groceries and later, wines and spirits, which were of a higher quality and more characteristic, both for taste and general excellence than anything she had previously bought at Harrods. But that is another story.

Then the last and certainly not the least of our friends in the village who were Cornish through and through were Sylvia and Michael Cock. Sylvia came four days a week for many years to look after Lower Cole for Sheila; her husband, Michael, was an experienced builder who did everything that needed doing to the house, including its plumbing; but more about them later.

50

Endings

"She left her lovely home in a wheelchair, brave to the last.
The night before she was playing bridge."

Wilfrid Russell

The last decade of the twentieth century was full of endings but I thank the Almighty that it was also full of one remarkable beginning, Robin and Fabienne's brood – Sheila's and my first grandchildren.

Taking the endings first, Paul Mellon died somewhere near the start of the decade. We had a card of exquisite taste giving us the date of the service in Washington Cathedral. A parking valet would be at the West Door of the Cathedral to take our car. The announcement was as modest, simple and solid as his remarkable life had been. Remembering him as the Anglo-American country gentleman it was impossible, at the same time, to imagine him as the greatest single beneficiary that any individual had been both to Cambridge University itself and to one single college, my own, Clare. A rough estimate put the figure at £57,000,000. More valuable than all that had been his friendship, his wit, his gifts and his hospitality. Sheila said nothing as she placed the funeral message upon our mantelpiece, but there were tears in her eyes. I looked at the table in the centre of our drawing room.

On it were several of the beautifully bound catalogues of the many exhibitions he had supported all over the world with his own pictures – Constables, Stubbs, Rowlandsons, (particularly apt for us because of Rowlandson's many visits to our district in Cornwall, Bodmin Moor, St

Kew and Hengar Wood). There were volumes of splendid photographs of Hindu temples in India, of the caves at Ajanta and the fabulous sculptures hacked out of the living rock at Ellora.

Paul gave a party in a nightclub in Berkley Square to celebrate the winning of the Derby by his famous, unbeatable and unbeaten horse, Mill Reef. At least a hundred of his younger friends were there. Each girl, including Sheila, was given a gorgeous silk scarf with the black and white outline on it of the jockey and the racehorse winning the very first Derby of them all in the late eighteenth century. We men each got a gold plated fountain pen.

When Sheila and I were greeted by him, I said, "I had five bob on Mill Reef."

His reply was, "You must have had a hell of a lot of five bobs on, even to pay for the entrance fee!"

Then there were others, of course, including Mark Ruck-Kean, husband of my niece, Susan, who was Sheila's goddaughter. I felt sad both for my brother Gilbert, his father-in-law, and for Patricia, his mother. She used to enjoy Sheila's curry suppers when she brought her family down to Rock for the summer holidays.

Then, there was Ban whom Sheila and I had first met on that fateful evening in August 1957. Her last post in a long life had been as housekeeper to Field Marshal Lord Montgomery. Her legacy to us was her home and her land, overlooking the Camel estuary.

The worst loss of all was darling Goopy, Venetia Marianne. Just before she was diagnosed a victim of cancer came the news from Suffolk that Leonard Cheshire had died of motor neurone disease. His memorial was the 250 Cheshire Homes in England and the 400 or more he had left behind him all over the world. Those two small asbestos huts in the grasslands of Bombay seemed a long way away. The bells of St Clements in the Strand, the RAF Church rang out for him. The Dambusters' crews mourned for him; all of those who survived him sat together inside Lincoln Cathedral. Sue Ryder followed him soon after. It seems strange but it is true that they were married in Bombay in Duggie and Dabeh's flat. Cardinal Gracias, the first Indian Cardinal, had officiated.

Robin had sent Sheila up to Winchester by car from Rock for several months so that she could sit with Thomas by Venetia's bedside. By this time

I couldn't even leave our house. I had just come home from Treliske hospital after my fifth hip operation. Sadly it was only after her death that I first appreciated to the full, Venetia's goodness, her painting and her poetry.

Thomas had looked after her with care and love for nearly twenty years. Her ashes were placed in the graveyard of their church in Winchester.

For me I can't remember any happier day in my life than July 14th 1951 – 'le quatorze Julliet' – sitting on the balcony of Bates Hill, gazing out over the blue stillness of the Indian Ocean, towards the West.

Sheila was driven home forty-eight years later on her last journey to Lower Cole by Robin, Fabienne, Sebastian and Bertie. When we met together outside the house where I had been waiting for her, leaning on the Zimmer frame, she wept, as she had done only once before when Duggie died, from a heart that was brave and a soul that was staunch.

Sheila's turn came on the 6th October 2002. Her ashes were strewn in the garden by Michael Cock. He planted a rose bush near the bottom gate, which leads down to the beach. It has blossomed ever since with the pale pink roses that she loved.

51

Sonny

*"I will work the mine of my youth to the last vein of the ore,
and then — good night, I have lived, and am content."*

Lord Byron

Sonny had decided soon after World War Two — the Japanese version came to its inevitable end at Hiroshima and Nagasaki — that he would resign his commission in the Indian Navy. It had been the mutiny of the ratings in February 1946, as much as anything else, which had caused him to make this decision, which had been a brave one since with a wife and two children to support he had to have a job. His only previous one, apart from commanding a destroyer in the war, had been selling second-hand cars in Bombay.

Fortunately one of Killicks' three regular buyers of our manganese ore was an American firm that felt it could increase the value of its purchases of this valuable mineral by opening an office of its own in India. This office, clearly, would have to be sited in Delhi; and with India's independence almost a reality it would have to be manned by an Indian. Preferably this Indian would have to be young, energetic, good at figures and with an appealing personality. Nepotism was not involved because Sonny met all these qualifications in full.

So I introduced him to the head of Golodetz & Company, a cultivated and vastly experienced American business house with Russian antecedents and a head office in Wall Street.

Overnight Sonny had found a job right up his street and suddenly earning twice as much as his boxwallah English brother-in-law. His office was to be on the ground floor of the house in Maharani Bagh, which he had only recently built somewhat recklessly. When I stayed with him from time to time I missed his lovely flat opposite the tomb of Saftar Jang but was recompensed by the proximity of his new home-cum-office to Humayun's tomb built in 1570 and considered by the experts to be superior to that of Saftar Jang. The important thing, of course, was that Sonny soon proved himself to be just the kind of person whom an exacting American employer wanted. He was a great success and the wheels of Killicks' mining business and those of our American clients became well oiled and profitable. Sonny was an instinctive businessman as well as being the best known socialite and raconteur in town. Years before he had been no slouch as a second-hand car dealer.

After five years of well-earned success and many Atlantic crossings things slowly began to go wrong. Phyllis fell ill; nobody seemed to know whether or not it was cancer. Sonny took her to innumerable doctors in different parts of the world, including some well known but unconventional chiropractors in the Philippines but sadly it was all without success. She died in Delhi.

Sonny carried on his business with one hand and searched for a new partner with the other. He found an American lady of a certain age who refused to live in independent India and somehow so arranged the marriage settlement that Sonny found it difficult to live up to the standard to which he had become accustomed.

They went to live in the middle of Long Island, a long way from Wall Street. Sheila missed him badly but not as much as she had done her beloved Duggie. She often told me, when we were alone and there was no one to see the tears in her eyes, how every week when she was a child Duggie used to give her all his sweets.

Sonny died in 1995 and Moneesha, his daughter, took his ashes to Delhi where they were buried next to those of Phyllis, whom Toots Williams had told me only the other day, repeating what he had told me before, that she would have lain flat all the Naomi Campbells of contemporary London.

It was moving to look back and realise that it had been Sonny, when he was a second-hand car salesman, who had introduced Sheila and myself to that famous writer, John Masters. The world became a poorer place for Sonny's passing,

52

Beginnings

> *"From quiet homes and first beginning,*
> *Out to the undiscovered ends,*
> *There's nothing worth the wear of winning,*
> *But laughter and the love of friends."*
>
> Hilaire Belloc

Somehow the only experience I have ever enjoyed in Germany and with Germans has been listening to a Mozart opera, any of them, although *Die Zauberflöte — The Magic Flute —* is my favourite, especially if it is played and sung in the eighteenth-century opera house of the royal palace in Munich. On the occasions when I did have that experience the pleasure was often diminished, since the main part was usually sung by Herr Kammersänger Heinrich Rehkemper, who was twenty years older than I was. He invariably took Susie von Shreck, my girl friend and a Baronnesse, off to dine and dance at the Vierjahrerszeiten Hotel while I slunk home to her mother's flat, considerably lighter in German marks for having bought two expensive seats in the stalls for the undoubted privilege of listening to him sing!

Apart from the occasional visit to Garmish and the Starnbergery, I wished that Leonard Cheshire had wiped the whole of Munich off the map except for Mozart's theatre and Nymphenburg, the home of the Bavarian Royal Family. As it was he dropped a flare two hundred feet above the Gestapo headquarters during the winter of 1944 so that the nineteen remaining Lancasters, waiting patiently at twenty thousand feet above him, could drop their Tallboys (11,000lbs each) of high explosive down the chimneys of the

Bavarian Sicherheits Dienst (Headquarters), which they did with accuracy and aplomb.

As opposed to that psychological quirk, there was scarcely anything French about which I was not passionately enthusiastic, from their food, their brilliant rugby football, and the poems of Paul Verlaine – also, of course, my first real girlfriend who used to invite me to stay with her parents in the imposing apartment in the Palais Bourbon, on the Quai d'Orsay – a long time before I met Sheila in the Meadow of Roses in Kashmir. This Francophile attitude to life was, I'm sure, why Sheila and I sent Robin for at least a month every summer holiday to stay with a French family in Languedoc.

In return they sent one of their boys to Rock from which visits he learned to dislike pretty well everything we put before him, from surfing to Cornish pasties.

Nevertheless by the time Robin had finished with Clare and had done his Articles with Price Waterhouse he was more or less bilingual in French. The latter firm of accountants, to whom my father had been articled in 1895, inevitably offered him a job, which equally inevitably somehow was in its Casablanca office in Morocco; equally inevitably, even before his first home leave, he was married to Fabienne Nucci (having side-stepped the old English custom of getting engaged before getting married).

The nuptials were performed by Her Majesty's Consul-General in Gibraltar. Fabienne's father was an engineer in Casablanca; his family came from Nice and all I had to do was to ask her father and mother's permission in as formal French as I could muster, if my son could offer his hand to their esteemed daughter. I thought it had to be the other way around (at any rate for daughters). But Sheila and I did at least escape the cost of advertising the situation in *The Times* and the *Daily Telegraph*. Sheila, I know, missed the church ceremony, the wedding dress, the flowers and the confetti.

Robin had always been a fast mover. More often than not he took his bride on the back seat of his current 700cc motorbike, if an aircraft was not immediately available. The Nuccis were a highly intelligent family, Madame Nucci, his mother-in-law, was one of the top French Scrabble players.

Fabienne was bilingual in English long before I asked her parents if Robin could become their son-in-law.

Several years passed before they threw in the sponge – it was unlikely that Fabienne would have a child of her own. We used to see them every summer in Rock where Robin became a skilful sailor of our Wayfarer, *Pickereel*, Registration No 221. They used to disappear quite often on behalf of Price Waterhouse into the French African bush before Robin joined a French Merchant Bank whose head office was in Paris, somewhere near the Avenue Malesherbes where I had once spent a miserable Easter vac in 1932 trying to understand what on earth a chap called August Comte had meant by writing unreadable books on French philosophy.

Robin and Fabienne found a flat in the suburb of Meudon where Sheila and I visited them several times. While Sheila learned how to handle French supermarkets, I was able to study the sculpture of Rodin in his Meudon house. I always thought *Le Baiser* the loveliest sculpture in the French artistic canon.

I think it was in 1986 that Robin transferred from Paris to a stockbroker's office in London and after that to Barclaycard in Northampton. He and Fabienne used to motorbike for hundreds of miles together, at least once as far as Casablanca, to see her parents. They also used to walk for miles in the Lake District, the worse the weather the better. Then Robin was headhunted by an American finance house – MBNA, the Maryland Banking National Association. Their head office was in Wilmington, Delaware where I had stayed in 1933 with Bill Marvell, the first Mellon scholar to Clare from Yale, where once so long ago I had flown with Alice du Pont from her parents' summer place on Cape Cod to Nantucket Island.

Wisely the MBNA founders – when they came to open their first office across the pond – chose Chester rather than the City of London as their foothold in the European financial jungle.

In the meantime Robin and Fabienne had adopted two small Moroccan boys and had brought them to their home in North Wales. From Fabienne's description of the corrupt and potentially dangerous extraction of Sebastian and Bertie out of Morocco, it was hard to tell which country made it more difficult to register these little boys as citizens of the United Kingdom – Morocco or England – the patronising red tape of the Northamptonshire County Council or the suspicious and corrupt manoeuvres of the Moroccan secret police.

Suffice it to say that by 1990 they were both visiting at Rock at least once a year and Sheila was able to hold her first grandchild in her arms. She never sought to conceal her joy. I used to think they were the two luckiest boys alive.

53

The Indian Impressionists

"For the twenty years immediately succeeding India's Independence, in 1947, one city alone — Bombay — was spawning thirty or more brilliant but penniless young artists who could and did paint with the freedom, confidence, imagination and skill of Monet, Manet, Gaugin, Cézanne and the lame duck, Toulouse-Lautrec."

Wilfrid Russell

There was one German, Rudi von Leyden whom I liked and admired enormously, as did Sheila. After all, he had been our Best Man and had helped me to bury her still-born child.

Rudi came from an aristocratic Prussian family. His father had been a senior civil servant in the Prussian government who had married into a Jewish Rhenish family. His eldest brother, Albrecht, since well before World War Two, had made his career in the well-known German photographic firm of Agfa. He had in fact started up their Indian business, in Bombay, in 1932. Rudi who had a penchant towards England had naturally asked Albrecht and through him Agfa if he could join the big German firm. Both brothers spoke English well. Agfa in Germany gave the von Leyden brothers their blessing. Rudi arrived in Bombay in 1934, one year ahead of me. It was their sister, who was spending the cold weather of 1935/36 in Bombay, whom I had met playing hockey in the Bombay gymkhana team who had introduced me to Rudi. Almost immediately we became friends. We called each other "Der beste Freund". Rudi was intelligent and artistic. He painted well in oils but his outstanding intellectual characteristic was his passionate interest in and knowledge of all things Indian, both Hindu and Mohammedan, particularly their art and architecture.

The British as a race had never shown much interest in Indian culture, except for George Nathaniel Curzon who as Viceroy in the early twentieth century had rescued the Taj Mahal from both Indian and British neglect, thereby placing the whole world, not least the future independent India in his and Britain's debt. I suppose my lifelong friendship with Rudi and Sheila's too was based on his knowledge and scholarship about this amazingly rich cultural treasure house. Long before the RAF took me off in 1939 I had spent weekend after weekend climbing in the Deccan Hills behind Bombay to the forts of the Robin Hood – like Maharashtrian General Shivaji.

Ultimately in the second half of the eighteenth century he had deprived the Moghul dynasty of its last feeble exercise of political power, and which in its turn was taken over by the East India Company, which then booted out the French, leaving the two Wellesley brothers in charge of India, politically, diplomatically and culturally.

By the end of World War Two, Rudi, and to some extent Sheila, were in a position to assist a new and energetic school of artists to come into existence. Albrecht and Rudi von Leyden had been British citizens since 1939. Before 1857 there had been little Indian art to study. There had been the beautifully painted ceilings in the Ajanta caves, but the human beings depicted there are nearly all Hindu ladies who in the Anglo-Indian nursery world of Sheila's childhood are all "nanga panga" with large circular hips and even larger bosoms.

The number and variety of Hindu temples and sculptures and also Islamic mosques, including the Taj Mahal at Agra, are legion. Many of them date back to 3000BC. The most astounding of them all are probably the caves and statues carved out of the solid cliff face at Ellora, three hundred miles east of Bombay.

All that England left behind in the way of art or architecture are a few fine examples of late Georgian architecture in Calcutta, umpteen solemn statues of Queen Victoria sitting on her marble throne, innumerable barracks of Queen Victoria's British Army all of which were left in the culturally protective arms of Lockhart Kipling, father of Rudyard. By far the most impressive architectural relics which the British have bequeathed to India in my view and that of Sheila's too, are Lutyens' fine Government of India buildings in New Delhi, the apex of which is the Viceroy's House now known as Rashtrapatti Bhowan. There are also a number of early Georgian buildings in Calcutta which were built in about 1800 for the Wellesley brothers (of whom the Duke of Wellington was the youngest). The most imperialistic and pompous of them all was the Victoria Memorial sited in the Maidan (Calcutta's Hyde Park). Appropriately it was completed in 1897 (Queen Victoria's Diamond Jubilee).

Yet for the twenty years immediately succeeding India's independence in 1947, one city alone – Bombay – was spawning thirty or more brilliant but penniless young artists who could and did paint with the freedom, confidence, imagination and skill of Monet, Manet, Gaugin, Cézanne and the lame duck, Toulouse-Lautrec. There were two young men in Bombay at that time, Karl Kardalavala, a Parsee, and Rudi von Leyden, who recognised their promise. Rudi von Leyden with some help from Sheila did scrape together enough money to rent a largish room in Rampart Row, which served as an informal club where they could talk about their main interest in life without having to pay an entrance fee or subscription. There were a few old deckchairs, but most of them preferred the lotus pose and sat cross-legged on the floor. Tea and Nescafé were cheap and one, if not two, of them were even sent to Paris for a year.

Ara worked as a car cleaner to one of Sheila's English friends who, having married the head of Swedish Match, bore a Swedish name. Ara used to practise his drawing skills in the pool of motor oil which dripped from the Volvo's sump and was dried by him with sand from Juhu Beach. A short twig supplied by the Swedish Match Mali was his brush. Sheila bought one of his early impressions of Juhu Beach for a derisory sum. Then there was Maneshi Dey, a Bengali, who might have become a great Indian artist had not his taste for Scotch whisky drowned his remarkable gift of an Indo-French style of painting.

I was lucky enough to buy in 1955, from Husain himself, a portrait of a Muslim girl in a green Shalwar Kamiz for the equivalent of a hundred pounds. Sheila bought several Aras, which now hang in our drawing room overlooking the Camel Estuary.

My favourite of our small collection is a Gade, a yellow ruin of a Goa-like convent with a worn searchlight-shaped tower and its red capsule, with a solitary dancing figure skipping in the foreground. The picture shines and talks. Its character is Portuguese and it overlooks the Indian Ocean somewhere on the Malabar Coast between Bombay and Goa. Manek Dalal, so long a faithful member of the Tata empire, now living in London near Hampton Court, told me the other day on the telephone of the unbelievable figures which these brilliant young men, most of them now dead, command, in what I imagine is a totally new market overflowing with rupees and a love of art in general together with the capacity to pay the prices their creators so well deserved.

But have they a name? Are they a school? They deserve to be. The artist in this group whom we knew best and who taught Sheila to paint was K K Hebbar. He contributed twelve watercolours to a book I wrote at that time, which were beautifully printed by Thackers. I still have several of the originals – the Dal Lake in Kashmir, Mahableshwar in the monsoon, Bundi City in Rajasthan. Sheila loved most his powerful, colourful views of the Moghul Gardens and scenes of Kashmir near her home.

54

À la Recherche du Temps Perdu

"Sheila never looked back."

Wilfrid Russell

6th October 2003, the anniversary of Sheila's death, will have come and gone by the time I write these words, on 18th October 2003. I am alone in Lower Cole, looking across the terrace with its geraniums and lobelia, over the mile-wide stretch of sand between Rock and Padstow. At low neap tide a few brave people walk across, there are only two places where you have to raise your arms above your head for a few yards, that is, of course, if you are carrying anything. You must, in any case, wear swimming trunks or a bikini if you want to cross the sand all the way past the dozens of Crabbers and Wayfarers, which lie stranded with their bottoms on the sand, disconsolate and temporarily useless.

It has been the best summer in the garden that I can remember since Sheila and I came to live here for good, thirty-one years ago. Day after day from mid-August the sky has been azure blue and Rock, being the magic place that it is, has had, every eighteen hours or so, a gentle rainfall, a sort of natural iced mint julep, to freshen up the wisteria and the roses, the hydrangeas and the California poppies, since there has been no drought here such as the frogs have had across the Channel.

Robin told me on the telephone from his holiday house in the Alpes Maritimes that a swimming pool this year is no luxury. Perhaps it was because I have lived for so long in the East that I have hardly noticed the heat. Sheila would have loved the garden this year and especially the view, even without the distant rumble of the Waterloo train crossing the Iron Bridge on its last few yards into Padstow Station; but all that was long ago when the branch line from Bodmin Road had been alive.

I can only see the garden, myself, by hanging onto a Zimmer frame and the strong arm of Marion Hawken, my strongest carer, who has heaved me onto the terrace and escorted me round the house, leaning on its gentle slope. Sometimes Jane Comer who commands the gracious platoon of carers who look after me and many other octogenarians who have finished up in this magic corner of this magic land heaves me by herself all round the house. Together with Henry and Rosemary Grattan, Jane has helped in the typing of the manuscript of this book. She runs the best nursing home in the county.

Sheila had always been a late riser, in England as well as in India. When we were together, which was for most of the sixty years covered by this story, I would take "chota hazri" (coffee and toast) to her in bed so that her day usually began at ten o'clock. She was often trailed by a Pekinese who had spent the night on her bed. After a session on the phone with Di Dunkerly of Di's famous Dairy, planning lunch and supper, there would be a more serious conference with Sylvia Cock. Sylvia, together with her husband, Michael, had looked after the house ever since I can remember. He had been for many years, in my view, the best builder in the Rock and Wadebridge region of North Cornwall. By this time it was about eleven o'clock. Her eczema and smoking had been a hidden, almost automatic reaction, a semi-neurotic admission of her resentment of other women's (they had been mainly English) unfair, inhuman dislike of her country, India, and her brown skin. This, together with her weak heart, had put paid some years previously to her morning drive up to the village to do her shopping, and was replaced by a morning walk around the garden. Keith Champion and then his son Nick would come once a week. There were no conferences about the garden. She knew what she wanted and father and son Champion usually carried out her wishes.

In the afternoon, after lunch, there would be an hour's sleep, stretched out on the drawing-room sofa, a Peke wrapped round her shoulders. Then, usually at about half past three, one of her bridge-playing friends would drive up to the front door and she was away in her favourite world, with her favourite friends and her favourite pastime. By the time she came home at about eight I had been heaved on to my bed. The days when she didn't play bridge we watched *Countdown*. She always beat me hollow, especially in the mental arithmetic. Richard Whitely and Carol Vorderman, even if only shadows on a screen, had been our lifelong friends.

The western wall of the sitting room carries at its centre a large piece of the oak keel of the old sailing ship, *Isabella*, which had been rescued by Venetia and Ken Duxbury from its resting place below Cant Hill. Its sturdy appearance was a perfect support for the large oil painting above the fireplace. This was a modern kind of still life in oils painted by Sheila when she was under the influence of her original English teacher in London. Either side of this oil painting were two Moghul miniatures we had bought in Delhi years ago and which probably date back to the middle of the eighteenth century. And then you complete a clockwise expedition by reaching the western end of a large glass French window which stretches the whole length of the south-west side of the house and gives on to the terrace with its summer decorations of Sheila's geraniums and lobelia.

Below the terrace there is a lawn which is skirted by a hedge beyond which lies the whole of John Betjeman's favourite Cornish view stretching across to Padstow and the Iron Railway Bridge. When we first came to Rock, steam trains brought all the emmets, including us, from Waterloo Station to Padstow Harbour. It was Sheila's favourite view in the whole of England and she was able to see it up to her last day with us.

Envoi: Goodbye, Darling

"I have seen much to hate here — much to forgive,
But in a world where England is finished and dead
I do not wish to live."

Alice Duer Miller

And now it is almost three years since her death — she had been playing bridge less than twenty-four hours before I saw her leave Lower Cole in a wheelchair for Treliske Hospital in Truro where she left us for good.

When I asked Sue Walsham, her best friend in England, "What would you say was Sheila's greatest virtue?"

Without hesitation she replied: "Her delicate courage."

FINIS

Postscript to *The White Sari*

When my father decided to write this tribute to my mother, he threw himself into it with the boundless energy that characterised his last years. He cheerfully and unscrupulously dragooned a range of people to help him, notably Henry & Rosemary Grattan, the kind ladies of Trewiston Lodge, Joanna Lumley for a foreword and Jane Tatam to help publish it. He spent many an hour on the telephone to old friends, checking details, reliving his life with Sheila. This would be a fairly daunting project at any age, let alone at ninety-three, but his will power was still intense.

Deep down I had a feeling that this was my father's way of setting everything in order before he died. As well as being a tribute to my mother, it became clear as we went through successive drafts that it was a testimony to a generation, a way of life, a certain way of looking at things.

Daddybar as we affectionately knew him died on 15th December 2004. He had almost finished this testimony to Sheila when he died, and so it has been an easy filial duty for me to have it published posthumously, thanks to the support of the Grattans and Jane. So there are a number of goodbyes in this book. But Daddybar would not want us to dwell only on the past, so may I ask all you who read this to get out and vote at the next general election so that the black flag Daddybar raised outside Lower Cole on Tony Blair's re-election can be finally lowered.... . Politically irascible to the last, this would be the best posthumous gift we could make him. For Mummybar and Venetia, who were somewhat disdainful of politics and would occasionally wind Daddybar up on his favourite topics, this book is their monument.

6 th November 2005